Introducing Australia

BOOKS BY C. HARTLEY GRATTAN

INTRODUCING AUSTRALIA

THE THREE JAMESES: A Family of Minds (*Longmans, Green & Company*)

WHY WE FOUGHT (*Vanguard Press*)

Introducing Australia

C. HARTLEY GRATTAN

ILLUSTRATED

THE JOHN DAY COMPANY, NEW YORK

Typography by ROBERT JOSEPHY

MANUFACTURED IN THE UNITED STATES OF AMERICA
BY THE CORNWALL PRESS, CORNWALL, N.Y.

FOR FREDERICK P. KEPPEL,

Last sea-thing dredged by sailor Time from Space,
Are you a drift Sargasso, where the West
In halcyon calm rebuilds her fatal nest?
Or Delos of a coming Sun-God's race?
Are you for Light, and trimmed, with oil in place,
Or but a Will o' Wisp on marshy quest?
A new demesne for Mammon to infest?
Or lurks millennial Eden 'neath your face?
The cenotaphs of species dead elsewhere
That in your limits leap and swim and fly,
Or trail uncanny harp-strings from your trees,
Mix omens with the auguries that dare
To plant the Cross upon your forehead sky,
A virgin helpmate Ocean at your knees.

BERNARD O'DOWD

CONTENTS

PREFACE   xiii

Part One: TO BEGIN WITH

1. *AS I SEE AUSTRALIA*   3

2. *AS AUSTRALIANS SEE IT*   9

Part Two: THIS IS AUSTRALIA

3. A CONTINENT   29

THE GREAT CITIES — A LAND OF VAST DISTANCES — THE CONTINENT DEFINED — THE GREAT BARRIER REEF — THE BUSH — THE KANGAROO, THE KOALA, AND OTHERS — BRIGHT-COLORED BIRDS — GAY FLOWERS — TREES: THE "GUMS" — WHY THE TROPICS ARE EMPTY — THE ABORIGINES.

4. THE MAKING OF A COMMONWEALTH   41

NEW HOLLAND: SITE FOR AN ENGLISH JAIL? — THE FIRST FLEET, 1788 — SLOW GROWTH — AN UNKNOWN CONTINENT — THE MILITARY AS MONOPOLISTS — JOHN MACARTHUR *vs.* WILLIAM BLIGH — WORLD INFLUENCES ON DEVELOPMENT — RISE OF WOOL GROWING — TECHNOLOGICAL CHANGE AND AUSTRALIAN DEVELOPMENT — END OF CONVICT TRANSPORTATION — THE GOLD RUSHES — RISE OF AGRICULTURE — BASIC POLICIES EMERGE — THE AMAZING NINETIES — THE COMING OF THE COMMONWEALTH — THE FIRST WORLD WAR — STATE POWER PROMOTES PRIVATE ENTERPRISE — RISE OF MANUFACTURING — THE GREAT DEPRESSION — AFTER 150 YEARS: REASSESSMENT AND REDEDICATION.

5. WHAT AUSTRALIA LIVES BY   57

LOCATION OF INDUSTRY — THE GREAT ESSENTIALS — THE CRITICAL RAW MATERIALS — A SHEEP STATION — SHEARING — SUGAR CANE GROWING — IRRIGATION ON THE MURRAY RIVER — WESTERN AUSTRALIAN TIMBER — RISE OF THE STEEL MONOPOLY: THE BHP.

6. FINANCE AND TRADE   84

FINANCIAL TIE TO UNITED KINGDOM — BORROWING FOR DEVELOPMENT — THE GREAT DEPRESSION AND FINANCE — J. T. LANG: BOGEYMAN — INTERNAL MONEY MARKET — LOAN COUNCIL — THE COM-

MONWEALTH BANK — FOREIGN PRIVATE INVESTMENTS — THE GREAT
COMPANIES — THE HEAVY EXPORT TRADE — DESTINATION OF EXPORTS
— . ORIGIN OF IMPORTS — THE PROTECTIVE TARIFF — PROTECTION FOR
FARMERS — PASTORALISTS AND THE TARIFF — OUTLOOK OF MANUFAC-
TURERS — EFFICIENCY OF INDUSTRY — FUTURE OF FOREIGN TRADE —
COMING CRISIS IN PRIMARY INDUSTRY.

7. THE STANDARD OF LIVING   116

THE FIRST LABOR FORCE — THE GOLD RUSHES AND LABOR — EUREKA
STOCKADE — RISE OF TRADE UNIONS — GREAT STRIKES OF THE 1890'S
— THE BHP STRIKE OF '92 — LABOR TURNS TO POLITICS — RISE OF
ARBITRATION COURTS — TRADE UNION RADICALISM — STRUCTURE OF
TRADE UNION MOVEMENT — HOW ARBITRATION COURTS WORK —
SCOPE OF AWARDS — STRIKES ARE LEGAL — DETERMINING WAGES — THE
BASIC WAGE — "MARGINS" — SOCIAL SERVICES: A PUBLIC ISSUE.

8. GOVERNING THE COUNTRY   149

THE FEDERAL CONSTITUTION — THE KING AND AUSTRALIA — THE SEN-
ATE AND THE HOUSE — HOW THE PRIME MINISTER IS SELECTED — THE
CABINET — POLITICAL PARTIES — ELECTION CAMPAIGNS — STATE POLI-
TICS — LOCAL GOVERNMENT — THE FEDERAL-STATE CONFLICT — GOV-
ERNMENT EMPLOYEES.

9. CULTURAL LIFE   165

LITERATURE: THE BEGINNINGS — THE AUSTRALIAN CLASSICS — THE
MEN AND WOMEN OF THE NINETIES — CONTEMPORARY POETS — CON-
TEMPORARY NOVELISTS — PAINTING: THE CONSERVATIVES RULE — IM-
PRESSIONISM WITH AN ENGLISH ORIENTATION — THE MODERNISTS
SCORNED — THE PAINTER'S PROBLEM — SIXTY YEARS OF AUSTRALIAN
ART — THE GREAT NAMES — BLACK AND WHITE — MUSIC — THE THEA-
TER — FOUNDING CULTURAL INSTITUTIONS — UNIVERSITIES — LIBRA-
RIES — ART MUSEUMS — TOWARD THE FUTURE.

10. ODDMENTS AND REMAINDERS   188

THE AUSTRALIAN OUTLOOK — WHAT DO AUSTRALIANS LOOK LIKE? —
AUSTRALIAN SPEECH — FOOTNOTE TO BARTLETT — FOOD — CLOTHING
— SHELTER — TAXES — LAND HOLDING — RELIGION — SPORT — MOVIES —
EXPORT OF TALENT — C.S.I.R. — THE FLAG — THE NATIONAL CAPITAL.

Part Three: AUSTRALIA IN THE WORLD

11. THE TIE TO BRITAIN   211

A BRITISH DOMINION — STRUCTURE OF BRITISH WORLD COMMUNITY —
THE KING: SYMBOL OF UNITY — THE BALFOUR FORMULA — THE DO-
MINIONS AND FOREIGN AFFAIRS — OUTBREAK OF WAR, 1939.

Contents

12. THE FIRST WORLD WAR 218

AUSTRALIA'S "FOREIGN POLICY," 1914 – THE "ISLAND" POLICY –
WHITE AUSTRALIA – TRADE ROUTES – THE ANGLO-JAPANESE ALLIANCE
– INTEGRATION WITH BRITAIN – AUSTRALIAN DEFENSE POLICY – THE
AUSTRALIAN IMPERIAL FORCE – GALLIPOLI – FRANCE – PALESTINE –
RISE OF WILLIAM MORRIS HUGHES – CONSCRIPTION REFERENDA –
HUGHES AT PEACE CONFERENCE – "ANNEX" THE GERMAN ISLANDS?
– RACIAL EQUALITY – REPARATIONS – COST OF WAR.

13. THE SECOND WORLD WAR 235

AUSTRALIA'S WORLD OUTLOOK, 1938 – THE INDUSTRIAL WAR EFFORT
– THE ARMY – THE NAVY – THE AIR FORCE – DOMESTIC POLITICS –
THE NATIONAL WAR COUNCIL – ECONOMIC CONTROLS – TRADE UN-
IONS AND THE WAR – AUSTRALIA AND JAPAN – END OF THE ANGLO-
JAPANESE ALLIANCE – THE WASHINGTON TREATIES – AUSTRALIA'S
EASTERN TRADE – AUSTRALIA'S PACIFIC OUTLOOK DEFINED – NEW
GUINEA – THE BRITISH EASTERN GROUP – NETHERLANDS EAST INDIES
– DARWIN – NEW CALEDONIA AND NEW HEBRIDES – NEW ZEALAND –
AMERICAN FAR-EASTERN POLICY AND AUSTRALIA – AUSTRALIAN VIEWS
OF U. S. A. – U. S. A. VIEW OF AUSTRALIA.

Part Four: AUSTRALIA'S TOMORROW

14. AUSTRALIAN DEMOCRACY 279

COUNTING AUSTRALIA'S BLESSINGS – POSTWAR REHABILITATION AND
RECONSTRUCTION – THE VARIOUS APPROACHES – A SCHEME FOR THE
SERVICES – NUTRITION – THE OUTLOOK OF THE CATHOLIC BISHOPS
– THE LABOR VIEW – PUBLIC WORKS – THE MANUFACTURERS AND
ECONOMIC NATIONALISM – CONTINUANCE OF GOVERNMENTAL CON-
TROLS – POSITION OF THE PRIMARY INDUSTRIES – STRUGGLE FOR A
TRADE POLICY – THE POPULATION QUESTION.

15. INTERNATIONAL POSITION 294

THE DEPARTMENT OF EXTERNAL AFFAIRS: ITS EVOLUTION – DIPLO-
MATIC REPRESENTATION ABROAD – PROBLEMS OF FOREIGN POLICY –
AUSTRALIA FOREVER IN THE PACIFIC – AUSTRALIA'S PRAGMATIC OUT-
LOOK – AUSTRALIA AND INTERNATIONAL ORGANIZATION – TOWARD
PEACE.

APPENDIXES 301
   a. Chronology
   b. Statistical Notes
   c. Reading List

INDEX 324

ILLUSTRATIONS

PLATES

Business section, Sydney—and The Bridge! 16

St. Kilda Road, Melbourne 17

The Three Sisters, Blue Mountains, near Katoomba 32

The mighty gums of Australia 33

Australia's own fauna: platypus, koalas, kangaroo, emu 64

Iron Knob, near Whyalla, a mountain of iron ore 65

Sheep station in the dry outback 65

A "mob" of sheep in charge of a mounted man and two dogs 80

Section of BHP works, Newcastle 81

Eight leaders of Australian life 160-161

Bondi Beach, Sydney 176

Snow—at 6,000 feet 177

Hume Reservoir, Murray River, key to irrigation 177

MAPS

PAGE

Australia 58

Australia and the World 210

OTHER ILLUSTRATIONS

The shearers accept "open shop," 1891 122

The Australian flag 204

PREFACE

THIS book is based upon my experiences and activities during three visits to Australia. My first visit was made in 1927 and extended from early February to late October; my second and longest came almost ten years later, when I spent from December, 1936 until September, 1938 in the country on a grant from the Carnegie Corporation for travel and study; while the third and shortest visit was made in 1940, when I spent September and October there collecting data for a report on Australia's reaction to the Second World War for the Institute of Current World Affairs.

Sometime between my first and second visits—I forget just when —I agreed to myself that one day I would write a full-dress study of the evolution of the Australian Commonwealth from 1788 to whatever contemporary year provided a convenient stopping place. After my first visit I began to write for the American press about Australian affairs whenever opportunity offered. My first article appeared in October, 1927. Others have followed, somewhat irregularly, down the years. When the Carnegie Corporation made me a liberal grant, I thought myself well on the way toward realizing my larger aim. I spent my twenty months in Australia collecting and studying material, acquiring a wide acquaintance, even building up a reputation among Australians as a commentator on their affairs, and—equally important—traveling widely within the Commonwealth to familiarize myself with the environment in which Australian events take place. I returned to the United States with the idea of writing two books, the first to be a short introduction to the Australian Commonwealth today, the second to be the large historical study.

This book is the introduction I had in mind. When I shall be ready to publish my large study, all properly documented, I cannot say. As I am (reluctantly) a free-lance writer, I have painfully little time for labors of love. My big book is, most decidedly, a labor of love.

In writing a short book the problem of what to put in and what to leave out is bothersome. Here I have tried to include what I thought would be considered important and interesting by American readers. I am well aware, therefore, that Australian readers may find what seem to them curious omissions and oddly foreshortened discussions of matters we have discussed together at length on other occasions, as well as odd inclusions. If I had written this book exclusively for Australians it would have included a slightly different range of material and far more detail. I am as conscious of what I have by design left out as of what I have chosen to put in. But a short book must be short. I have not always detailed the war-time changes brought about by regulations under the National Security Act because I doubt that they will invariably be permanent. Constitutional amendments will be required to retain some of the most important, and such amendments are not readily made.

This portrait of Australia has been painted as Cromwell requested the artist to do his, "warts and all." I am convinced that plastic surgeons of the pen, who try to present prettified versions of their subjects, do them a profound disservice, for the portrait is not realistic; sometimes it is hardly recognizable; and the conclusions drawn from it are often false. Australia is a land of human beings; and to assume that they, any more than my fellow Americans, have conducted their affairs in an antiseptic atmosphere to uniformly beneficent ends is something I have found it impossible to pretend. Nevertheless it has always been my intention to be fair. I have tried to give the extenuating facts and arguments when I have indulged in criticism. I am well aware that much against which I have directed criticism may not appear to all readers to deserve criticism. I have my own ideas, prepossessions, and bias. My mind is not a *tabula rasa*. When I was last in the Commonwealth a paper which has never been too friendly to me noted that I was back again and then added, "Apparently he likes us after all." After all? I have always liked the Australians and Australia. But one can fall out of patience even with those one likes best. Fortunately many Australians share my views, though not necessarily in detail, as the letters quoted in Chapter 2 well illustrate. Australians know they aren't perfect, but they have a very human dislike of being told so by outsiders. Perhaps they have, after putting up with me off and on for fourteen years, ceased to regard me as a complete and utter outsider!

In this book I have tried to see Australia whole. I have not ground the ax for any particular state or city. My conclusions about the relative positions of states and cities follow from Commonwealth statistics, not from my personal whims and subjective likings.

Since I have been concerned with things Australian for so many years, my obligations are enormous. Every Australian mail increases my indebtedness. I cannot, in all decency, fail to state here that I am tremendously grateful to the innumerable Australians who have done me courtesies in times past and will, I know, continue to do them in the future. I must, on this occasion, specifically thank all those who replied to the letter I circulated in 1940. Their replies add a touch to this book which, I think, makes it unique among books on Australia. Instead of the outsider doing *all* the talking, here some Australians get a few words with the reader. I wish also to express here my indebtedness to those Australian writers (and their publishers) from whose books and articles I have made short quotations. Often they are friends who will, I am sure, bear with me for levying on them once more. I owe special thanks to Mr. Brian Fitzpatrick, the brilliant economic historian, for a copy of his unpublished study quoted in Chapter 6. The longer quotations from Australian sources are mostly from government documents, government statements, and political speeches. All figures, unless otherwise indicated, are taken from official Australian sources.

I must also thank the editors of *Harper's* and *Asia* for permission to use without quotation marks articles contributed by me to those magazines. Finally, I must thank Messrs. Reynal and Hitchcock for permission to quote Professor Paul Birdsall's characterization of William Morris Hughes.

An Australian friend who prefers to remain anonymous kindly read my manuscript and made numerous valuable suggestions with a view to clarifying some of my statements.

My wife has helped me with this book in ways too numerous to specify. Above all, she strongly urged me to write it at this particular time and cheerfully endured my intense preoccupation with it.

C. Hartley Grattan.

Flushing, N. Y.,

note: A few minor revisions were made in the text on January 12, 1942.

C. H. G.

Part One

TO BEGIN WITH

1. AS I SEE AUSTRALIA

AUSTRALIA is not the home of any "Middle Way," nor the seat of an ideal commonwealth of workers and peasants, nor are its political and economic arrangements destined for a life of a thousand years. Australia is, like our own country, a democracy, and democracies are justified, not by achieved perfection, but by the fact that they offer men an opportunity to work toward better conditions than those in which they find themselves. The Australian story is replete with efforts in that direction. I see in Australia the opportunity to build a version of European-American civilization which will be unique and perhaps possessed of virtues we are little likely to achieve in our own country. I do not think that Australia will ever be one of the Great Powers. I do think that the Australians will one day, if fate favors them, be a great people.

I began my study of Australia by reading as widely as I could in Australian literature, which is not negligible in either bulk or quality. That seems to me the best possible approach to any country; for from a good novel, or a first-rate poem, one can gain an insight into the innermost thoughts, feeling, and character not only of the particular author, but also of the people about whom he is writing. The ideas about Australia and the Australians I got from reading Henry Lawson, Tom Collins, Bernard O'Dowd, Shaw Neilson—even Marcus Clarke and Rolf Boldrewood—are still the foundation on which whatever understanding I have of Australia really rests. Over the years I have modified and corrected my first impressions, and I still find myself revising my ideas. After all, Australia is and always will be a foreign country to me, and I shall never see it exactly as the Australians see it, or accept unquestioningly ideas which they think are axiomatic. I shall never become a complete Australian. But, insofar as one can have a second country in this world where primary loyalties are so very important, my second country is Australia.

One reason why I am interested in Australia—to some it may seem rather abstract—is that within the hundred and fifty-odd years of its history the country has gone through an extremely rapid evolution which has carried it from the absolute autocracy of a penal colony to the freedom of a modern social democracy. Although not embellished with bitter wars of liberation or many soul-stirring personal martyrdoms, the story of the Australians has a fascination of its own. When you think that in 1788, when the first Australian settlement was planted, there was nothing of Western European civilization on the continent and no indigenous civilization from which white men could draw much usable wisdom, while today the land supports a complex, Western, modern, free society, you begin to wonder how the job was done. It was done, of course, by fallible men following what light they had at the moment.

As Americans we are, I think, rather better prepared to understand the story than other peoples, even the English. We know something about building a society from scratch in a virgin land beyond the seas. And when, further, we discover that the Australians have accomplished this extraordinary job on one of the most recalcitrant of the continents, compared with which our own is uniformly a land flowing with milk and honey, our respect for them mounts. They are still building, and so, I hope, are we.

That is not to say that I shall tell the Australian story in romantic and moralistic terms. There is no occasion for doing so, and a realistic presentation will make it far more understandable than any amount of idle patter. But it is to call attention to the fact that in a century and a half the Australians discovered how to make a difficult continent support a modern society. In fifteen decades they outlined a system of exploitation which, in the next fifteen decades, will not, I think, be modified in any essential particulars. It is rather a question of balancing, elaborating, and intensifying the activities now under way and the better use of the resources for the benefit of all those who make their homes in Australia. How anyone who is at all interested in the human adventure can fail to be interested in the Australian chapter of it—a continental chapter, by the way—is something I don't understand. For my part, I am fascinated by it, in its historical, contemporary, and prospective phases.

The Australian environment is not lush. Nor is the continent one which makes the appeal of the exotic. At one time or another I have visited every type of Australian environment: the sugar-cane country of northeastern Queensland, the timber country of southwestern Western Australia, the great commercial and indus-trial cities of southeastern New South Wales and Victoria, isolated mining towns like Broken Hill in western New South Wales and Mount Isa in western Queensland, irrigation settlements along the River Murray, Alice Springs in the center of the continent, Dar-win in Northern Territory, the tiny seaports like Wyndham and Broome on the forbidding northwestern coast, vast sweeps of farm-ing and grazing country in every state and the tiny towns they support from Hughenden (Q'land) clear around to Katanning (W.A.). I have been in these places and many more, but I cannot testify that Australia is a paradise for those incorrigible sightseers who must be fed a new marvel every hour of the day. I am afraid the average sightseer would often agree with the comment of an Englishman who, after traveling for hundreds of miles in the sheep country of western Queensland, remarked, "It all seems so unnecessary." The tourist will be charmed and amused by a koala; he will enjoy the great beaches; he will get pleasure out of the Blue Mountains back of Sydney. But he can see all he will want to see by visiting the capital cities and their environs, going over-land from one to the other to get an idea of what the countryside is like. I don't think the average tourist will get any fun out of going to Broken Hill.

Much of Australia can support only a very sparse population, and that fact complicates many Australian problems. There is nothing more remarkable about the Australians than their ability to make a "go" of it under environmental conditions which hardly favor them. They even get to like conditions which to an urban-ized stranger seem appallingly dull. I remember talking to a young lady in western Queensland—the "unnecessary" country—who had recently been to Tasmania, the well-watered, hilly island off the southeastern coast, on her wedding trip. She told me that the Tasmanian hills oppressed her. She was happy to be back in the great-open-spaces which were home. On the other hand, there are Australians who simply cannot endure life outside the coastal cities and who resent it mightily when they have to go "out back." It should be remembered that one-third of the nation is crowded into two cities, Sydney and Melbourne.

To me it is part of the fascination of Australia that the Australians have been able to make so much out of their difficult continent. It is not only the time element which I emphasized when insisting that their history is fascinating; it is also the environment in which that rapid evolution has taken place. In one sense, Australia is a paradise for the geographical determinist. Such a man would have a lovely time demonstrating to his satisfaction that the Australians got the way they are because the rainfall in Bourke is so-and-so many inches a year, while in Cairns it is so many more inches a year. And he would, in a very important sense, be quite right. The first question to ask about any part of Australia is, "What is the annual rainfall?" If you know that and have an appreciation of the months during which it falls and the rate of evaporation—Australia is a warm country with a high evaporation rate—then you can make a reasonable guess about the worth of the country. If you are interested in how men adapt themselves to hard environments, then Australia will interest you.

Although Australia is a western Pacific country, it partakes not at all of the character of Asia or the South Sea Islands. It has a European-American civilization, like the United States and Canada. If you like compounds, you may prefer to call it, geographically speaking, an Indo-Pacific country, for its eastern shores are washed by the Pacific and its western by the Indian Ocean. Australia inherited its geographical nomenclature from Europe. It speaks of the Far East. Yet if you go east from Australia you come to South America. And if you go west you get to Africa. It is only when you go north and northwest that you get to Asia. In recent years, as the political problems of Asia have become more and more difficult for the Western powers, with which Australia must be classified, thoughtful Australians have tried to substitute the term Near North for Far East. But whatever the terminology, Australia is an important Pacific country. It is strategically located in the southwestern portion of the Pacific Basin and cannot fail to be of interest to Americans for that reason. American possessions stretching southward from Honolulu reach their extreme limit at Samoa. Pago Pago, the Samoan naval station, is only two thousand miles from Sydney, the largest Australian city. The Far Eastern problem is sufficiently difficult that no angle from which it can be approached can safely be overlooked. From the American point of view, Australia is a logical collaborator in Pacific politics, both in fundamental outlook and also from the viewpoint of naval and air strategy. Looking at the United States, the Australians reach much the same conclusion from their standpoint.

The Australians are a people of British origin. They frequently —often sententiously—say that they are 98 per cent British, a statistical monstrosity. Although I myself am 100 per cent British by origin—using the Australian criterion of the nationality of one's forebears—I find this boast rather irrelevant. I like the Australians better when they get off on the other track and talk about their character as Australians—not Englishmen in exile nor pseudo-Americans, but Australians. After all, nine out of ten of the people now living in Australia were born there. But the fact remains that to a degree far surpassing the American nation, Australia is a country whose origins and traditions are British. I have referred to their European-American civilization to indicate that they belong to the cultural world of which we Americans are also a part. But if I were to refine my reference, I should have to say that the British elements in the European complex are of overwhelming importance to the Australians. Far less than the Americans have they been influenced by Continental traditions and customs. No one would ever think of trying to define Australian culture in pluralistic terms. It is simply a case of a British theme with Australian variations. But it is important to emphasize the Australian variations if you really want to understand the country and the people.

Even the American half of my hyphenated term is chiefly useful to indicate that Australian civilization is like the North American in contrast to that of Asia or even South America. The American influence in Australia is not of overwhelming importance. It runs a poor second to the British, but it is conspicuous because it is almost the only non-British influence at work. Moreover, it is growing and may play a much larger role in the future. Australians, however, are given to saying that they are very like Americans, as you will discover when you read the next chapter. Their reasons for thinking so are fairly convincing. But when I am driven to try to define them, I say that while they are like Americans in many of their emotional reactions, the cultural content of their minds is far more British.

In short, a people fairly like ourselves have in a relatively short time built a Western-type civilization on a difficult continent in a far corner of the Pacific Basin. Perhaps on closer acquaintance we will find that they appeal to us to a greater extent than peoples of whom we are today far more acutely aware and about whom we are much better informed.

2. AS AUSTRALIANS SEE IT

ALTHOUGH Bobbie Burns sang of the great importance of seeing ourselves as others see us, there is also merit in seeing others as they see themselves. This is particularly true of nations. Friendly as the intentions of a foreigner may be, he inevitably sees and interprets a country not his own in a fashion passing strange to his hosts. He sees them "as others see us"—and often the results are not happy. The only worth-while corrective is to ask how they see themselves.

After expressing my views of Australia and the Australians for over a decade, that is just what I did. On my last visit to the country I solicited the views of a representative sample of articulate citizens. "Faced with a request to give a talk, or write an article, explaining Australia to Americans," I wrote each one, "what ten (or eight or twelve) points would you wish to make?" What follows epitomizes, with liberal use of direct quotations, what I was told. This is Australia as Australians see it.

"There is not a fixed type of Australian," wrote a distinguished judge. "The type has varied rapidly from decade to decade, and there are important variations between the different cities. The type now developing is not English and is not American, it is Australian." Nevertheless, one of the points which recurs again and again in the letters I received is that the Australians are like the Americans (though not exactly like). "The people make Australia what it is today. What sort of people are they? Like Americans? I think so," wrote a leading novelist. "Not so energetic, self-confident, and resolute, perhaps," she added, "but courageous, independent, and democratic." And, said a lawyer, with a touch of humor, "both countries are developing their own versions of the English language, each of which is equally horrifying to the English."

Why the Australians have become like Americans when the direct American influence has never been very strong is a point for which many explanations were suggested. Of these, two most often recurred—isolation from European influences and the experiences of pioneering a new continent. (But the same explanations were also given by some who did not feel that Australians were like Americans just because they were "not Englishmen.") "Australia," says a clever young economist, "is a 'fringe' country: the population is all on the fringe of a continent, on the fringe of all the great world movements, on the fringe of considerable industrial opportunities, on the fringe of disaster—from the East." His immediate superior called this "protected insularity." "I have added 'protected,'" he wrote, "because of the encouragement given to insularity until recently by our secure position in the British Empire—economically and politically." In their isolation, or "protected insularity," or position on the fringe, the Australians, so the argument goes, have had a chance to develop unique characteristics which make them "not Englishmen," like Americans—or Australians! In their isolation, they pioneered a continent.

This is not the place for a systematic review of Australian history, so it will only be used here as my correspondents used it. "The Australian population has been recruited mainly from the wage-earning or lower income sections of the British Isles," wrote an historian. Thinking of Australia's reputation for experimental social legislation, a high government official said, "No one can properly understand the Australian outlook unless he realizes that this community sprang from the fermenting English community of the period between 1830 and 1880," a point supported by a leading member of the Labour party thus: "influx of Chartists, Irish rebels, etc., last century, is the basis of the militant trade unionism of this century." This approach may surprise many Americans whose only knowledge of Australian history is the fact that the nation began as a convict colony. What about that? The matter is succinctly handled by a novelist:

Little has been heard of transportation to the American colonies before the settlement of Australia. Nevertheless convicts and political offenders were transported in conditions practically of slavery to the American colonies. The same system was applied to Australia. In

America, the free settlers arrived first: the convicts followed. Convicts arrived first in Australia: free settlers followed.

The convicts, setting aside superior types among them who showed great enterprise after completing their jail sentences, did not pioneer and develop Australia, even in the early days, in the sense of planning and executing the necessary agricultural and pastoral experiments. Their contribution was as a labor force. It was the early free settlers of Australia, the first of them being the military guard set over the convicts, who discovered Australia's potentialities. While it is impossible to forget the convicts, it is easy to exaggerate or misstate their significance. Although foundations were laid in the time when their slave-labor was available, it is still essentially true, as another novelist remarked, that:

Effective settlement of Australia began in the eighteen-fifties with the discovery of gold. Within a decade the balance of population was entirely changed. A new type of settler predominated in numbers—the political rebel, the adventurer, the man of will and enterprise who had left Europe to better himself.

In short, the types to which reference has already been made. These men, my correspondent continued, found stimulation in Australia's isolation from the old world and, another adds, they profited by the almost complete break with "the aristocratic tradition." "Many settlers came here," said a Labour party leader, "with a strong sense of social injustice in England," and were determined to prevent the growth of similar conditions in Australia.

In this fashion the Australians explain the genesis of the most admirable Australian tradition, the one which, they feel, best reflects their character as a people. It is the tradition composed of "utopian, republican, national, democratic ideas." This tradition was most intensely alive during the last four decades of the last century. Many of my correspondents pointed out that the people lost their grip on it early in this century. This sense of a "lost tradition" gives the present-day Australian outlook a nostalgic quality which must intrigue and puzzle foreign observers who have not the time to tarry and discover its origin.

It accounts for the self-criticism in the letters I shall now quote.

An academic economist wrote me that, "Australians are a people without a philosophy." "The environment and history of the Australian people," wrote a Jesuit Father, "have so accustomed them to security and ease that they have become lazy, particularly in the region of the mind and the spirit. They are, accordingly, moved more by sentiment than by reasoning. Their contentment has grown into self-satisfaction, often touched with arrogance. Their scale of values is materialistic." A newspaperman said, "Social ideals: vague, almost wholly wage-and-salary desire; little conscious of more." "Australians," wrote a judge, "seek material comfort, but they acquiesce in makeshifts. In social, political, and artistic affairs there is too little variety and too much opposition to new ideas." These remarks illustrate both my earlier point and its complement, a critical view of Australian accomplishments of recent years in all fields but the sphere of production for the market. Listen to a clever poet on his own people:

Their cultural standards are low. Severe criticism is always considered ill-natured. More of it would improve them greatly. Their moneyed people are "near the ground" and patronize obvious charities with no sense of ultimate values. They have grown up during the most materialistic period of the world's history. They are far more generous in act than in thought, and this is the basis of their hearty and unpolished manners.

And then he takes some of the edge off this by declaring:

They have bright and penetrating intelligences and are intolerant of shams and humbug; suspicious of high motives; generally sceptical.

They are indifferent to the claims of religion. "Since the settlement of the Irish question," said a librarian, "there has been no great religio-racial cleavage amongst the people." That such a cleavage once existed is suggested today when the Catholics ask that public funds be granted for parochial schools and are brusquely opposed by the bishops of the Church of England. The religious situation is stated with temperateness by a Jesuit Father: "Outside the Catholic Church organized religion plays but a small part in national life. Measured by the standard of church attendance in normal times, religion has but little hold on the people, and the state educational system combined with the materialistic outlook of the people seems likely to end in the growth of an almost pagan race." Of sun-worshipers? An economist lists as Australian characteristics, "Sun-worship and preoccupation with sport." After all, Australia is a sunny land, and outdoor sports can be played the year around.

But, in spite of the inadequacies, a novelist quoted earlier concludes that, "Australia remains at the core self-reliant, forward-looking, convinced that she has an individual contribution to make to the world's future. The present desperate crisis has to some extent stimulated her. She knows she cannot go back to the old idea of isolation, the dream of a utopia removed from the world, that nourished her infancy, but, on the other hand, she will not be inhibited by the idea of dependence that paralyzed her in later years."

The Australian continent itself is one of the major problems confronting the Australians. Many of my correspondents said they would tell the Americans that, contrary to the impression cultivated for many years, Australia is a land of limited resources. Lack of rainfall is the outstanding handicap. A distinguished scientist wrote:

Declining rainfall as one passes inland and lack of any large river systems have, and will for all time, limit settlement and population to east, southeast, and extreme southwest. Australia has a dead heart in the center of 1,000,000 square miles and another 1,000,000 square miles capable at best of sparse pastoral occupation. The tropics climatically are quite dissimilar to the neighboring fertile tropical areas (Dutch East Indies) and are incapable of supporting a large population.

This is a quite different Australia from that envisaged by those who have taken the population figure of 7,000,000 and the area figure of 2,975,000 square miles and concluded that Australia is dangerously underpopulated and underdeveloped. "Limited resources," notes an economist. "Hence the fallacy of inferences based on comparisons with the United States in terms of area."

That is not to say that the development of Australia has reached a peak. It is simply to discipline optimists. An historian commented:

Nearly all Australians are conscious that the area of Australia is roughly the same as that of the United States. In the past they tended to draw false deductions from this fact and look forward to a growth of population and wealth in Australia similar to what has taken place in America. . . . Most of them know better today and realize that our inferior resources make such a development quite impossible.

This long-held belief has nevertheless led us to making efforts to undertake the effective occupation of the whole of our continent, desert, tropical jungle, and all. We have spent God knows how much money on trying to develop the Northern Territory and the interior. We would do better to concentrate on the more valuable areas, and I think we are coming to realize that.

What is the continent like? "Similarity of much of Australia to California and Arizona," wrote a professor of education. Perhaps western Texas should be added to the list. But surprisingly few of my correspondents felt an urge to write of the scenic beauties of the land. They are not absent. They are, perhaps, rather more difficult to appreciate than those of New Zealand, for example, especially for people from the well-watered sections of the Northern Hemisphere. But it is rather remarkable that, other than the romantic gentleman who said to "tell them about our blue skies and our golden beaches, tell them about our beautiful girls and our suntanned men," the only extended comment on the scenery I received was this from a woman novelist:

. . . elaborate the predominant similarity of flora, fauna, and topography throughout Australia as compared with the greater change in other continents. The prevalence of eucalypts throughout, so that, east or west, the bush is still merely the bush with a difference and the shapes of the Blue Mountains (in the east) are the same as the shapes of the Kimberley hills (in the west). Query: does this general and universal similarity help to account for less divergence of type and opinion amongst Australians than among other people of equal sized countries?

That question in geographic determinism is impossible to answer offhand!

Perhaps one reason the Australians don't talk about the scenery is that they are not acutely aware of it, except as a kind of backdrop for their rural economic activities. They are, seven out of ten of them, resident in what the census calls "urban areas," and almost half of them live in half a dozen big "metropolitan" centers, of which the best known are Sydney and Melbourne. I find that this always surprises Americans who think of Australians as riding madly over vast areas after sheep, living in the wilds among black natives and kangaroos.

Australia is a highly urbanized country. Many people regard this in itself as one of Australia's problems. An economist offers this explanation of urbanization:

There has been too much muddled thinking in regard to urbanization in Australia. There are solid reasons for the high urban population: (a) Importance of the wool industry, which requires very little labour. (b) Large-scale farming with machinery. (c) The high standard of living prevents the growth of subsistence farming.

Reverting to the first two factors, there are in the cities numbers of people connected with the finance, transport, and marketing of the products of the country population, and in attending to their wants. It has to be kept in mind that the dry climate over huge sheep, cattle, and wheat areas, prevents the farmers from providing their own food to the extent that this is done in many other countries. Many of these farming areas even have to use condensed milk and canned fruits. The hard fact remains that the finance of town development is much more attractive to financial concerns than rural mortgages.

A further point to keep in mind is that brought forward by another economist: "Primary industries dominate in export returns, but not in national income. Secondary [i.e., manufacturing] industry provides a larger share of employment and income." Naturally the manufacturing industries are in the cities. As a civil servant pointed out, "The trend in the proportions of total breadwinners employed in primary industries has been downward since the beginning of the century . . . and there is every reason to expect the trend to continue after the present war."

But there are plenty of people who object to the cities in Australia, even while living in them! The urban-rural conflict is a political fact of considerable magnitude. For political purposes, the issue is defined in terms different from those employed by economists. A spokesman for rural interests puts it this way:

Growth of large capital cities has been stimulated by an unbalanced political and economic policy. City voting power has played a dominant part in the first thirty years of federation, resulting in advanced social and industrial legislation at the expense of the great primary industries—the real wealth producers. Protection, through tariffs, coastal navigation act, embargoes, etc., has brought about an increase in city population through artificial stimulus causing higher costs to the export primary producers who are unable to pass them on. Struggle between city and country constitutes the nation's basic problem.

A rural political leader states the point of view in slightly different terms:

There are really two Australias—one in urban, commercial, and manufacturing Australia, in these great cities, maintaining a strong, rich, and dominating press, which renders that population articulate; the other an Australia engaged in tremendous industries, like the wool, wheat, butter, sugar, fruit, and mining industries, producing the major part of the wealth of the country, yet, by reason of the magnitude of the area in which it operates, unable to concentrate its efforts on a single object, and largely inarticulate.

Many Australians will find the assertion that the rural interests are "largely inarticulate" rather amusing. But here we are not rehearsing facts; we are merely letting various Australians speak for themselves.

The big point which is of interest to Americans is that Australia has, in the last quarter-century, and with increasing rapidity, developed manufacturing industries. As a leading industrialist put it:

In other countries Australia tends to be thought of mainly as an agricultural country, and its achievements in manufacturing industry are underrated. This misconception should be dispelled. . . . Emphasize the general efficiency of Australian industry and also the important limitations imposed upon mass production and industrial specialization by the size of the population.

With varying emphasis and in words which run the gamut from pride to disapproval, other correspondents also expressed these ideas. Australia today, then, must be thought of as a country which still depends upon the export of raw materials and foodstuffs to pay her bills abroad, whether interest on past borrowings or for

Business section, Sydney—and The Bridge!

St. Kilda Road, Melbourne.

goods currently required, but which at home has developed its manufacturing industries to the point where they are not only of considerable magnitude and complexity but are also the principal employment resource. Before the present war broke out it was generally believed that manufacturing development was the true road forward for Australia; the war has played directly into the hands of those who hold this belief; and in the postwar period it is quite certain to be the basis of economic policy.

Practically all my correspondents had something to say about the place of the labor movement in the national life. Almost to a man they stated their conviction that that place made Australia in some way unique. Some thought that the far-famed social legislation and the court system for handling employer-employee relations somehow made Australia a paradise for the workingman. Some expressed the view that the standard of living was high and that no extreme contrasts of wealth and poverty existed. That this was true was, by some, attributed to the influence of the labor movement. And many implied that the injustices of modern society were, in Australia, considerably tempered by the power of the Australian labor unions and the Australian Labour party. Yet only the conservatives were complacent either about the condition of the workingman or the outlook of the Labour party. Among the liberals and radicals there was much disappointment and dissatisfaction with both. Again and again correspondents played variations on the theme that the labor movement has become sterile. It holds its past gains, but it doesn't have a vital program for the future. Viewing the matter historically, it is likely that the disappointment with the labor movement is a phase of the general disillusion which has overtaken many thoughtful Australians as a result of the course of events during the first four decades of the present century.

Perhaps, as many correspondents suggested, it was the rise of the wage-and-job psychology that destroyed labor's creative idealism. A newspaper editor wrote, "Socialism in Australia has no 'mystique' except since the depression among a labour left-wing minority . . . majority labour prefers to leave the risks to the capitalist and do the best possible for itself by twisting his tail." An employer felt that much of the trouble arises from the "misuse of leisure—the drink problem, the problem of gambling on horse races—by a general inability to use the leisure presented to workers by the short working day in most industries." Another newspaperman felt that the difficulty was in some fashion related to what he called "advanced monopolization aided by imported capital," which had got out of labor's control.

It should be recalled that, quoting a journalist, the "growth of trade unions preceded industrialization" and that they became "strongly established as a result." Thinking of this he pointed out that during the same years in which the trade unions and the political labor movement got started, the Australian spirit of independence was articulate. A few years later the country moved toward industrialization, at first over British objections. To meet this situation, he suggests, there was an increase in Imperial propaganda to combat republicanism and an interlocking of local with Imperial capital, further strengthening Imperial ties. This analysis will arouse the ire of many good Australians. I am quoting it as an expression of opinion. I should like to link it with the views expressed by a respected novelist who is a close student of Australian history:

The first four decades of this century marked the decay of "isolationism" as a spiritual force. But a limiting factor in the new external contacts was that they applied largely to Great Britain, not with the outside world as a whole. Marketing, means of communication, transport, and news-services, fear of Japan—these were often used to tie Australia to imperial policies with which she had small concern. And a sense of economic and military dependence sapped the strength of the creative forces that were plainly evident in Australian life towards the end of the last century.

Since labor was the principal carrier of the creative forces, and its organizations the vehicles of its economic and political expression, it naturally follows that labor was the chief victim of their recession.

Yet I cannot help feeling that there is something wrong with this picture even though it emerges clearly enough from the letters I received. Labor isn't as moribund as these opinions would lead one to think. It is the most powerful single organized force in the Australian community, "the magnetic pole by which all political ships must set their course." In a sense, my correspondents have heaped on labor's head faults for which the Australian community as a whole must bear responsibility. I myself see little evidence to support the implied thesis that labor, acting alone, could have changed the direction of social evolution by any action or series of actions of its own. True, it might have evolved wiser and better policies. But to influence the evolution of the nation it has to carry with it the nation, or at least a majority of its members. If a majority could not be found to support labor, naturally labor could not act. And it is certainly to labor's credit that those who feel that Australia must once more take the high road of emphasizing social welfare after a long tramp along the low road of building industries instinctively relate this task not only to Australia's Great Tradition but also to the revivification of labor.

My correspondents often expressed critical views of politics and politicians. It was stated by a woman leader that there is a "dislike of politicians as a class" running through Australian life and "a disinclination to take an active part or interest in politics." She expressed the idea that "voting was made compulsory in order to get Australians to vote" at all. "Politically," wrote a poet, "they have never been called upon to make up their minds in an irrevocable way about anything vitally important, and accordingly they take their politics in a holiday spirit. Their privileges have come easily. . . ." Said a librarian, "The people are politically minded, but in a party sense rather than in the sense of being strongly conscious of what is essential for the maintenance of free democratic government or that eternal vigilance is the price of liberty." This suggests that the people are indicted for tending to vote party tickets rather than to study issues, but I believe that this is a universal fault in democracies, not peculiar to Australia. It is, perhaps, a bit exaggerated in Australia by compulsory voting. Politics in Australia will revive and engage the best minds when vivid and compelling issues come before the people.

It was frequently suggested that Americans would be interested in the fact that the Australian constitution was modeled on the American, with elements from the British parliamentary system superimposed. The country is organized on a federal basis, there being six huge states. Many writers expressed the conviction that the federal system was in a state of crisis in Australia and that the crisis would have to be resolved in the postwar period or chaos would ensue. The distribution of powers as between the states and the Federal government is thought faulty, and a redistribution in favor of the Federal authority was often suggested. Related to this is the widespread conviction that Australia is suffering from overgovernment; that seven million people do not require thirteen houses of parliament. (Every state has two houses, excepting Queensland which has one; and the two Federal houses are set over these.) A banker suggested the reorganization of Australia into four huge zones, each occupying roughly a quarter of the continent, the whole to be run under a unitary rather than a federal system. "This," he said, "would give the opportunity of bringing the best political leaders together in one parliament and, similarly, have the beneficial effect of amalgamating the various Civil Services." Even those who don't suggest as drastic a solution as this clearly see that changes must be made. A distinguished civil servant wrote: "The attempt to solve our major problems with the existing constitution is well-nigh impossible. Attempts to solve production and marketing problems and social security problems must be largely futile under the present constitution. Australia, like most other countries, is trying to solve the problems of a neo-technic age with an eo-technic organization." Thinking along the same lines, a man who has made a career of public administration wrote of "the problem of administering large modern developments of government policy in the economic field in a federal structure based on eighteenth-century ideas of laissez faire."

These ideas are familiar to Americans, though the problems which suggest them are more obvious in Australia than here, for the Australian governments are charged with the responsibility for a greater variety of services than the American. The tradition of calling in the state to carry out projects of all kinds is very old in Australia. Some of those who commented thought it originated in the paternalism inseparable from the administration of a convict colony, but others attributed it to the character of the continent, which made railways, for example, hopelessly unattractive to private enterprise since they had to traverse huge areas which would never be closely settled. Australia has gone far along the road toward the bureaucratic state, and even the rise of private enterprise in industrial affairs has failed to temper the tendency as signally as private enterprise in the pastoral and farming industries failed earlier. The people look to the state for aid and comfort, for railways and electricity and old age pensions. A distinguished judge was one among several correspondents who said that "The relation of men to the state is entirely unsatisfactory. There is too little sense of obligation and at the same time too little sense of individual self-reliance." A woman novelist put it differently: "The tendency remains to let the state help on all possible (and impossible) occasions, without at the same time creating a society in which the state is freed from private competition." A librarian summed up, "As a result, largely, of geographical and economic conditions, Australia is—and has been from the first—accustomed to a high degree of state paternalism—hence the tendency to use the government as a leaning post."

It has been suggested that within the last half-century the Australians have moved from a sense of isolation from the world to a sense of dependence on Great Britain. It would be wrong, I think, to say that either emotion was ever an absolute principle. As yesterday's isolation was supported by a sense of security within the British Empire, so today's dependence is tempered by self-reliance. A lawyer puts the present position thus: "The two conflicting 'pulls' on Australia: toward Britain and toward independence." The relative strength of the "pulls" depends upon the world situation. Today, due to the war, the former is the more important.

As a nation with a civilization European in character, Australia feels herself closer, in spite of her geographical position, to the great centers of that civilization than to neighboring non-European countries. A woman novelist wrote:

. . . The average Australian feels much closer to London (and New York) than to Durban or Singapore. . . . It would be almost safe to say that we never really imagine ourselves as cut off by many miles of dark countries or wide seas from the rest of the English-speaking world. It still gives us a shock to be thought far-away either by Britishers or Americans.

The tie to London—the strongest overseas tie—is composed of many elements, well analyzed by a civil servant whose field is foreign relations:

Australia's ties with Britain are imperial; racial and sentimental; cultural; economic, the United Kingdom has always provided the major market for Australian primary production; defense, Australia rightly regards the British navy as the first line of Australia's defense; and legal, the final court of appeal is still the Privy Council.

But, however strong the tie, it would be wrong to assume that all Australians delight in it. A vigorous opposition statement is the following:

Mental vassalage to London is resented by a few independent souls who would dispense with the feudal officials and snobs wished on us by Great Britain, but it would be futile to replace them by native exploiters with worse manners or by American bagmen [i.e., travelling salesmen] with chewing gum and ingenious but superfluous gadgets, which is what would happen inevitably under a continuance of the present system of economics, no matter who emerges from the war.

With all possible reservations taken into account, Australia's tie to Britain is the determining factor in her outlook. It has increased in strength lately because of the war. But the events of the war are also forcing a reassessment of the Australian position, particularly in the Pacific Basin.

The rise of Japan was cited as a factor in breaking down Australia's sense of isolation. Today the Australian view of Japan is mixed, as is shown by two quotations, one from a newspaper proprietor, the other from an editor:

Australians are very touchy on the question of Japan's southward movements but would welcome friendship.

In the Pacific we have leaned towards appeasing Japan through fearing and distrusting her. This is due mainly to geographic fright. . . . Australia is probably the chief cause of weakness in recent British Pacific policy. This could be altered by firmer confidence between Australia and the United States.

The Australians know themselves incapable of meeting Japan on an equal footing and therefore are seeking outside support for their firm desire to escape the Japanese net. This, among other things, leads them to look hopefully toward the United States, a powerful Pacific nation holding views similar to their own.

The expressions of desire to move closer to the United States were many and varied in the letters I received. Some writers recalled that Australians have not always been friendly to the United States, a librarian stating:

> Over all there is a growing tendency to turn to the United States, and this is rapidly extinguishing the previous ignorant and ill-informed pro-British, anti-Yankee attitude which was common amongst all classes.

How strong the desire of today can be is reflected in the proposition of a veteran labor journalist:

> That our country and America must inevitably draw ever closer together in the international sphere, until this trend culminates in an alliance so powerfully cemented by common interests that its dislocation will come to seem unthinkable.

Even those who are uncertain as to how to draw closer still want to move toward the United States. A newspaper editor dwelt upon some of the difficulties:

> There is a widespread feeling of the danger of relying on American policy. Firmness in the Pacific must take into account the possibility of war, and the question for Australia is whether the U.S. will be there with "the goods." Australians recognize the dislike of commitments in advance in the U.S. and their necessity for Australia. Australians are troubled by the fear of instability in American foreign policy due to the dual control by the Administration and the Senate. . . . Congress very close to the emotional movements of public opinion . . . the permanent isolationist trend . . . suspicion in the U.S. lest America should be used to serve the interests of other powers. . . .

This editor went on to remark that "there is now a feeling in Australia that this country has little to hope for economically from America" but added that "economics are not the primary consideration." What, then, is the consideration? A newspaper owner stated it as follows: "The strategic importance of Australia to America if the *status quo* between Australia, Japan, and the Indies is threatened or cannot be enforced by Great Britain owing to defeat or preoccupation on the Continent." Quite apart from the current difficulties in the Pacific, many Australians expect the United States to play a larger role in the Australian future than she has in the Australian past. One political leader suggested how by saying, "In seeking opportunity the American slogan has always been 'Go West, young man.' Now that the western United States is so highly developed, Australia is still a western land of opportunity."

Many articulate Australians take little satisfaction in the immediate past of their country. I think that a healthy sign. And that it is, is shown by the high resolutions expressed about the future. I have quoted the statement that Australia still feels "that she has an individual contribution to make to the world's future." I have also hinted that the Australian Great Tradition provides an ideology for future advances, adjustments being made to take account of changed circumstances. A conservative politician stated that even from his angle the Great Tradition is a fixed point of reference:

Our ideal is a community without great class distinctions, or distinctions of rank, or great differences of wealth. A community free from the hatreds of the old worlds, but tuned to the best in European as well as American culture . . . we intend to participate in a just peace settlement, and we intend to plan reconstruction here with wider social justice and greater opportunities for all.

With much the same purpose in mind, a civil servant stated, "The Commonwealth should be vested with full powers so that plans for Australia as a whole may be evolved, but many of the powers should then be delegated to provincial bodies whose personnel is in close touch with the groups affected by any action taken." Plans require research. A librarian declared:

Australia is not so much poor in persons capable of research as in the equipment and provision for it. As I see it, Australia's development would be greatly helped by the development of postgraduate research in our universities, of industrial and scientific research, and of research in the social sciences.

Suggested fields of action were:

There is room for investment of possibly £100,000,000 by the governments . . . over a period of say twenty to thirty years, to conserve water.

Full scale attack on soil erosion, coupled with afforestation.

Exploitation of the wealth of the waters around the continent by a fish canning industry.

Solution of the internal transport problem by eliminating the railway gauge breaks. (The railways of no two Australian states completely interconnect because of differing gauges.)

The extension of manufacturing.

Further improvements in the social services, health services, and housing.

Extension and elaboration of educational facilities and cultural institutions generally.

All, it may be added, motivated by the purpose of raising the standard of living in Australia, both in material terms and culturally—this to be done in the light of the egalitarian principle which has inspired so many social movements in the Commonwealth.

What the Australians appear to be groping for is a way to utilize their resources for production in a fashion which will benefit the masses of the people, thus insuring a firm economic basis for democracy. My correspondents in no instance suggested that the answer is to be found by allegiance to any socialist program. They appeared to feel that while vast administrative changes are necessary, and also perhaps a changed attitude toward money and credit, no revolutionary shift in social power was required. It was even implied that the bureaucratic state can do the job if given its head and not hamstrung by constitutional obstacles and vested economic interests. What is really needed is a return to the ideology of fifty years ago, tempered and redefined in the light of subsequent internal developments and the place of Australia in the world. She will then, it is suggested, realize her ideal.

The unanswered question is, "Will she get a chance to do this?" Only if the war is won. A labor leader wrote, "A peace-loving people, Australians are fighting this war because they see the liberties, privileges, and standards of living won by political and industrial battling threatened by the triumph of Fascist ideology."

This is how Australians see Australia. How do you see your country?

Part Two

THIS IS AUSTRALIA

3. A CONTINENT

THE American traveler who sets out for Australia from San Francisco or Los Angeles first sees Australia at Sydney, the capital city of the state of New South Wales. As one approaches the coast it looms up in stern, rocky cliffs. The ship sails directly at them and goes, with dramatic suddenness, between two imposing headlands—"The Heads"—into Sydney Harbor, officially called Port Jackson. "Our Harbor" is the pride of all true-blue Sydneyites and their devotion a subject of quiet amusement to other Australians. "Our 'arbor which art in heaven . . ." Its innumerable arms—sunken river valleys—extend in all directions, and hardly a visitor ever sees them all frequently enough to name them on sight. On every harbor journey he makes—speedy ferries dart about everywhere—he sees a new vista that lifts up his spirits. From the water's edge rise tiers of red-roofed single-family houses or, in certain quarters, tall blocks of flats, usually buried in the green of trees. The blue of the water, the green of the foliage, the red roofs—these compose the color symphony of Sydney, a symphony most brilliant when bathed in the extraordinarily vivid Australian sunshine. Arching across the harbor is a tremendous bridge which connects the old city with the north shore and its many residential suburbs, symbolic perhaps of Australia's conquest of nature and certainly the object of an enthusiastic admiration second only to that devoted to the harbor itself.

Over a million and a quarter English-speaking people, who follow British customs modified by local circumstances into Australian ways, live on the shores of this magnificent sheet of water—nearly a fifth of the people on the continent. They work in factories, banks, offices; they are employed by merchants who deal in locally produced and imported goods; they handle the wool, wheat, meat, butter, fruits, and minerals that go overseas to market. Railways radiate out from Sydney all over the huge state, six thousand miles of them, and drain the produce to the coast. The trading, manufacturing, and banking, the intellectual and social life tend to concentrate around a single focal point in each state—in New South Wales, Sydney. Victoria, to the south, supports the great city of Melbourne with a population of a million; Queensland, to the north, Brisbane with 325,000; Tasmania, the island state off the southeastern coast, Hobart with 60,000; South Australia, Adelaide with 320,000; and Western Australia, off by itself facing the Indian Ocean, Perth with 220,000. The pulse of Australia beats in its cities, but the lifeblood is drawn from far and wide, and only as it is pumped back and forth along the railway lines and highways is Australia economically healthy. The 7,000,000 Australians live mostly on the edges of the continent, almost half of them in the great coastal cities. That is why the amazing Australian beaches are the real playgrounds of a continental nation.

Australia is a land of vast distances. Like the Americans, the Australians can travel thousands of miles in a straight line and still be within their own country. Their continent has an area about the same as continental United States. But, whereas the Americans have carved forty-eight states out of their country, the Australians have thus far found need for but five, plus a huge federally controlled territory on the mainland, and a sixth state on the adjacent island of Tasmania. In order of economic importance the states are New South Wales, Victoria, Queensland, South Australia, Western Australia, and Tasmania. The Northern Territory is a problem area. In every case except Tasmania, the political divisions include vast sweeps of dry country in which intensive development is forever unlikely. (The lakes which usually are shown on Australian maps are mostly dry.) If the really good parts of Australia were gathered together in one block, it would include about a fourth of the continent. Professor Griffith Taylor, whose realism often offends superpatriotic Australians, divides the continent according to its economic utility as follows:

About 42% is arid, of which 20% is almost useless for stock and 22% of which is fair pastoral country, except during bad droughts.

About 34% is good pastoral country under normal conditions.

About 21% is fair temperate-climate farming country, suitable for close settlement, of which 13% receives over 20 inches of rain per annum and 8% receives less than 20 inches. It is in this area, chiefly found in southeastern Australia, that the bulk of the population has always been found and probably always will be found.

About 3% is tropical with a uniform rainfall throughout most of the year and capable of intensive agricultural development.

It is predominantly a warm country. Snow falls only in the highlands of the southeast and in Tasmania. Only one or two towns of any significance have to wrestle with it. Centrally heated homes are uncommon. There is much more use for air conditioning than for heating. The country is unlike northern Europe or northern North America. The climate is, to a great extent, Mediterranean, or, in American terms, like Southern California.

On a continent as vast as Australia there are many types of scenery, and while the varieties may not be as extraordinarily numerous as in North America or Europe, they are sufficiently diverse to escape any casual generalization. Australia is a pastel country. The landscape is a medley of half tones in greens, browns, yellows, and reds. But even to the observation that the green of the foilage is not deep but gray-green, which is true in the main, there is the exception of such areas as the Queensland coastal tropics where the green is as gratefully normal to Northern Hemisphere eyes as anyone could wish.

Though Australia lacks a vast mountain range with sky-piercing peaks, still it has Mount Kosciusko, on which snow piles up. Only 5 per cent of the Australian land surface has an elevation of over 2,000 feet. The maze of precipitous hills, with deep valleys running every which way and leading nowhere, which lies back of Sydney —the Blue Mountains—is truly Australian, though perhaps untypical. So, too, is the range of low hills which runs north and south just west of Cloncurry in Queensland. Apparently the final stand of what ages and ages ago was a fine mountain range, they are today a wilderness of mounds of all shapes and sizes. This country looks very old, old and weary. One of the pilots on the plane in which I flew over it asked me if I had ever flown over an older country. The truth is that while a young country historically, Australia is an old continent geologically, and many of its plants and animals have forms which elsewhere in the world have passed permanently into the fossil stage.

Most of the attractive photographs of Australian scenery which are seen in America are of vistas on or near the seacoast; and, as remarked before, only the traveler who is more interested in man and his works than in the extravagances of nature can profitably travel far and wide in Australia.

A striking exception to this generalization is the Great Barrier Reef off the coast of Queensland. It extends for twelve hundred miles and is probably the best known abroad of Australia's natural features. It is equally attractive to the tourist, the fishing enthusiast, the geologist, and the ichthyologist. It is unique of its kind in the world and of inexhaustible interest. The face the Reef turns to the sky and to the curious humans who stare at it from a glass-bottomed boat or tray held alongside consists of a fascinating conglomeration of coral formations, colored in all the rainbow hues and shaped as variously. In and among the coral swim vivid fishes of all shades of blue, red, yellow, green, and purple. In the learned and popular books of scientists all this life is named and its extraordinary functioning told in detail. I cannot say that it is helpful to have such knowledge in one's head when looking at the Reef, though the books make interesting reading and the pictures create anticipatory pleasure and revive the memory in after days. It is rather as a spectacle, a wonderful and vivid picture, that amateurs should view it, a superb *tour de force* of nature, as charming and unforced as a field of vivid flowers, made perhaps more startling because the medium is the water, not the more familiar air and earth. It is the most lovely thing in Australia.

But what is *typical* Australian scenery? It is, I think, "the bush," but the bush varies! The term is one which has a most elastic meaning, stretching to cover almost any area outside the towns and cities, no matter where located. Two fairly distinct kinds of bush characterize Australia reasonably well, however, the hilly bush and the interior plains.

The Three Sisters, Blue Mountains, near Katoomba.

The mighty gums of Australia.

The former is chiefly found near the coast, and good samples of it can be glimpsed on a journey between the great cities of Sydney and Melbourne. It consists of low, rolling hills, grassed to the top, interspersed with large grassy valleys. Trees are scattered about in fair profusion, and the total effect is of a land which has at some remote time been tamed by man but which has escaped him to go its own way once more. This is not, of course, the case at all, for when it is pasture country it is just as man found it, except that he may have "ring-barked" some of the trees to give the grass a chance. The ring-barked trees have had a narrow belt of their bark chipped away at a convenient height from the ground that they may bleed and die. In the dry Australian climate they do not quickly fall once they are dead, but continue to stand in gray and haunting majesty, giving the countryside where they are numerous a ghostly character which can be unpleasant to sensitive persons, as several Australian writers have made clear.

The interior plains differ from the hilly bush chiefly in their flatness and, when you get far into the inland country, by their dryness. In western Queensland I traveled for many miles through bush country which was, to my inexperienced eye, indistinguishable from the country in western New South Wales far to the south. This bush is reasonably well grassed and dotted with trees, occasionally in quite dense clusters, but not infrequently there are patches of bare ground, either sandy earth or clay. The patches of clay, known as clay-pans, are often extensive enough to be natural airports—I have boarded planes on such ports—and traveling by automobile over this roadless country the motorist can pick up considerable speed when crossing them, say fifty miles an hour. The bush can, when one is in the right mood, be compared to a park. Indeed the pioneers frequently used the word park to describe the country. I am told that during the great droughts the grass disappears and the red or black soil is all that one can see, barring the trees—a true desert. I am also told that when the rains come and the grass springs up fresh and green and flowers bloom by millions, the park-like nature of the country is even more obvious. I have never seen it in either extreme.

In the bush I have seen, the grass is, where Mitchell grass prevails, straw-colored like cured hay. It is dry and will burn like tinder if set alight. Flinders grass, the other common type, dries red, and from an airplane it is difficult to distinguish it from the red earth. Imagine, then, the Australian bush as country consisting of flat to gently rolling land, dotted with trees and carpeted with straw-colored grass.

What is beautiful about the bush? That is what the early pioneers frequently asked themselves, and frequently their reply was, "Nothing! It is simply good sheep country." Even some of the early, British-born Australian writers and painters reacted unfavorably to it. They found it gloomy and oppressive and cursed it. "What is the dominant note of Australian scenery?" asked Marcus Clarke. "That which is the dominant note in Edgar Allan Poe's poetry—weird melancholy," he replied. Today this strikes the native-born Australians, especially those from the bush itself, as queer nonsense. In spite of being a foreigner, but not an Englishman, I have never reacted adversely to the bush. The bush is beautiful in an eerie way; it is never, to my mind, melancholy; it is rather almost unbearably and unreasonably cheerful when bathed, as it usually is, in incredibly bright sunshine. Really to see the beauties of Australia—and especially of the bush—one must retrain one's eye. Only when native-born painters appeared did the true appeal of the country get transferred to canvas. When clearly seen —when intruding memories of other beauties are put aside—it is magical. It is beautiful. And it is Australian. There is even an occasional surprise. Sometimes one will see a tree apparently covered with large pink and white flowers. As one approaches, the flowers take wing; they are galahs.

Australia is the home of the marsupial animals that are so uncommon on other continents, the animals that carry their young in pouches until they are mature enough to fend for themselves. The most famous of these is the kangaroo, the symbol of Australia; but wallabies, wombats, and koalas are just as strange. It is the koala which sat as a model for the world-famous teddy bear. Even more outrageously strange than any of these is the duck-billed platypus. This queer beast which grows only to the length of two feet is considered by scientists the most primitive of living mammals. Its body is covered with fine fur; its snout looks like the bill of a duck; it lays eggs; and it suckles its young. No wonder that on discovering such animals as these the early settlers wondered what kind of place they had gotten into.

It used to be said, and sometimes still is, that Australia is a land of bright-colored birds that cannot sing and bright-colored flowers that have no smell. This statement has just enough truth in it to be annoying. There are many birds of brilliant plumage that can't sing and many striking flowers that lack perfume, but Australia has her share of native songsters and pleasantly perfumed flowers. Scientists have identified 616 species of bird that breed in Australia, and few of them are found in all parts of the continent. Those the visitor will want to see are the lyrebird, an extraordinary mimic; the bowerbird, which builds a decorated playground and solemnly dances in it; the numerous parrot-like birds, some of which are gayly colored; the emu, which resembles the ostrich and appears with the kangaroo on the national seal; and the kookaburra, popularly known as the "laughing jackass," which instead of singing emits a raucous "laugh" at the most disconcerting moments. The ornithologist, amateur or professional, will not lack occupation in Australia. For one thing, he can entertain himself distinguishing local from introduced birds, among which is the omnipresent sparrow.

Flowers are present in profusion. It is hard to think of Australia without thinking of them. Among the native flowers the wattle is perhaps the best known. Akin to the mimosa of America, several hundred varieties have been identified. The commonest are yellow, consisting of clusters of little balls of fluff, delicately scented. The boronia is also an exceedingly well-liked flower, growing in greatest profusion in Western Australia, the home of an extraordinary variety of wild flowers. The most common boronia has small, cup-shaped blossoms, usually a brown outside and golden green inside, with a dark-green leaf and stem and a pungent perfume. The fragrance of a small bunch is to some tastes almost overpowering. (A delightful sweet perfume is made of the boronia.) Other striking wild flowers that have common fame are the waratah which, in eastern Australia, consists of a huge ball of red gathered up in a kind of cup of petals markedly larger than those forming the center; the flannel flower, so named from the texture and color of the petals and center; and the extraordinary banksia, a favorite with painters who do flower pieces, which, to put it crudely, resembles a huge purple-colored pine cone! Flowers are extremely popular among all classes as decorations for the home. The Australians have become, in recent years, great gardeners. Only a few of the wild flowers have been domesticated, so the introduced varieties are the objects of intense solicitude.

Among the trees, the eucalyptus family predominates, and three hundred and fifty different species have been described. There may be more. Some of them have beautiful flowers, the most striking being the flowering red gums of Western Australia. (Not all red gums have flowers!) They usually grow—the species that are true trees—to the height of 100 to 150 feet. Broadly, five kinds are commonly distinguished, the ironbarks, the stringybarks, the woolly-butts, the bloodwoods, and the smooth-barked gums proper. All the eucalyptus trees are loosely called "gums." The best-known scrub eucalypt is the mallee which has given its name to a rather poor belt of wheat country which extends through New South Wales, Victoria, and South Australia. The wood of the eucalypts that have commercial importance is hard; it is put to a wide variety of uses, and it often has a beautiful grain. The continent of Australia has the smallest percentage of commercially valuable forest lands of all the continents, and it is notably deficient in soft woods. Lumbering is carried on in all the states, and scientific forestry is practiced to some degree by all of them. For example, in south-western Western Australia, where hardwoods known as karri and jarrah flourish, the state authorities have taken charge of the forests and, using modern methods, have worked out a scheme for permanent production. Considerable efforts have been made in various parts of the country to apply modern afforestation methods, especially to develop a softwood supply. Of course there are many trees in Australia other than the gums, but the gums are so completely characteristic that the smell of them, which is pungent, will make an Australian homesick if he encounters it abroad. They are found in numbers in Southern California, southern France, Abyssinia, and many other places, being a most adaptable tree. On the other hand, many foreign trees have been acclimatized in Australia, some of which have run wild, like the weeping willow.

Many early settlers in Australia determinedly introduced not only trees, but also flowers, birds, and small animals from overseas in an effort to make the country familiar and hence livable to them. In the case of plants and animals of commercial importance, like wheat and sheep, such adventures in acclimatization proved a great boon, and those who carried them out became heroes. But some imported things of no particular value liked the new environment too well and increased and multiplied to such an extent as to become pests. This is true of rabbits among the animals and the prickly pear among the plants. Immense amounts of money are spent annually in trying to control and exterminate the rabbits, which are very destructive of pastures, but no really successful method of dealing with them has yet been discovered. Large sums have been spent in fighting the prickly pear, which overran large areas of rich land. The scientists say that when settlers invade a new land with new plants and animals the "ecological balance" is upset. Sometimes that leads to disaster, and those responsible for unprofitable upsets have no honor in the history books.

Probably no part of Australia is the subject of more widespread misinformation than the tropical portion. It is empty. But it is not empty because of any dog-in-the-manger policies followed by the Australians. Its existence as an empty area is not a provocation to any but the ignorant. It is not rich. It is terribly poor.

Tropical Australia is divided between three administrations, the states of Queensland and Western Australia, and the Commonwealth, which controls Northern Territory. It includes about 40 per cent of the territory of the Commonwealth, well over a million square miles. Only Queensland has a tropical area which can be developed intensively. Along the northeastern coast, facing the Barrier Reef, is a narrow strip of country which, all told, makes up 3 per cent of the entire continent and less than 10 per cent of the area within the tropics. It alone of all the tropical country of Australia has a regular rainfall the year around and is well adapted to tropical agriculture. In this region Australia's cane-sugar industry has been developed and something like close settlement of a white population achieved. This small fraction of the Australian tropics is chiefly a one-crop area, for perishable fruits, a logical crop, cannot be easily handled over long distances in quantity—though some are grown. Moreover, Australia is such a warm continent that fruits like oranges and lemons can be grown far to the south, even in Victoria, South Australia, and Western Australia. (In southern Western Australia I have seen apple orchards and orange groves side by side on the same farm.) Perhaps the Queensland papaya-growers will experience a boom in the postwar period, for an extract of that fruit has been found important to the preparation of unshrinkable woolen goods. Where conditions are favorable, the Australians have brought their tropical country into fairly intensive production. It carries two-thirds of all the population in tropical Australia, or upwards of one hundred fifty thousand people. Practically all the rest of tropical Australia is unfavorable to intensive production; it is grazing country, an exception being the Atherton Tableland back of Cairns in north Queensland (twelve thousand square miles) which is adapted to dairying, timber, and mineral production, and the growing of corn. The Tableland did not appear to me, when I traveled through it, to be as rich as enthusiasts represent it. Tropical Australia outside the Queensland coastal plains is predominantly poor country.

The rainfall is strictly seasonal. There are two seasons, the "wet" and the "dry." This makes tropical agriculture most difficult, barring the building of expensive irrigation works, and, when coupled with the fact that good soil is found only in patches, practically rules out agriculture as a basis for development.

The country is believed to be rich in minerals, but only a few spots have been "proved" and fewer still are under exploitation, notably at Mount Isa in western Queensland. Mount Isa is in the midst of those old, old hills of which I spoke earlier. The silver-lead mine was discovered in 1925 and brought into production in 1931. The American Smelting and Refining Company holds a 30 per cent interest, and all the principal figures on the technical staff are Americans. The mine is connected with the seacoast by railway, a distance of six hundred miles. In most parts of tropical Australia, however, transport is poor and expensive, and only highly valuable minerals are apt to be produced. It is alleged that there are deposits of gold, silver-lead-zinc, copper, tin, scheelite, etc. If all the deposits could be brought into profitable production, that would indeed transform the picture, but this is unlikely in the visible future. No responsible Australian authority has ever said that the *basic* activity in most of tropical Australia will ever be anything other than grazing.

I have purposely kept clear of the question of white men living and working in the climate of this region, for all competent observers are inclined to discount its significance as a crippling handicap. Although Griffith Taylor has stated that "except for a portion of the Sahara the Australian tropics are hotter than any other region of the world," it should be recalled that heat in itself is not a menacing factor, however uncomfortable it may be. White settlement throughout the Australian tropics is a matter of adaptation, of housing and diet especially.

Speaking of the prospects of the Northern Territory portion of the tropics, the last full-dress commission to study the area said,

We suggest . . . that with wise administration the population may, within about a decade, be increased to fifteen thousand white people or about three times the number which now exists. Within twenty-five years the population might possibly grow to 40,000 persons.

That does not imply richness. But from all I can learn from a study of the copious literature, it seems to be the truth about tropical Australia, at least about that nine-tenths of it which sprawls across the continent from Queensland's coastal hills to the Indian Ocean.

The aborigines of Australia came off badly in their contacts with the white invaders. They were nomads, living off the country, having developed neither permanent dwellings nor agriculture. It is customary to say that they were low in the scale of civilization, but as is so often the case with such people, their adaptation to their environment was intricate and in many respects remarkable. Professor A. P. Elkin, the distinguished Australian anthropologist, states that, "In view of the differences which exist between the aborigine and the other great divisions of mankind . . . the Australian aborigine is now classified in a special group, the Australoid." They are utterly different from the native people of the islands near Australia, like New Guinea and New Caledonia, who were broadly classified as Melanesians, and equally unlike the Polynesians farther east. Anthropologists still find the tribal customs of the Australian natives a fascinating study, especially the conception of kinship and the ritual dancing and decorative symbolic art. While neither numerous nor well-organized enough to offer much forcible opposition to the white men, after the fashion of the American Indians, they nevertheless did resist and consequently suffered hard treatment at the hands of some of the early settlers and occasionally were brutally slaughtered as one might slaughter vermin. Today the few that remain are a perennial problem to prick the conscience of the white population. Only lately have any well-founded plans for their welfare been formulated, in spite of the fact that the anthropologists and interested laymen have been prodding the governments for years. Probably as pathetic a native people as the world contains today, the Australian aborigines are yet men and worthy of intelligent and careful treatment at the hands of those who took their homeland from them. The casual visitor to Australia is not likely to see aborigines, least of all chance upon any living as their forefathers did. Those who are in contact with the whites usually live precariously on the fringes of the national economy, often under conditions it would dignify to call "slum." The half-castes are an especially pathetic people. The aborigines flourish best when their contacts with the white people are fewest. In recent years some Australian artists have tried to put aboriginal designs to modern uses. The boomerang is, of course, a native weapon which is also a symbol of Australia in the minds of thousands of foreigners.

4. THE MAKING OF A COMMONWEALTH

IN THE year 1786 the British government decided to take definite steps to solve a problem in penology that had been kept in abeyance since the outbreak of the American Revolution. That war had put an end to the accepted practice of disposing of British criminals by transporting them to the American colonies. Not only did the severe criminal code of those days multiply the number of offenders against the law of the land, but also the internal social turmoil of England occasioned by the Industrial Revolution so unsettled the population as to "make" criminals at an astonishing rate. There was a widening gap between the actual social conditions of the land and the law and policy under which it was governed. The "carnival of crime" which jaundiced observers thought they saw in England was a symptom of maladjustment. With dogged persistence the authorities tried to cure the disease by drastic action against the symptom. A phase of their policy was transportation of certain classes of criminals to the British possessions beyond the seas.

Since the American outlet was blocked, the authorities decided, after considerable discussion, to follow the advice of Sir Joseph Banks, first proffered in 1779, and establish a new penal colony in the land along the eastern coast of which he had sailed in 1770 while serving as botanist under Captain James Cook. Specifically, Banks recommended Botany Bay in New Holland as a suitable place for a settlement. In definitely planning to execute Banks's suggestion, the British authorities were undertaking to plant a European colony on a continent about which they, in common with all peoples, knew very little indeed. The continent in its entirety was then called New Holland, while the coast to which Captain Cook had laid claim in the name of his king was designated New South Wales. The name Australia was not generally applied to the continent until after 1820.

The command of the expedition to Botany Bay was entrusted to Captain Arthur Phillip, and an excellent choice it was. On January 20, 1788, after a voyage of eight months and one week from England, the First Fleet, consisting of six transports and three supply ships, was assembled in Banks's Botany Bay. The Bay proving on examination to be an unsuitable place for a settlement, Captain Phillip ordered explorations to be undertaken. What a member of the exploring party called a "noble and capacious harbour" was found. On its shores the foundations of the city of Sydney were laid, the first settlers leaving the ships on January 26th. Exactly how many individuals took part in establishing the English settlement in New South Wales is a matter for dispute. It is certain that they did not exceed one thousand, two hundred of them military men assigned to guard the others who were still technically in jail. Many of the prisoners were old, sick, and feeble, so carelessly had they been assembled by the prison authorities.

A more unfavorable beginning for a colony can scarcely be imagined, and many years elapsed before it could stand on its own feet. The growth of the population was spasmodic. In 1815, after over a quarter-century of existence, there were but fifteen thousand individuals in the settlement. It was not until 1835 that the numbers rose above one hundred thousand, by which time there were other settlements on the continent in addition to that at Sydney; and not until sometime between 1850 and 1855 were as many as five hundred thousand persons to be found in Australia. After that level was reached events conspired to accelerate the rate of growth, the million mark being passed by 1860, the two million mark twenty years later, the five million mark during the First World War, leading to the present population of a little in excess of seven million. These bare figures conceal a good deal of history.

The continent on which Captain Phillip landed was more suspected than actually known to exist for close to two hundred years before the English decided on settlement. The Dutch had sighted the west coast of the land mass while on voyages to the East Indies via the Cape of Good Hope, and there is an authentic record of a landing by them in 1616. It was the Dutch also who first touched on the northern and southeastern coasts, but they did not connect their isolated contacts in a fashion which would have allowed them even to outline the continent, nor did they attempt settlement, since they almost uniformly touched on inhospitable coasts. The Portuguese explorers had similar experiences, as did the earliest of the English adventurers, William Dampier, who landed on the barren northwestern shore. When Captain James Cook sailed along the eastern coast in 1770, he made known more of the new continent than any previous explorer, and he had the good luck to find the very best part of it. But he did not join his discoveries with those of the Dutch to form a coherent conception of the whole. Indeed, his explorations were so incomplete that he failed to establish such an elementary point as that Van Diemen's Land (Tasmania since 1853) was an island. This was not made clear until 1798, ten years after Sydney was founded. And of course what the interior might hold was only slowly revealed.

The unveiling of the mysterious interior could best be illustrated by one of those animated maps used sometimes in the newsreels. Briefly, until 1813 when the incredible jumble of mountains back of Sydney was crossed, very little progress was made in continental exploration, though a good deal was done by sea. Once started, the exploration of the interior went forward rapidly. Between 1813 and 1875 practically the whole continent was traversed, but even today there are minor isolated areas, probably of small economic importance, that are still to be trodden by white men. Long before intrepid explorers ceased to strike out into the unknown, most of the "good country" was known and occupied. A surprising amount of the detailed exploration of Australia was done by pioneer pastoralists seeking new pastures.

The early years of the settlement at Sydney were overshadowed by the Napoleonic Wars which prevented the Imperial authorities from taking much interest in or positive action with regard to it. Nevertheless it was impossible for the community to be without a history. In the original instance, the Imperial plan, apart from the primary purpose of establishing a jail, was to develop Australia on the basis of a small-holding peasantry recruited largely from convicts who had served their terms or been pardoned. This program was rudely shattered during the period of neglect. During the years that elapsed between Governor Phillip's leaving the colony in December, 1792, and the arrival of his successor in September, 1795, when the colony was under the control of the military, the officers brought their own plan into full operation. They contrived to gain economic control of the community by establishing a trading monopoly which enabled them mercilessly to exploit the entire population, especially since they used rum as the principal medium of exchange. The few small holders were almost all driven into debt, bankruptcy, and servitude. By forcing the landholders to forfeit their property and by obtaining grants for themselves direct from the governing authorities, the military men became great landholders as well as monopolist traders. They solved the problem of labor supply by arranging that convicts be assigned to them to work on the land and generally serve as a cheap source of labor supply. In this fashion the settlement was milked for the benefit of a tiny minority.

John Macarthur, who had originally arrived in New South Wales in 1790 as a member of the military, was the prime mover in establishing this monopolistic system, though he was technically a free settler. He was also engaged in experiments in sheep breeding designed to improve the quality of the wool produced. He was thus bringing some of the wealth he was wringing from the community to the service of the community (and of course himself!) by feeling his way toward what was to become the basic industry of the continent, wool growing. The monopoly was a retrogressive economic step, but the experiments in wool growing proved astoundingly dynamic. To be successful, wool production required the holding of large areas of pasture lands by individuals, a small but subservient labor supply, and a steady market abroad. The natural pastures of Australia, especially those found across the mountains in 1813, proved admirably adapted to sheep grazing. Those interested in extending the industry carried on a lengthy political struggle for a system of land tenure suited to their purposes, and the English woolen mills proved capable of absorbing all the wool Australia could supply. It is one of the little ironies of Australian history that Captain William Bligh—he of the *Bounty* fame—was sent to Australia in 1806 to break up the monopolistic system which Macarthur favored. The clash of wills between Macarthur and Bligh produced, in 1808, the so-called "Rum Rebellion" in which Bligh was deposed from his governorship. Though in the immediate instance Bligh lost and Macarthur won, the irony arises from the fact that only when the monopolistic system finally collapsed could Macarthur's pastoral schemes really flourish; and it was the dynamic character of those schemes which in the end made the monopoly untenable. It should be added also that, on the record, Bligh was right and Macarthur wrong in the Rum Rebellion. Dr. Herbert Vere Evatt in his study of the episode convicts Macarthur of treason.

As early as 1804 Macarthur was able to interest English wool dealers and manufacturers in the Australian product, though they did not agree with his optimistic forecast that Australian wools would free England of dependence upon Spanish and German supplies. Indeed, most of what Macarthur had to say in 1804 was based upon optimism, but he was proved later to have made a correct guess as to the possibilities. In any case he was able to induce the Imperial authorities to change their land policy to the extent of making grants sufficiently large for sheep runs. When the Napoleonic Wars were concluded, English capitalists began to appear in Australia to engage in the new industry. Especially after 1825 English money flowed freely into Australia, reaching such a volume in the eighteen-forties that a land and stock boom was engendered, followed by a collapse and a disastrous and discouraging depression. By 1847 the graziers achieved what they wanted by way of a land policy, and since wool had then been the chief Australian export for almost twenty years, they were the most powerful group in the community.

From the many factors which must be taken into account in any rounded study of the Australian background, I shall select but two for emphasis here, *time* and *technology*. It is these factors which make the Australian story so significant.

In thinking of Australia, it is always necessary to take notice of the general world drift. In spite of the fact that Australia is peripheral and not central in relation to world affairs, it has always been profoundly influenced by events overseas. Australia was born at a moment when the old mercantilist system of merchant capitalism was breaking up and the new industrial capitalism, with its political and economic effects, was taking its place. It was born immediately following the collapse of the First British Empire, caused by the defection of the group of North American colonies which eventually became the United States. That defection was in large measure provoked by the fact that the terms of mercantilism proved too onerous to be borne with complacency. The Second British Empire was slowly taking shape all during Australia's formative years, and it was an empire based on industrial capitalism. Finally, the early years of the Australian story were overshadowed by a great upheaval, the French Revolution, most accurately defined as the coming to power of the French middle class. This revolution set in motion a variety of forces and ideas, some repressive, some progressive, which gradually worked themselves out, when taken up by the middle classes of other nations, especially the United States, into what we know as democracy under industrial capitalism. These events and tendencies were almost inextricably intertwined and interlocked, mixed with traditions differently based, clarified and distorted by cross-currents in the world, the British Empire, and Australia, weaving that subtle but illogical argument we call history.

Certain men in Australia, bent on nothing more noble than getting rich, turned first to erecting an exploitative monopoly of land, labor, and trade, and secondarily and quite incidentally, to the growing of fine wool. It was this latter experiment which provided the key to Australia's future, but it would not have turned in the lock if it had not been inserted at the very moment when the manufacture of wool was following that of cotton along the great highroad of technological change. It was the discovery of ways and means for applying the technique of factory machine production to wool that opened up the English wool market to the Australian product. Machine production of woolen cloths rapidly expanded the consuming power for the cloths, and this ratified in strictly commercial terms the vast increase which took place in the production of wool in Australia. Thus Australia was deeply influenced by technological change very early in its history. This particular change reoriented Australia and England, bringing the two countries into the relation characteristic between industrial and primary producing countries under nineteenth-century conditions. It is under these conditions that the Australian story has continued down to the present day.

Grazing, on which Australia's first upward surge was based, is one of man's oldest occupations and, superficially viewed, has changed little since the dawn of time. When it became general in Australia the conditions were not so utterly different from those described in the Bible. But within the last one hundred years, the Australian industry has been revolutionized, and the end is not yet, as the experts assure us. The basic machine used in wool production, the sheep, has itself been transformed. The nature of the fleece, the weight of the fleece, the nature of the carcass—all have been changed. The Australian stud masters have been extremely successful innovators. The methods of running sheep have changed to an almost equal degree. The unknown genius who invented the system of confining sheep in fenced paddocks, but giving them free range there, instead of assigning them to the care of shepherds, effected a revolution in station economy. The labor force necessary for operations was reduced by this change, the capital costs of a station somewhat increased, but on balance the cost of wool production was lowered. The methods of taking the wool from the backs of the sheep have radically changed. Following 1868 the progressive improvement of shearing equipment revolutionized this phase of the industry. So, too, the method of preparing the wool for market has been transformed. Shipping wool in the grease was a significant innovation at the time. So also was the shift from bullock dray to railway as a means of getting the wool from the sheep station to the seaboard and from dray to motor-lorry in getting wool to the railway. There was, again, the change from sail to steam as a means of getting it overseas. The speeding up of transport and communication made it possible to establish wool auctions in Australia, a major advance for the local producers. The experiments in the refrigeration of seagoing vessels carried out by Harrison and Mort made possible a frozen meat trade and gave animal carcasses a value to the grazier hitherto unknown. In short, within the last hundred years, the technology of grazing in Aus-

tralia has been completely changed, and the changes have all contributed to or encouraged increased production.

Even when the graziers were unquestionably the dominant
group in the community, they were not undisturbed masters. Moreover, their position was to be quickly challenged. They were
frequently defeated on issues of great importance to them. It was
the opposition to them of the traders in the towns who preferred
free labor to convict labor and the men of good will of all groups
that forced the abolition of transportation to Australia. This move
cut off the supply of cheap, virtually slave, labor, on which the
pastoralists had come to depend. The system was brought to an
end in the different colonies at different times, from 1840 in the
mother colony of New South Wales to 1868 in the isolated and
underdeveloped colony of Western Australia. (Some colonies
never received convicts, South Australia for example.) This move
eventually forced the working of the sheep stations with free
laborers, a class which had begun to appear in the colonies as
immigrants in the twenties and in increasing numbers from the
early thirties on. Most of the immigrants were brought out with
government assistance, the funds being supplied in part by land
sales. The whole question of immigration, assisted or otherwise,
has been one of the most constant of Australian problems from
that day to this.

The exploitation of the continent on a pastoral basis necessarily
made for a widely scattered, small population in the grazing areas,
coupled with sizable towns at the ports which served as distribut-
ing centers, receiving the wool for shipment overseas and handling
the manufactured imports, as well as financial dealings. It was
also in the towns that the small amount of elementary manufacturing which such an economic system encouraged was carried
on. When in due time manufacturing became more complex and
extensive it further accentuated the concentration of population in
the coastal cities. Thus it was very early made obvious that in spite
of a small total population, Australia was to have cities of considerable size. The tendency toward exceptional urbanization soon
precipitated that struggle between the cities and the countryside
which is a persistent feature of Australian politics. The struggle

was not in the least abated, though it has taken new shapes from time to time, when farmers in considerable numbers were added to the rural population and factory workers to the town populations.

By the late eighteen-forties Australia had a population of upwards of half a million scattered over the entire continent, perhaps a maximum under the conditions of a strictly pastoral economy. Yet this population was able, perhaps just because of the urban concentration, to win a measure of self-government and in the fifties the basic privileges of representative government. But representative government should not be confused with democracy.

Suddenly Australia was "precipitated into nationhood" by the discovery of gold. From 1850 to 1860 the country was in flux once more, and adventurous men from all over the world flocked to the gold fields of New South Wales and Victoria, not a few of them arriving from California. In the fifties the population more than doubled, until in 1860 it was 1,145,585. The remnants of convictism which had an importance in a small society were effectively subordinated. But while the decade was full of dramatic incidents, including a miners' rebellion to which labor has given symbolic significance, in a fundamental sense the gold rushes did not interrupt the basic trends of Australian development. When the tumult and the shouting died down the problem was to find routine economic activities to support the increased population. The logical outlet was on the land—to develop commercial farming in Australia. But the land was "locked," to use an Australian word; it was held in large blocks by the pastoralists, especially the areas best suited for cultivation. Thus there was precipitated a new struggle over land policy comparable in importance and intensity to that waged by the graziers when they were the rising economic interest. In the event, the political success of the advocates of unlocking the lands was not immediately followed by an economic success on the part of the farmers. It required a combination of factors to get the Australian farmers on their feet: railways to the ports, knowledge of dry-farming techniques, suitable seeds, notably of wheat, refrigeration of ocean-going vessels, and so on. And it must not be overlooked that the rise of farming did not mean the decline of grazing. Wool growing still remained the basic Australian industry. It would be quite wrong to convey the impression that agriculture *replaced* grazing in the Australian economy. It would be more accurate to say that agriculture was expanded from very small beginnings in the years after 1860 into one of the great activities of the Commonwealth.

Australian farming, in the beginning, was crude, actually on a lower level than that in England. It dragged along on a low level for almost a hundred years. Then a cumulation of technological innovations, together with changes in the laws governing land holding, completely revolutionized the position. The experiments of John Wrathal Bull, John Ridley, and the Mackays with mechanical harvesting equipment, of R. B. Smith and others with new kinds of plows, of Mullen with methods of clearing land, of William J. Farrer and Baron Ferdinand von Mueller in the field of economic botany, of various hands with chemical fertilizers, especially superphosphate, the coming of the railways, the devising of water conservation and supply schemes, the application of refrigeration to the overseas transport of perishable products, the introduction of the cream separator and the butter factory, all figure in the story. The productiveness of Australian farming rose in a steep and fairly continuous line once its problems were really tackled, and the improvements continue.

Three other major policies date from the period of the gold rushes and their aftermath. These are the White Australia policy, designed to exclude yellow, black, and brown peoples from settlement on the continent, the foundations of which were laid in the conflicts of white and Chinese miners on the gold fields; the practice of building manufacturing industries behind a protective tariff, first used by the colony of Victoria in the late eighteen-sixties and applied to the entire Commonwealth after federation was achieved; and the working-class policy of building trade unions. These three are still vital today. A fourth, which dates from the early seventies, seems to have received a permanent revision during the recent depression. It is the policy of heavy governmental borrowings overseas for public works of a developmental character. The emphasis in recent years has been on internal borrowing for works. The policy of depending upon the government for the provision of fundamental services like transport and electricity supply is, of course, too deep-seated to be abandoned at this stage.

The Australian story rises to a climax in the eighteen-nineties. In the early nineties the inflationary policies of the colonial governments, plus a reckless speculative trend in private business, especially land trading—both encouraged by the free flow of investment money from London—led to a tremendous financial panic which brought economic life almost to a halt. On top of that came a devastating drought—droughts, major and minor, constantly menace production—which, when combined with falling wool prices, further depressed enterprise. In this decade also the conflict between capital and labor, which had been brewing since labor began actively to organize and make demands in the 1880's, resulted in a series of rough-and-tumble strikes involving maritime workers, pastoral employees, and miners. The workers suffered grievous defeats, especially since the power of the state was enlisted against them.

On the other hand, the nineties are also of crucial importance on the constructive side. During the decade there was a great upsurge of creative idealism among the masses and the intellectual classes. Australian literature flourished as never before. The painters, under the stimulation of impressionism brought home from Spain by Tom Roberts, for the first time began to get the Australian scene on canvas. Almost all the articulate people were in some measure influenced by a powerful desire to build a better society in Australia, though a few gave up the job and tried to establish a utopian community in far-off Paraguay. The desire expressed itself in all kinds of schemes, from straight-out utopianism to extremely practical suggestions for immediate reforms. Nationalism flourished as never before or since, and republicanism had its adherents. These ideas were important in giving the people the resilience to act even after the decisive defeats on the industrial front.

Labor turned to politics and by framing platforms broad enough to appeal to the liberal members of the small middle class, and to the struggling farmers, quickly won important positions in the colonial parliaments. From stray labor members, the progress was to labor parties which quickly became the official opposition and then began to form governments. The reforms labor spoke for, many of which had active middle-class advocacy and support, began to be put on the statute books. The whole tone of Australian life changed. From this period should be dated Australia's world-wide reputation for social legislation of an advanced character, especially the development of the industrial court system for dealing with industrial disputes and the fixation of wages and conditions of work. This is when Australian social democracy was born. The Australian Labour party has ever since been a powerful force in politics, state and Federal, often as influential in the formation of policy when it is the official opposition as when it is holding office.

Nor did all this exhaust Australia's creative energy. The long-mooted plan for federating the six colonies of Australia was brought to final form in 1901, when the Commonwealth of Australia was proclaimed, with a constitution considerably influenced by the American, though with a political system basically British in structure and character.

The creative tide ran unequally in the several colonies and ran nowhere without encountering formidable obstructions. Australian history is difficult to summarize accurately in broad generalizations as is here attempted. The tide continued to run, but with diminishing force, until the outbreak of the First World War. Although customarily referred to as "the nineties," Australia's most seminal period, to which many people now look back nostalgically, really extended from the early nineties to 1914.

The Commonwealth government has initiated surprisingly little that is truly new by way of policy. Its signal contribution seems to be co-ordination of existing services and the extension of them to include the whole nation. In recent years also the tendency has been to centralize more and more power in the hands of the Commonwealth, a drift which first became important during the First World War, was accentuated during the Great Depression especially with regard to finance, and is once again powerfully active during the Second World War. Under the present constitution many fundamental activities are left largely in the hands of the states, or are duplicated, with resulting confusion. The states still have primary power in dealing with agriculture, carry on most of the social services and public utilities, and have an important say about labor affairs. It is one of the curiosities of Australian government that there is no Federal ministry of agricultural and pastoral affairs, and no Federal ministry of labor; this in a country where these are basically important matters. (There is, however, the Agricultural Council, consisting of the State Ministers of Agriculture and the Federal Minister of Commerce, which discusses national policy questions; and the war-time Ministry of Labour and National Service, which deals with labor disputes and the allocation of man-power.) Two striking examples of the use of the Federal power to achieve uniformity, setting aside such an obvious move as the consolidation of the postal services, are the extension of the White Australia principle to the entire Commonwealth and the extension of the protective tariff to the entire nation. Federation also made possible a national defense policy, the felt need for which played a part in bringing about the system.

By and large, however, the fundamental pattern of contemporary Australian life was apparent in the nineties. Federation did not essentially change it. To be sure, the social emphasis has shifted from time to time and will continue to shift in the future. The fundamental change which came over Australian life after 1914, a change necessarily reflected in politics, was a shift of emphasis from betterment of conditions to the use of the state power to encourage and support private enterprise in all fields, especially agriculture and manufacturing. In this line of policy the Federal authorities took the lead, since the tariff is a Federal measure. Labor was persuaded by the argument that if it supported the tariff, the government would see to it that labor got full social benefits from the new industries in the form of good wages and working conditions through the industrial courts or whatever other measures might be necessary. As a result, labor is today perhaps more protectionist than its opponents. The emphasis in its mind always falls upon the creation of jobs, rather than on the building up of private capitalist enterprises, and upon the standard of living the job-holders must be guaranteed. This general attitude brings to its support, on many occasions, sections of the urban community normally opposed to it, notably the organized manufacturers, though these same sections will oppose labor on other issues where its stand is more plainly liberal. Labor began its political career by framing platforms which included appeals to the small farming interests which ran counter to those of the large landholders, chiefly pastoralists. Today, when governmental assistance to exporting farmers is popular, labor follows along, even though the farmers have become in considerable measure a conservative interest in Federal affairs.

It has thus come about that the gap between the Labour party and the conservatives is not as wide as many observers are prone to assume. What the laborites call "ratting"—the desertion of labor leaders to the conservative side—goes on constantly without undue violation of any principle except loyalty. The fact that labor has given so many hostages to conservative fortunes has facilitated the process; and only a sharp redefinition of labor's outlook will sharpen political issues. In recent years, therefore, labor radicalism has chiefly found expression in the trade unions. Only a minority of labor politicians can be said to represent the leftist union position in the parliaments, state or Federal.

The First World War did not fundamentally change the direction of Australian economic development. It did, of course, cost the country a tremendous lot in men and money. No really new economic element was injected into Australian life. But as farming came forward in the years following the gold rushes, building on small beginnings, so during and after the war manufacturing steadily increased in importance. The building of manufacturing industries is, it seems to me, the most significant Australian activity in the last quarter-century. To my mind the turning point came when the Broken Hill Proprietary began steel production at Newcastle, N.S.W., in 1915, an objective toward which the company had worked since 1911. Manufacturing went forward most rapidly during the First World War, during the Great Depression, when the idea of a "balanced" economy (i.e., balanced as to primary and secondary production) gained widespread acceptance, and during the present war. Australia should emerge from this war with a fairly comprehensive manufacturing establishment capable of adaptation to its basic peace-time needs; and the signs indicate

that many will advocate that its further elaboration and extension
be a primary postwar task.

There is, therefore, nothing surprising in the fact that Australia's
various schemes for meeting the problems of the Great Depression
were far less radical in relation to the social context in which they
were evolved and applied than were the parallel policies of the
New Deal in the American context. It is not unfair to say that the
basic idea in Australian policy was to make the economy work
profitably by an all-around reduction of costs to meet the lower
prices the depression had brought about. Many and ingenious were
the schemes applied to achieve this end, some of them permanently
valuable to the Australian nation. But no more than the American
New Dealers did the Australian leaders discover the answer to
unemployment, and no more did they satisfy the people that the
ideal commonwealth was to be found down the road they were
persuaded to take. It is impossible, except for purposes of argument, to say how far Australia "recovered" because of the planned
action of the government and how far because of rises in export
prices and increases in manufacturing activity. Certainly rising
prices and new investment have been traditional factors in recovery.

But the fact is that the Australian liberal and working-class
spokesmen were in 1938, on the eve of the new war, somewhat
disturbed by the situation in which they found themselves after
a hundred and fifty years of history. The hundred and fiftieth
anniversary of Captain Phillip's landing was celebrated with appropriate pageantry, but the country was also interested in a wide
variety of ideas for improving the well-being of the masses: free
public libraries, with which the Australians are the poorest supplied of all English-speaking peoples, the forty-hour week, housing,
universal unemployment and health insurance, and better school-
ing, including the raising of the compulsory age limit above 14
years where it came to rest many years ago.

It was earlier remarked that Australia is a democracy and that
democracies justify themselves not by achieved perfection but by
giving the people a chance to improve their condition by their own
concerted action. On that basis Australian democracy must be

reckoned a success. For while it cannot be denied that the Australians are unclear about *what* domestic steps should now be taken to realize their ideals, the search for ways and means goes on. It has been intensified by the outbreak of war. The testing time for Australian democracy—like all surviving democracies—will be the postwar period. With the fighting over, the task of dealing with reconstruction will put the leaders and the people on their mettle. If the Australians rise to their job and handle it with their traditional dexterity and good sense, their future will be assured.

5. WHAT AUSTRALIA LIVES BY

IF IT were possible to see all of Australia at once from an airplane, most of the people would be seen in the southeastern portion, the true heart of the continent. Keeping in mind the long finger of good country extending northward along the Queensland coast, and the "island" of good country in Western Australia, it is still true that most of the land capable of intensive use is found in the southeast. This is made clear by shading on the map on page 58. Not only are the agricultural industries chiefly confined to these portions of the continent, but the records show that most of the sheep, beef, dairy cattle, and pigs are found within them also. The pastoral industries are, of course, responsible for most of the utilization of the dry outlying parts of the country. Although they cover an area enormously larger than the good portions, their carrying capacity is so low that the number of sheep and cattle they support is decidedly smaller than one might suppose offhand. Mining is the only other significant industry carried on in the dry country, with a few readily explained exceptions like smelting, a necessary part of the mineral industry. By great good luck the principal Australian coal fields, including the very largest, are within the area of good rainfall. Although minerals must be brought from the dry country, the presence of coal really determines the location of the industrial development. It is found in or close to the large cities. This further promotes the concentration of population in the southeast.

While the states vary in productive capacity—they differ decidedly in area and rainfall distribution—their productive activities are surprisingly similar.* In order of area under crop, they should be listed as follows: New South Wales, South Australia, Victoria, Western Australia, Queensland, and Tasmania. Taking an all-

* Figures on production are given in Appendix B.

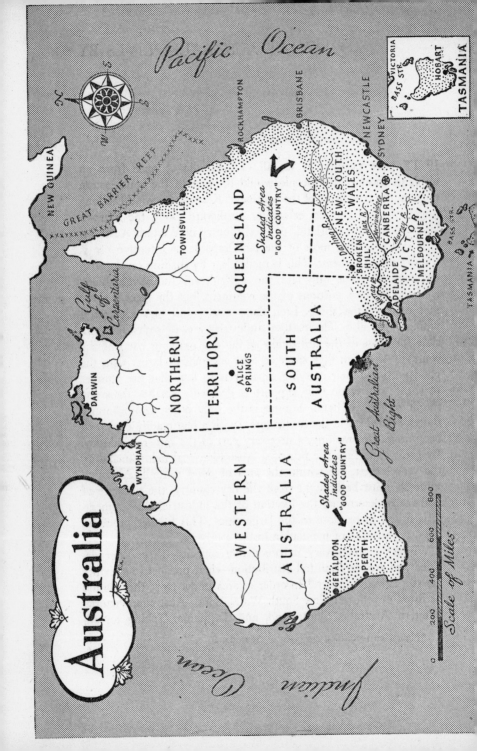

around view, New South Wales is the most productive state in the Commonwealth, though she does not lead in all fields by any manner of means. Wool, mutton, lamb, beef, and pork are sent to market by every state. All have large numbers of horses. They all produce wheat, hay, oats, and potatoes. Five out of six grow barley. But only two grow sugar cane, Queensland completely dominating the industry, and only three grow corn, Queensland again being the principal producer. Queensland also produces all of Australia's cotton. New South Wales produces all the rice— along the Murrumbidgee River under irrigation. Victoria leads in the growing of tobacco. Tasmania is predominant in the production of hops. Irrigation agriculture for the growing of citrus fruits, grapes (both table and wine), peaches, apricots, etc., as well as pasture grasses for fat lamb production is widely scattered but most highly developed along the Murray River in New South Wales, Victoria, and South Australia. Citrus fruits and temperate climate fruits are also widely produced without irrigation. Every state has a dairy industry, though Victoria's is the most productive.

All states produce some of the minerals used in modern industry, but New South Wales leads in black coal, zinc, and lead, Victoria in brown coal (for generating electricity), South Australia in iron and salt, Queensland in copper, and so on. Western Australia is by an overwhelming margin the leading gold producer. The beautiful opals for which Australia is famous (and the principal gem stone found in the country) are chiefly produced in northwestern New South Wales, especially at Lightning Ridge, and in the far west of South Australia at Cober Pedy, in "sun-scorched, harsh, and waterless environments."

Queensland has the greatest output of sawed native timber, including beautiful veneers for furniture; but all states except South Australia have important lumbering industries, recalling, however, that Australia is poor in commercial forests. Western Australia is notable for skillful forest management, designed to preserve her superlative hardwoods, karri and jarrah.

Fishing is decidedly the cinderella industry of the Commonwealth. The largest take for food is in New South Wales. Queensland and Western Australia contribute most of the pearl shell.

In manufacturing, New South Wales predominates by every

statistical measurement. Above all, it has the basic heavy industry—steel. Victoria, however, is close on its heels. Secondary industry is least developed in Tasmania.

Every continental state should be understood to have an area of good country of varying extent situated close to the sea. In this area production is always concentrated. In the dry outlying parts production is dispersed, often to a fantastic degree. The island state of Tasmania also follows this pattern, but with a difference; her outlying area has the rainfall, but it is rough and mountainous.

The position of Australia with regard to essential and critical raw materials has never been scientifically studied, but I should like to present a rough assessment of it. In the following tables I have followed the classifications of raw materials used by Dr. Brooks Emeny in his classic study, *The Strategy of Raw Materials*. The notes, including those in the prefatory remarks, give the situation as accurately as the material at my disposal allows.

I am well aware that Australia has known resources which are not today being exploited. If these were brought into production, her position would be even stronger than it appears here.

For example, sources for aluminum exist but to date have not been used, though laboratory scientists at Sydney Technical College have successfully experimented with the low-grade New South Wales deposit of bauxite. In July, 1941, however, it was announced that the Commonwealth government had registered a large company called the National Aluminum Mining and Smelting Company. Meanwhile Australian processers are dependent upon imported ingots. The alunite deposits at Lake Campion in Western Australia, believed to be enormous, are a reserve which can only be exploited in the most dire emergency because the technical difficulties of handling them, including transport, will raise costs to a prohibitive level.

It should also be said that some important materials are produced but that the facilities for their complete utilization are not present. Australia produces tin but currently lacks the facilities for making tin plate, though they may be imported as a phase of the war effort in manufacturing. The situation with regard to nickel is worth special mention. The French island possession of

New Caledonia, off the eastern Australian coast, is rich in nickel and is, after Canada, an exceedingly important source of the world's supply. Given the facilities for handling this ore, Australia will have an abundant supply of nickel.

On the other hand, Australia has at Newcastle the world's most comprehensive single plant dealing with the alloys of steel.

All told, while the indications are that Australia can support a modern industrial economy out of her own and near-by resources, it should be remarked, by way of a caution, that I imply nothing here about the extent of the reserves of the various metals I shall mention, and I hazard no opinion whatever about the prospects of new discoveries, either on the continent or in the near-by islands. Little is known about the extent of the reserves, even with regard to deposits now being worked, let alone the deposits not being used, and if new discoveries are made, the position will be revolutionized overnight. Faster transportation is going to extend the Australian "resources area" to the surrounding islands.

THE GREAT ESSENTIALS

FOOD — Extremely strong position; heavy exporter in many basic lines; and importer chiefly of tropical products like tea (mostly from Netherlands Indies) and of specialty products and luxuries.

POWER — The basic power resource is coal, water power necessarily being secondary, though still capable of considerable expansion. In this field the chief problem is to provide the power-generating facilities and transmission lines.

IRON & STEEL — Strong position, and production is being expanded.

MACHINERY — Heavy importer, but the position is being rapidly strengthened during the present war.

CHEMICALS — Heavy importer, but the industry is rapidly getting on its feet, both in industrial chemicals and medicinal drugs.

COAL	Very strong position; reserves in 1930 were estimated to be equivalent to the world's total production of coal for 50 years in the future.
IRON ORE	Strong position, but the location of some known reserves raises a problem in transportation which, however, can probably be readily solved since the most isolated deposits known (at Yampi Sound off the northwestern coast) are allegedly phenomenally rich.
PETROLEUM	No natural flow oil of commercial significance has been discovered on the continent. Deposits of oil shale have been located at various places, and those in New South Wales are in production. In Victoria low-pressure oil sands may shortly be brought into full production. But there is little hope of meeting Australia's needs from continental sources. However, the Australian mandate of New Guinea is a potential source of flow oil and experimental drilling is under way, but no reports on results have been made public.

CRITICAL RAW MATERIALS

(States listed in order of importance as producers)

COPPER	Sufficient; Tasmania and Queensland. Wartime shortage.
NITRATES	Importer, from Chile.
COTTON	Importer, chiefly as cotton manufactures, but some raw cotton; Queensland.
ZINC	Exporter; Tasmania.
MANGANESE	Sufficient; New South Wales.
CHROMITE	Small production; New South Wales.

WOOL	World's greatest exporter.
PHOSPHATES	Little in continental Australia, but ample supplies available from the island of Nauru, of which Australia is a joint mandatory, with the United Kingdom and New Zealand.
TIN	Small production; Queensland, New South Wales, Tasmania, Victoria, Western Australia.
LEAD	Exporter; New South Wales, Queensland, Tasmania.
SULPHUR	Importer; a bounty is paid on the production of sulphur from Australian pyrites.
ALUMINUM	Importer; but has undeveloped resources of bauxite and alunite.
RUBBER	Importer; small production in the Australian colony of Papua.
NICKEL	Importer.
TUNGSTEN	Sufficient; from wolfram, Northern Territory, Tasmania, Queensland, New South Wales; from scheelite, New South Wales and Queensland.
POTASH	Importer.
ANTIMONY	Sufficient; Western Australia, Victoria, New South Wales.
MERCURY	Importer.
MICA	Sufficient; South Australia and Northern Territory.

Before Australia became a great wool-producer, hundreds of experiments were made. The same is true of wheat growing, dairying, fruit growing, and the rest. The problems involved soils and seeds and especially the availability of water for the growing crops. The fact that Australia is a warm country created special problems in butter manufacture. Americans will be interested to know that many suggestions useful in developing Australia came from the United States, directly or indirectly, but the American contributions are so deeply entangled in purely Australian developments that to specify them would probably exaggerate their significance. It would be unprofitable to review each industry in detail, specifying its particular problems and the unique solutions of them the Australians have found. I will, however, describe a few of them.

In the dry outback the sheep stations lie along the bush tracks away from the small towns. As a rule, too, they stand well back from the tracks, and in going across country between towns they are only occasionally to be seen. Gates in the fences tell where one should turn off, but the station buildings are often miles from the main road. The idea is to get them as near the center of the run as possible for convenience in working, the conditioning factor being permanent water. Failure to find permanent water at the desired point frequently leads to the location of the home far off center.

The station buildings are few. Ordinarily the house is a low, squat affair of one story, a collection of essential rooms surrounded by a wide veranda. The houses are so built that the rooms all open onto the veranda, the living rooms running through the house to give them spaciousness. This scheme assures ventilation in a country which is hot most of the year, frequently extremely hot, but it fails lamentably in the brief cold winter. Sleeping rooms are usually approached from the veranda, interior halls being rare, and the only living rooms customarily open one into the other. The kitchen is set apart from the main house to do away with the man-made heat. Frequently the dining room is also, so that it may be effectively screened against the millions of flies of all imaginable kinds that flourish at certain seasons. A good station home is lighted by electricity, has some kind of mechanical refrigeration—electric or kerosene—and a septic tank sewage system, though these are counted as luxuries.

Scattered about near the house are a minimum number of small buildings, a garage, a fowl house, a tightly screened meat house, a blacksmith shop, and an odd shed or two. There are no barns,

Platypus.

Koalas.

Kangaroo.

Emu.

Both photographs by Wallace Kirkland, courtesy *Life*

Iron Knob, near Whyalla, a mountain of iron ore.

Sheep station in the dry outback.

the horses being kept in the open the year around. Sometimes close by, but often a considerable distance away, is the most important structure on the place, after the house. This is the wool shed where the sheep are shorn, the wool baled, and the result of the year's labor started to the railway and market.

How big is a station? It depends upon the quality of the country, and they therefore vary from around ten thousand acres to an equal number of square miles and more. Where the country is too dry for even the most obstinate farmers, the sheep runs are held on lease from the state governments, the average outback squatter—the term has no invidious implication, being synonymous with affluence in many contexts—having no freehold land whatever. Pick up a map of Australia showing how the land is held, and you can deduce the quality of the country and the use to which it is put with fair accuracy.

An outback squatter's capital, not being in the land, is, sheep excepted, in improvements. After the house, the outbuildings, and the wool shed, these are of two major kinds—fences and water conservation schemes. The squatter not only has to run a wire fence around his holding, but he has also to divide it off into manageable blocks called "paddocks" no matter how big they are. Only in the far outback where cattle are chiefly run, do you get into unfenced country. Fencing is a very expensive business, and the squatters watch the price of fencing wire like hawks.

Water conservation schemes are also expensive, but they are basic to the carrying capacity of the station. On the elaboration and success of them depends the success of the squatter. In the old days the feed—the natural growth of grass and herbage—frequently outlasted the water, but today the reverse may be the case. Over wide areas, especially in Queensland, the cause for this is the use of "bore water" as much as anything. In the 1880's the practice of putting down artesian bores, introduced from America, was begun. The water from the bores is distributed through earth-channels. As a rule, this water, while acceptable to stock, is useless for humans, since it is heavily mineralized. Supplementing the bores are dams and tanks. In many areas, dams and tanks alone serve the purpose. A dam is an earthen obstruction placed in a water channel, dry most of the year, at a point where a natural water hole is found, with the idea of increasing its capacity. A tank is a huge earthen construction dug in relation to the prevailing slope of the watershed to catch the surface water that might otherwise run to waste. Such works cost money, but once they are done they are fairly permanent and enhance the value of the station. It is toward water conservation that the best energy of the squatters is now directed.

Enough rain to bring up the feed grass and fill the dams and tanks, and the squatter is secure, from everything except the vagaries of the wool market! Since the feed remains green but a few weeks out of the year, anyway, following which it is naturally cured by the sun and remains standing almost indefinitely, too much rain can be a disaster, for it may lead to destructive floods. A little rain at the wrong time is bad, too, for it can ruin the cured feed and so throw the station economy into confusion. What the squatter wants is the right quantity of rain at the right time. That quantity may be incredibly small, as little as five inches a year in some parts.

The shearing shed is really the focal point of the station. It stands in splendid isolation for much of the year. At the proper season, when the weather is right and shearers are available, sheep are brought to it from all parts of the run to lose those marvelous fleeces for which they are world-famous. A shearing shed is ordinarily a long building with a pitched roof. Timbered with wood, it is covered with corrugated galvanized iron. The sheep are brought to yards at one end of the shed and are counted and sorted on the basis of age, sex, or other characteristic. This is done by an experienced person, either the station owner or manager, by having the sheep driven through a narrow-fenced lane to a point where, by manipulating a complicated group of easily swinging gates, the sheep can be directed into the proper pens. As wanted for shearing, the sheep are driven into the wool shed itself and there into a long oblong pen extending two-thirds of the length of the shed along one wall, or down the center. Along an outside wall (or walls, if the shed is large) is the shearing equipment, each unit of which is called a stand. One man works at each stand. The shears resemble nothing so much as barber's clippers and operate on exactly the same principle. They are power-driven. Ex-

tending from one end of the line of stands to the other, is a long
shaft driven by a steam engine for which wood is the fuel. At
each stand is the necessary arrangement for attaching the individual shears to the shaft by means of a semi-rigid tubular affair
which has several flexible elbows and which drops naturally to
a level at which the shears can be conveniently operated when
the shearer is bending over a sheep. The shearer has complete
control of the powering of his shears by means of a cord which
dangles within easy reach of his hand and connects with the
mechanism attaching his shears to the shaft. A slight jerk of this
cord puts the shears in or out of gear.

From the long pen within the shed, the sheep are let into a series
of square pens leading off it. Two shearers are assigned to each
of these pens, and they secure the sheep for shearing, usually catch-
ing the sheep under the forelegs, turning it on its back, and dragging it on its hindquarters to the shearing stand. The shears are
then brought into play, and by a series of carefully calculated
movements, long since determined by experience, the fleece is
taken off and the wool removed from the head, the legs, and the
crutch. The trick is to remove all the wool with as few unnecessary movements as possible, for shearing is paid for per hundred
sheep. Shearers naturally differ considerably in the speed and neatness with which they can take off the wool. A champion with
whom I once shook hands had a record of three hundred in a
working day. A routine worker does one hundred and fifty.

The shearers do not handle the wool once it is off the sheep. The
fleece proper is gathered up by a roustabout, who tosses it flat on
a table, the top of which is a series of rungs about three inches
apart. The loose bits of wool fall between the rungs to the floor.
Men working at this table pull off the coarse, dirty, and otherwise
undesirable parts, roll it up again, and another roustabout carries
it to the wool-classers' table. Wool-classing is an art and a science,
and the classers are aristocrats of the sheds. With incredible rapidity a good classer determines the quality of the fleece and indicates
its proper disposition. From his table, or from the floor behind
or beside him, a roustabout gathers up the fleece and tosses it into
the proper one of a series of huge bins extending crosswise in the

shed. Meanwhile, roustabouts sweep up the loose wool from about the shearing stands and carry it to the end of the shed.

Behind the classfying bins is a team of men baling the wool according to type with the aid of hand-powered presses. It emerges from their hands neatly and securely wrapped in burlap and properly marked as to type and station of origin. It is now ready for trucking to the railway, which will carry it to the auction rooms. From the ports it will go to the world.

The shorn sheep, sorry, nude-looking animals, are forced through an opening in the shed wall behind the shearing stand and into a small pen. From this pen they are let into a larger pen, counted as they go, and the tally entered in a book to the credit of the shearer who handled them. In due time they are returned to the grazing paddocks to grow new fleeces.

When shearing is in progress a wool shed has all the bustle of a busy factory, but when the day is done it is a gloomy and deserted place. The men go to their quarters. A shearers' camp usually consists of a number of bunkhouses, several mess halls (one for the wool-classers and other "aristocrats," one for the shearers, and one for the roustabouts), each with a separate kitchen, and, finally, a small structure which houses a temporary office and a store. An ordinary menu for dinner (on a Friday, as it happens) is tomato herring, salmon, cold lamb, fresh tomatoes, toast, butter, treacle, tea, and oranges. About the same menu was served in all three halls. After eating, the men usually gather around the open fires and talk, visit the store, do as they like. A rough and ready life, but during the season a decidedly nomadic existence, for the men must visit station after station to make a decent year's income.

The workers in the pastoral industry of Australia are highly unionized. Some of the most violent, prolonged, and disastrous strikes in Australian labor history have centered around the wool industry. To the fore in all union matters are the shearers, originally gathered in a separate union but now in the Australian Workers Union. The A. W. U. determines, via the arbitration courts, the conditions under which the men will work in the sheds, and also lays down specifications for the food and lodgings provided for the workers. It thus plays a principal part in controlling shearing.

In the beginning the Australian tropics were exploited according to the traditional pattern: large plantations and imported colored labor. The Kanakas from the Pacific Islands were used. The traffic in them led to "blackbirding," and the laborers were reduced to something unpleasantly close to slavery while on the plantations. Under the pressure of the White Australia sentiment of the south, the Queensland authorities made several attempts to regulate and then to abolish the traffic in the islanders. But the sugar-cane growers always resisted, contending that they could not go on without Kanakas. With the coming of the Commonwealth in 1901 the argument ended in favor of the White Australia advocates, and in a few years almost all the Kanakas were repatriated. The sugar-cane industry was reorganized, and small holdings owned and worked by white Australians were substituted for large plantations manned by colored labor. In northern Queensland today one sees a rare experiment—the exploitation of a tropical area exclusively by white men. But whereas cane growing has been planned to give a chance to the individual small holder, sugar refining is in the hands of an enormously wealthy private monopoly, the Colonial Sugar Refining Company, Ltd., of Sydney.

The region is a one-crop country. The sea of cane is crisscrossed with narrow gauge railways on which the harvested cane is carried to central sugar mills. It was possible at the season when I visited the region to see the industry operating in all its phases, from the plowing of the earth to cane cutting. The cutting is undertaken by gangs of itinerant laborers. They are employed on each farm for but a short time each season, work at rates determined in the arbitration courts, and are housed and fed at standards similarly established.

The cane fields are defined on one side by the high, dark-green hills of the coastal range and on the other by the sparkling blue of the sea. Because the area is so clearly defined, one gains the impression of immense activity and mastery of the country. The domineering hills, the light green cane fields, and the blue sea make this one of the lovely parts of Australia.

In the old days the Murray River carried a flourishing steamer traffic. Unfortunately, it did not produce a Mark Twain, but one day an inspired writer will do a book about the steamboat days which will be highly entertaining reading. C. E. W. Bean's story of the Darling River, *The Dreadnought of the Darling,* is an indication of what we may expect. The Murray and its principal tributaries flow through low rainfall country, and contradictory as it may seem they have but little natural influence upon the character of the country along their banks. They are fed by the torrential rains which fall occasionally even in the driest parts of the Commonwealth and by melting snow of the eastern highlands. It is one of nature's paradoxes that water can roll down to the sea and yet leave the land on either side of its course thirsty and parched. So completely was this the case with the Murray that the banks were originally used, not for farms but for sheep stations. Even today this is true of the Darling River, which cuts across the semiarid portion of western New South Wales.

Beginning in the eighteen-eighties, when the Chaffey brothers arrived in Victoria, the scene slowly changed. These men, born in Canada but trained in irrigation in California, brought modern irrigation methods to Australia, and while they, themselves, suffered severe reverses, both financial and technical, they laid the foundations upon which the Australians are still building.

The Chaffeys are identified with Mildura in Victoria and Renmark in South Australia. These are still outstanding centers of irrigation activity, though many new settlements were subsequently formed and entirely new districts opened up. Mildura is ordinarily approached through a woefully dry area known as the Victorian Mallee, which is utilized, rather precariously, for wheat growing. Emerging out of this country into Mildura is like bursting out of a desert into an oasis. All about Mildura the countryside is covered with grapevines, citrus, and other fruit trees. Wherever water has been scientifically applied to the soil and wherever the soil has been correctly assessed as to its irrigability—for disastrous errors have been made—the effect is truly magical. The holdings are usually small, calculated to provide family livings; but they are closely linked in production control and marketing schemes.

Australia is a paradise for irrigation engineers. The unsolved problems there are of stupendous proportions and require equally stupendous schemes for their solution. Australians who have seen the tremendous works being constructed in the American West return to their own country convinced that in spite of their size, the irrigation problems of Australia can be solved. What the Americans are doing today, however, far outruns the financial resources of the Australians, but if they could discover ways and means and the economic warrant for building the necessary works, the capacity of the Australian continent for carrying population could be multiplied several times.

At Manjimup, Western Australia, near where the jarrah timber meets the karri, I spent a day in the forest with a ranger. For hours we traveled along rough roads between stately rows of mature trees. Under the state conservation scheme the ground we were traveling will always be forest, for the holders of cutting licenses are carefully supervised to insure that they take only trees marked by the forester for their use and are reasonably careful in felling them. Immediately a patch has been cut over, it is surveyed and a plan for its rehabilitation made.

The timber-getters actually at work seemed rather far removed from Paul Bunyan. After extending a narrow gauge railway to the site of operations, they put a huge, wheeled steam engine in place and use its power to drag the fallen trees to the railway. Oxen haul the chains from the engine to the trees. The fallers work in pairs on small platforms placed to leave a minimum stump, notch the tree with axes, and then fell it with a crosscut saw. The logs go to a central mill around which a permanent town has been built.

The Western Australian forests are a superb example of how to exploit properly a basic resource which can readily be exhausted if carelessly handled.

Far out on the western plains of New South Wales stands one of the most remarkable cities in the world. Its name is Broken Hill. If it is taken as a symbol of Australia's social development, Broken Hill becomes charged with deep meaning. In spite of its splendid isolation—there is no town of comparable size within three hundred miles in any direction—it has had a profound influence on the development of the entire continent. Out of the mines which produce silver, lead, and zinc, millions of pounds have been earned. The words Broken Hill are today in Australia almost interchangeable with "basic economic power." The workers who have delved in the mines for wages have made history of a kind that has given Australian labor a reputation for militancy the world around. The compromises these opposing forces have achieved are, in essence, the compromises characteristic of the nation as a whole. Out of the struggle the masters have emerged in triumphant power, even though the workers have achieved and maintained the safeguards characteristic of a social democracy. From isolated Broken Hill, the trail leads all over Australia into all the significant economic activities of the nation. After all, its silver-lead deposits are the richest yet discovered in the world and the Broken Hill mines have been the greatest source of Australian industrial capital.

One of the ablest of the early explorers of Australia was Captain Charles Sturt. He it was who discovered the Darling and Murray rivers. In 1844, Sturt was commissioned by the colony of South Australia to make an exploration toward the center of the continent, then an absolutely unknown quantity but suspected to contain a vast inland sea! On this expedition Sturt confirmed the existence of the Barrier Ranges, hills hitherto only known by aboriginal report, and he ascended a curiously shaped "broken" hill to make a drawing of the surrounding country. He had chanced into the area in a season of extreme drought, and he and his men suffered horribly from heat and dust. The party weakened rapidly, and in the desperate struggle to get back to the settlements they jettisoned, among other things, all mineral specimens. The true nature of the "broken" hill remained unsuspected.

Within a decade of Sturt's visit to the hill, however, the pioneering pastoralists had pushed into the vicinity and established sheep runs. One, called Mount Gipps, fourteen hundred square miles in extent, included the "broken" hill in its area. The hill gave its name to a paddock of fifty thousand acres. In 1866 the Mount Gipps station was taken over by a pastoral company in which the senior partner was Sir James McCulloch, Australian partner of a firm of British importing merchants and premier of Victoria. To the newly acquired property Sir James sent his nephew, George McCulloch. It was a dreary post, made drearier by recurring droughts, and McCulloch all but abandoned the station on several occasions.

Ten years after George McCulloch arrived at Mount Gipps a storekeeper named Paddy Green, who did prospecting on the side, found some silver-lead ore on a near-by station called Thackaringa and got a good report on it from England. Green died in 1880, but his discovery directed attention to the area, hitherto only prospected unsuccessfully for gold. Prospectors located what seemed to be rich silver-lead deposits all about the district, and a settlement of three thousand persons grew up at a place which the natives called Umberumberka but which the whites named Silverton. For five years Silverton flourished on the basis of mines imaginatively called Day Dream, Maggie's Secret, Terrible Dick, and so on. The prospectors looked over the broken hill and assessed it as worthless—in their parlance, "a hill of mullock."

A rank outsider proved to be wiser than the men of experience. In September, 1883 Charles Rasp, who was working for McCulloch as a boundary rider at a pound a week, caught the mining fever and bought a prospector's manual. What followed can be told in his own words: "I was employed at Mount Gipps Station as a boundary rider. My business during shearing time was to go to the different paddocks and find a sufficient number of sheep for shearing. This enabled me to know pretty well the whole run. At the time of the shearing, in 1883, some mines were started in the neighborhood, particularly the Day Dream. The whole country was in a simmer of excitement, and knowing the peculiar outcrop on one corner of the Mount Gipps run, now called Broken Hill, I thought it might be worth my while to go prospecting there. I had no idea of minerals, and was green as could be." Because of the skepticism of the professionals, Rasp's ideas about the broken hill were viewed dubiously by his associates on the station, but in the end six others were good enough gamblers to join in pegging claims, and the seven associates thus got control of what appeared to them to be a mineralized reef. They were right. They formed a syndicate and put in about $350 each to finance development. All were associated with Mount Gipps station and included besides Rasp and McCulloch, the storekeeper, the overseer, another boundary rider, and two men then engaged in sinking dams on the station. Trading in shares began almost immediately, largely because the hill seemed chiefly remarkable for the money it absorbed in developmental work. Within a year the group was reformed on the basis of shares of one-fourteenths, thus initiating a process which has gone on down the years. This move brought into the syndicate men who remained associated with Broken Hill for many years. The new-comers included a surveyor, a station hand, a station manager, a station owner, and a rabbit inspector. The latter was a government employee who checked up on the methods employed to control the rabbit pest.

So rapidly did prospects improve that again a year later, on August 12, 1885, the Broken Hill Proprietary Company Limited—popularly known as the BHP—was floated; and a name of almost mystic significance in industry and finance appeared for the first time in Australian history. The company issued 16,000 shares of $100 each (paid up to $95) of which 14,000 were allocated to the members of the second syndicate and 2,000 offered for sale to the public at $45 each, subject to call at the rate of 25 cents per week until $95 was reached, when all 16,000 shares would be liable to a call of $5. Out of the $90,000 realized on the shares offered for sale, $15,000 was to be paid to the members of the syndicate to reimburse them for their outlay thus far, and $75,000, less expenses, was to be paid into the company treasury and used for further developmental work. Thus the fourteen members of the syndicate got their shares "for nothing" and a little more, and as from this point on there was no turning back—development was for years financed out of earnings, not even the $75,000 being used—the mine automatically enriched the original investors. Of the original syndicate of seven, four, including Rasp and McCulloch, reached this stage on the road to riches; but in the end only McCulloch rose to power and place in the BHP.

The extraordinary rapidity with which the BHP boomed is some-thing to marvel at. In the first report, dated December 15, 1885, the directors congratulated "shareholders upon possessing a silver mine of remarkable richness and extent, the present development already revealing large bodies of valuable ore which it will take years to treat and reduce. . . ." (Incidentally, the BHP very early brought in American technical experts from the Comstock lode in Nevada to direct development.) In June of 1886 the first dividend of $5.00 a share was paid, and thereafter for many years they flowed like a river. Total dividends for 1886 were at the rate of $63\frac{3}{19}$ per cent, while in 1888 they had risen to 126 per cent! In 1937 one of the surviving mines at Broken Hill paid dividends of 120 per cent. Moreover, money poured in from all sides. In 1887 the BHP formed three off-shoot companies to exploit leases adjoining their own and floated them in London. One of these, the British Broken Hill, was based on 240,000 shares at $25 each, of which 80,000 fully paid up were distributed among the BHP shareholders, while the 160,000 remaining realized $4,000,000 in the market, of which $3,375,000 was eventually also distributed among the BHP shareholders, leaving the British company with $625,000 on which to commence operations. It made pots of money. Still not satisfied with operations of this kind, the BHP began to water its stock as early as 1889, a process which has gone on to this day, giving the company a huge capital structure on which to pay dividends. But so profitable is it that the dividend falls below 10 per cent only in the worst of times.

In 1888 a tremendous boom developed at Broken Hill, based on the supposition that since the BHP holdings were fabulously rich, the whole area in which they were located must be rich. Madness descended upon the community, and the most ridiculous and outrageous frauds were perpetrated. The fever was communicated to the stock exchanges in the capital cities, where the BHP directors did not disdain to participate in it; but the most reckless trading was done at the Hill itself. The next year, when the boom had collapsed, the *Silver Age* newspaper recalled that "In a small way Broken Hill was the Monte Carlo of Australia."

While the BHP mines were extraordinarily profitable, the exploitation of them from the technical standpoint posed difficult problems. Blast furnaces had been set up in Broken Hill in 1886, but, the problem of water supply proving difficult, they were transferred to Port Pirie, South Australia, two hundred miles away. But this difficulty was as nothing compared with the trouble that arose around 1900 when the exhaustion of oxidized ore, the treatment of which was well understood, made the matter of treating the lead-zinc sulphides very pressing indeed. Hitherto a gravity concentration had been applied to these, by which method lead and silver were fairly well recovered and the zinc-bearing "tailings" stored. In time the tailings made truly mountainous piles all about the mines. Both Australian and overseas metallurgists applied themselves to the problem, and eventually the Australians solved it. In 1902 a "flotation" process was introduced, and it has been progressively improved until today the percentage of recovery of the minerals is very high indeed. The solution of this problem was not confined to one method at first, and the utilization of different methods brought new organizations into the life of Broken Hill, specifically to deal with "tailings." Most of them interlocked either with the BHP or the other mines and thus became permanently associated with the Hill, ending up in some instances by controlling mines themselves.

Of far greater ultimate significance in the end was a move made by the BHP in 1911. Back in 1899, encountering difficulties in securing regular supplies of high quality iron stone for fluxing purposes at the Port Pirie smelters, the BHP had reached across the Spencer Gulf and secured leases on hitherto neglected iron deposits at a point now generally known by the name of the port, Whyalla. Within a few months they were under exploitation, and for a decade they served this lowly purpose only, though the high quality of the ore was well understood. In 1911, however, the predictable life of the BHP mine at Broken Hill was adjudged short, and the BHP hit upon a new world to conquer. It turned to steel production. The project was put into the hands of the hard-driving General Manager, G. D. Delprat, who had come to the BHP from the notorious Rio Tinto mines in Spain in the late eighteen-nineties.

When the BHP shifted its attention to steel, the principal ironworks in Australia was in the possession of the Hoskins family at Lithgow, in the mountains back of Sydney. The industry was not on a sound footing either technologically or managerially. In effect, the BHP had a clear field for its proposed operations. An American expert, David Baker of Philadelphia, was brought to Australia by Delprat, and after surveying the situation he suggested that Whyalla iron be brought to New South Wales coal at Newcastle. The layout still conforms with Mr. Baker's original suggestions.

The Newcastle plant was built on a vast swamp which was filled in at a place known as Port Waratah. It came into production in 1915, and the first steel was rolled on September 5th of that year. (A small piece of it can be seen at the Newcastle Club!) Since Australia was then cut off from the world steel supplies, a very valuable market was immediately at hand from the beginning. The BHP supplied the steel rails for the transcontinental railway which was then being built. Only when the steel-producers of the world came back into the international market after the war did the BHP have to fall back on government assistance to sustain its position. It turned to the Commonwealth which controls the tariff and related instruments for encouraging private enterprise. But behind the shelter afforded, the BHP achieved a very high order of efficiency, and on May 9, 1939 the first cargo of steel ever sent from Australia to England left Newcastle.

The BHP has never really turned back since it went into steel. What has it become? Fully to tell would lead us into a maze in which all clarifying light would disappear, and to present the case diagrammatically would bring into being a "spider-chart" of the most astonishing kind. It would, moreover, involve a fairly complete exposition of Australian production. Briefly, therefore, the BHP is, first and foremost, Australian steel, and since 1935, when it absorbed its last prospective competitor, it has had a monopoly. It is also deeply involved in controlling the materials it uses; it produces its own iron, limestone, dolomite, fluor spar, and coal. It has built a plant to handle the alloys needed in producing special steels. It owns the shipping necessary to move its materials to Newcastle, especially the iron ore from South Australia. It is closely interlocked, either directly by shareholders, by directorships, or by being the sole supplier of the basic material of the industries, with shops producing black and galvanized sheets, plain and barbed wire, wire netting, fencing wire, wire rope, nails, steel wheels, tires, axles, and so on, through the role of steel processing industries. It usually succeeds in tying up with any concern whose activities have to do with steel as, for example, the American Rolling Mill Company which recently built a plant in Australia to produce steel sheets. It is directly or indirectly concerned, through the utilization of the by-products of various phases of its productive activities (e.g., the making of coke), in supplying the Australian market with sulphate of ammonia (used on the sugar fields of Queensland), benzol (used as motor fuel), naphthalene, road tar, concentrated ammonia liquor, and so on. Naturally it is the principal Australian ally of Imperial Chemical Industries. It is interested in gold mining. In association with General Motors Holden, Ltd., a partly American concern, and the Broken Hill Associated Smelters Pty., Ltd., of Port Pirie, it began in 1937 "the biggest aircraft development in the history of Australia," a project of inestimable value to Australia when war broke out. (Incidentally, the United Kingdom government tried to keep the American interests out of the Australian airplane industry.)

And so the BHP is in on the ground floor, supplying indispensable, inescapable materials to the basic Australian activities of grazing, farming, manufacturing, mining, transport, and construction. Indeed where is the BHP not found? It is, said the Australian *Chemical Engineering and Mining Record* in 1937, "the apotheosis of Australian capitalism." Without it, Australia today would be an entirely different place. The BHP sits at the center of capitalistic power in Australia, a vertical and horizontal trust and a holding company. It also wields an unhealthy amount of political influence. Little did the seven men who gathered together a few pounds at Mount Gipps Station in 1883 envisage anything like that!

Where is the center of all this power? When the BHP was launched in 1885, its head office was established in Melbourne. However, the center of gravity soon shifted to London. It was there that the BHP directors went when they wished to turn into money some of the mining leases they held but could not conveniently exploit. At the Half Yearly Ordinary General Meeting of July 30, 1897, the Chairman declared, "The bulk of our shares are held in Europe and abroad. In fact we have 5,443 shareholders on the London register as against 3,850 on the Melbourne register." Sixteen years later, when the company was well advanced with its steel works, the *Mining and Engineering Review* brought out figures and ventured an explanation of the situation then existing. Of 960,000 shares outstanding, 714,110 were held in London, the balance being distributed, mostly in small parcels, in Australia. The *Review* said, "One reason for this is that the ups and downs of the field have played into the hands of speculators, who, in alliance with London houses, have made the mines the subject of extensive market dealings." The ups and downs were, of course, metal prices, water problems, metallurgical puzzles giving rise to depressing rumors, and labor troubles. The situation still exists, the BHP is still strongly penetrated with London money, and it has a London as well as an Australian board of directors. The subsidiary and associated companies of the BHP are in most cases intimately tied up with London also. Nevertheless today the Australian operating directorates have, in most instances, the predominating influence. Essington Lewis, Managing Director of BHP, is incomparably the greatest production man in contemporary Australian industry.

It is only necessary to reiterate that the good country in Australia is found along the coasts to make it clear that the transport and communication problem is difficult. The task is one of building coastal lines, with feeder-lines running out from it until they peter out in dry country. This is especially obvious in the case of the railways, but it is equally true of roads and telegraph and telephone lines.

A map of the Australian railway system shows that a main line starts at Cairns in northern Queensland and runs parallel to the coast clear around to Perth in Western Australia. It is as though the United States were served by a main line running from northern Maine around the coast to Los Angeles. From the Australian main line the feeder-lines branch off, being most numerous where the country is richest. Ordinarily the feeder-lines gather and distribute goods for a coastal port and, in all states except Queensland, mostly for a single port. In Queensland, because of the shape of the state, there are four ports which feeder-lines serve, Brisbane, Rockhampton, Townsville, and Cairns, their importance reflecting the economic activities behind them. How natural or inevitable is this bringing of the railways to a focus on a single port is the subject of dispute in Australia. It is freely alleged that it is not natural, but the result of political and economic pressure of the big city interests. If the railway systems had developed logically, the argument runs, produce would be fed to what are now very small outer ports. This dispute is but one of the many which go to make up the political struggle between city and country.

But even that is really an ideal statement of the railway problem, for it implies a unified railway system, which is precisely what Australia does not have. Not only does each state own and manage its own system, but also the railways suffer from the handicap of varying gauges. For this reason it is impossible to send a train around the coastal main line from Cairns to Perth. Such a journey would take this form: the train from Cairns to Brisbane would run on a 3 foot 6 inch gauge; from Brisbane to Albury in southern New South Wales on a 4 foot 8½ inch gauge; from Albury through Melbourne and Adelaide to Red Hill, South Australia, on a 5 foot 3 inch gauge; on the Commonwealth-owned transcontinental railway to Kalgoorlie, Western Australia, on a 4 foot 8½ inch gauge; and then to Perth on a 3 foot 6 inch gauge! The reason for this extraordinary situation, which is wasteful economically and which complicates the defense problem of Australia, is that the railway systems date from colonial times. Each colony developed its own, disregarding the possibility of linking its lines with those of its neighbors. The disaster of the gauges could have been avoided had the engineers and politicians of the eighteen-fifties thought in terms of a continental railway network. Such minor contributions to unification as have been made, like the short extension of the New South Wales gauge into Brisbane, or the linking up of the Victorian and South Australian lines in part, emphasize the problem without solving it. The idea of dealing with it by a gigantic works program is one which has been entertained in Australia for many years, but the job has never been tackled. Quite apart from the enormous cost, vested interests now interfere.

Much of the traffic in heavy freight between states is sea-borne. Whether this is because of lower charges or because the railway system is inefficient for this purpose is not certain, but probably both factors are influential. Certainly it is not because the coastal shipping concerns are free from legislative impositions of a kind which multiply expenses. But there it is. Another factor which keeps down the interstate railway traffic in heavy goods is the situation with regard to overseas shipping. Most of the overseas

A "mob" of sheep in charge of a mounted man and two dogs.

Section of BHP works, Newcastle.

vessels come from England, go to England, and are of British registry. (Japanese and United States vessels are successfully competitive on lines to their countries.) A vessel coming to Australia from England usually touches first at Fremantle, the port of Perth, goes on to Adelaide, to Melbourne, and then to Sydney, and perhaps up to Brisbane, discharging cargo at each port. On the outward voyage, the order of call is reversed. Of course some vessels go to but one or two ports. It is obvious that in either case it is possible for each state to assemble its exports at a port within its border, on its own railways, for dispatch overseas; and to receive its imports for distribution there also. This cuts down the need for interstate transport by rail. While the Commonwealth statistics show twenty-three ports at which the net tonnage entered, taking all classes, exceeds three hundred thousand per year, the capital cities are the most important ports by far, only four others handling over a million tons a year: Newcastle in New South Wales; Townsville in Queensland; Port Kembla in New South Wales; and Geelong in Victoria. Of the ports, Sydney is incomparably the busiest; it handles over eleven million tons of shipping a year.

The traffic which justifies the building of roads suitable for modern motor vehicles is naturally concentrated around the great cities. Therefore, around the cities one will find excellent roads which encourage motoring for pleasure as well as for commercial purposes. There are also excellent arterial roads along lines of heavy traffic between population centers. But in the outback the quality of the roads deteriorates until one reaches the point where they are mere tracks through the bush. In 1936 the state of Victoria, which is as manageable as any in this regard, had roads of the following descriptions: concrete or bituminous surfaces, 6,700 miles; water-bound macadam and gravel, 22,000; formed only, which means that scrapers had thrown up the form of a road and left it for the traffic to pound into shape, 25,000; and natural surface, which means bush tracks, 53,000 miles. In the other states the proportions are not materially different. But comparing the population and the area, the Australian road system seems remarkably good.

The Australian government railways are badgered by the road-rail competition problem, for in normal times the Australians are great users of motor vehicles, most of them of American make. The road-rail competition cannot be allowed freely to work itself out, for the railways represent an enormous investment of public money on which interest charges must be met. Many efforts have therefore been made to control road traffic, especially the hauling of freight, in such a fashion as to reduce to a minimum the competition of this new method of transport. The railways must, of necessity, be the primary consideration. But in a way it is unfortunate, for road transport might serve Australia's needs better than rail in many parts of the Commonwealth.

The telegraph and telephone systems are under the control of the Post Office, a Commonwealth function. The Australians send more telegraphic messages per head each year than any other people in the world. The telephone system is also highly developed, Australia ranking seventh among the countries of the world in density of telephones. In radio broadcasting there are two systems, the National System, which is a Commonwealth government enterprise, and a private system owned by various individuals and corporations. Both are dependent upon the Post Office for technical facilities. The government system derives its revenue for programs from the license fee paid by all owners of listening sets. It shares the fee with the Post Office, which thus has revenue for the development and maintenance of its technical equipment. The private stations obtain their revenue from advertising; and make a contribution to the Post Office in the form of a license fee. Australia ranks sixth among the nations of the world in the number of receiving sets per hundred of population.

A cable connecting Australia with England was opened in 1871; and one connecting the Commonwealth with Canada at Vancouver was opened in 1902. Australia is in direct beam wireless communication with the United Kingdom (since 1927) and other Empire points, as well as such Pacific islands as New Guinea, New Caledonia, Fiji, and others. A similar service to the United States depends upon action by the Australian government. In general, Australia is within the British Imperial communications system.

The Commonwealth is peculiarly adapted to the use of the airplane, and Australians make excellent pilots. There is an elaborate system of air lines covering about twenty-five thousand miles. Most of the planes are of American make. It is likely that the airplane is doing more to knit the country together than any other means save the radio. The airports are not as elaborate as in America, and in the smaller centers are amazingly primitive. But they serve the purpose. The Commonwealth is, in normal times, connected with England by a British-owned air line which runs via Singapore and India to London. A Dutch service runs to Sydney from Batavia. There are also lines to New Guinea and to Dilli in Portuguese Timor. An American line runs from Los Angeles via Hawaii, Canton Island, and New Caledonia to Auckland in New Zealand, where it connects with a British trans-Tasman service to Sydney. There is a prospect that this line will eventually go from New Caledonia directly to Australia at Brisbane, a logical course now made impossible by legalistic difficulties. Thus far no link connecting the Australian line to New Guinea (or the lines which operate within New Guinea) with the Japanese services which come down through the mandated islands from Japan proper has been established. But even today it is clear that the airplane will bring Australia into intimate contact with the whole world. Her isolation is rapidly disappearing.

The only direct communication between Australia and the United States is by radio telephone. Newspaper dispatches from New York, of which there are an increasing number, reach Australia via Canada.

FINANCIAL policy is the subject of constant debate in Australia, and there is a strong disposition to make it *the* political issue. Your opinions on public finance are often taken as an index to your general political outlook. Among the more dogmatic conservatives any show of weakness for the labor position is regarded as a weakness for sin; and among the sterner labor people any skepticism about their notion is taken as proof that it is accompanied by a belief in social oppression in general. The foreigner cannot help being amused by this, even when he recognizes the importance of the stake. Especially is this true when he notes that ideas labor has advocated at one time, to the accompaniment of angry catcalls and general execration from the conservatives, are later taken up and used by the conservatives. Labor's "sinister plots" have a way of becoming the "brilliant policies" of the conservatives. Americans are, of course, familiar with this political phenomenon.

A detailed exposition of the financial problem and the issues of policy would bog us down in a swamp of statistics and technical discussion. All that will be attempted here is an elementary statement of the situation.

The fundamental fact is the strength of the financial tie between Australia and the United Kingdom. This has been called the "financial nexus" between the two countries, but whatever it is called, it is a fact of overwhelming importance. A complete understanding of Australia's history is only possible when one relates events in Australia to the condition of economic affairs in England. There is a fairly exact correlation between Australian and English booms, between Australian and English slumps. For many years the flow of British capital into Australia played a large, if not decisive role in Australian internal economic conditions; and the existence of huge Australian debts held in Britain explains in considerable measure why the Australian export trade has been concentrated on Britain. The interest on the debts has had to be paid with exports of Australian commodities for which there was a demand on the United Kingdom market.

The Australian colonies began to borrow in London as early as 1842, but the really heavy borrowings took place in the six decades after 1870. Most of the Australian public debt was accumulated by the colonies (states, after 1901), and the outstanding excuse for it was the need of funds for development. Even under the Commonwealth the burden of development has fallen on the states. Much of the expenditure was for tangible assets and was justified by a feeling of optimism about Australia's future growth. Developmental schemes were undertaken because of a conviction that while the existing population did not justify them, the population they would bring in and the production for which it would be responsible would make the burden of them very light indeed. This did not always happen. Recent efforts to open up what are distinctly marginal areas have revealed the flaw in this line of argument. But Australians generally are still convinced that the final justification of their possession of the continent is the extent to which they develop it to the limits of its potentialities. Usually this conviction is stated in political terms. It is a reflex of the fear that some hostile nation—the Japanese, for example—will take the continent if they fail fully to develop it. There is, therefore, a very common type of Australian who argues for developmental investments regardless of whether any tangible economic ratification of the schemes can be found.

Since development has been the basic purpose, and since Australian governments for this and other reasons have assumed responsibility for services elsewhere left to private enterprise, an analysis of how the loans have been expended gives a result quite different from that found in other countries. As of June 30, 1936, the situation was as follows:

TOTAL LOAN EXPENDITURE, COMMONWEALTH AND STATES

General	£m.
Railways	367.73
Roads, Bridges, Harbors, Rivers	85.55
Water Supply	76.43
Local Gov't Loans & Unempl. Relief	43.50
Post Office, Teleg., Telephone	41.05
Public Buildings	37.36
Electricity Supply	25.62
Sewerage	22.75
Other Public Works	21.25
Housing	19.30
Tramways	13.76
Federal Capital Territory	7.78
Defense	7.65

Primary Production	
Land Settlement, incl. Advances	94.94
Water Conservation, Irrigation, Drainage	28.19
Agriculture, incl. Banking	22.28
Other Primary Production	6.74
Mines and Minerals	5.80
War Purposes	367.08
Other Purposes	27.84
Discount & Flotation Expenses	35.47
Funding of Deficits	82.03
Grand Total	1,440.10

This is not, of course, a statement of the existing debts but of the total loan expenditure. Even a casual reading of the table clearly indicates how Australia has spent its borrowed money. The heavy expenditure on railways, for example, fully supports the point about development being the primary reason for borrowings. A statement of the total debt as of 1936, including a statement of where it was redeemable, gives the following result:

Redeemable

Australia	£ 665,550,482
London	£ 544,960,662
New York	£ 45,259,837

Grand total: £1,255,770,981

To the figures given above, one would have to add the borrowings of local government bodies and statutory bodies with authority to borrow, as well as private debts, to get the ultimate grand total of Australian indebtedness. Such an elaboration would not change the relative position of the places of redemption. One can understand, therefore, why Australian financial and trade policy must be governed in relation to the general economic situation in the United Kingdom.

The nature of the financial tie to the United Kingdom was dramatized in a very unpleasant fashion during the Great Depression. While the prices for Australian exports sharply declined, wool taking the lead, the interest charges on overseas debts remained fixed. To meet them it was necessary to export more primary produce than formerly, at a time when there was an excess of supply and a minimum of demand. Where formerly one bale of wool paid a given amount of interest, it now required many bales to pay the same amount. Since the borrowing had been done on the unconscious assumption that commodity prices would retain a reasonably stable relation to interest charges, the Australians were naturally irritated by the situation in which they found themselves. There was a widespread feeling that they were expected to hold the dirty end of the stick regardless of the consequences. Hard things were said about the City of London and its representatives.

What to do became a major political issue. One leader, John Thomas Lang, Labour Premier of New South Wales, acquired permanent infamy by proposing to withhold all interest payments until the London bondholders agreed to a compromise. This was not done, of course, for it savored of repudiation, which British people hold in horror (except with regard to war debts). But the sharp struggle within New South Wales and between that state and the Commonwealth created the bitterest political situation in recent years. Mr. Lang was eventually decisively defeated, not by the most savory methods. The party which he led was driven into the political wilderness for a decade. It emerged, under new leadership, in 1941 to take charge of state affairs again. John T. ("Jack") Lang was, for all those years, the great bogeyman of the conservatives and an old man of the sea to New South Wales labor— indeed to all labor, for the allegation was that every labor leader was infected with his heresies, a monstrous fable. The struggle of the Labour party members to dislodge Mr. Lang from party leadership, a prerequisite to rehabilitating the party and winning office, is an epic of labor politics, replete with skullduggery and counter skullduggery, charges and counter-charges without end. Today Mr. Lang is still a member of the lower house in New South Wales and still a member of the Labour party, but his hold over leadership and policy seems permanently broken. The point is that this protracted, bitter row revolved around finance. Mr. Lang is, to an American observer, a singular example of the genus demagogue and a master of machine politics. He is a monotonous speaker, but he is a man of great native ability, a superb parliamentarian, and an excellent administrator, though these things are rarely said of him in Australia. It is somewhat startling to hear Mr. Lang begin a speech. His invariable salutation is, "My friends . . ."!

Instead of withholding interest payments, the Australian governments, under the leadership of the Commonwealth, carried through the program of bringing internal costs into closer line with external prices. The necessary technical advice was given by academic economists, the most conspicuous of whom was D. B. Copland of the University of Melbourne. The authorities put through a series of conversions on the London money markets, thus lowering total interest charges. They depreciated the Australian pound 25 per cent in terms of sterling. They lowered wages 20 per cent, cut by government fiat other charges by the same proportion, and loosened up the credit situation within Australia. These measures, among others, when combined with rising prices and increased investments in manufacturing enterprises, brought Australia out of the depression. But there was left a heritage of social maladjustments, including unemployment.

One of the permanent effects of the depression has been the development of the internal money market in Australia. This has enabled the Commonwealth to cut down its borrowings in London. The institution of crucial importance in determining how much loan money the states shall have is the Federal Loan Council. It consists of representatives of the Commonwealth and the states and was established in December, 1927. As of July 1, 1929, the Commonwealth, acting under the provisions of the financial agreement on which the Loan Council is founded, took over the unpaid "gross public debt of each state existing on 30th June, 1927," subject to certain additions and subtractions. For fifty-eight years from July 1, 1927, the Commonwealth will make a fixed contribution toward the interest payments on these debts, the states paying their pro rata share of the balance. The Commonwealth contribution is equal to the contribution which the Commonwealth made to the states from 1910 on, as compensation for their having relinquished customs revenues to the Commonwealth under the Federal constitution. An arrangement was also made whereby both the Commonwealth and the states contribute to a sinking fund to extinguish the debts and also all new ones contracted. With regard to the latter, the Loan Council co-ordinates all public borrowings. Each state annually submits to it a works program, giving the amount of money it deems necessary to carry it out. The programs are reviewed by the council and the states assigned proportions of the total sum it is deemed wise to borrow. The total sum is then obtained in the money market by the Commonwealth and the fixed shares handed to the states. In certain instances the states may borrow on their own account, the Commonwealth guaranteeing such bonds. In this fashion the Loan Council exerts control over the finances of the states. Its establishment is an excellent example of how the Commonwealth has increased its power in recent years at the expense of the states. A phase of the row between Mr. Lang and his opponents was a challenge of the right of the Loan Council to exact from New South Wales its share of the charges. The High Court ruled against New South Wales, thus establishing the constitutionality of the whole set-up. The Loan Council played a strategic role in implementing the plans for bringing Australia out of the depression. Its control of the public debt and new borrowings plainly made that possible.

Another financial institution which played an important role in the depression is the Commonwealth Bank. It was established by the Labour party, the act authorizing it having been passed in December, 1911. In June, 1912, it started operations without capital, transacting government business and accepting savings accounts from the public. The following year it entered general banking. It was quickly successful, carried on extensive banking operations on the Commonwealth account during the First World War, and took control of the note issue in 1920. Its powers have been variously defined by successive governments, and the intent of the Labour founders has been the subject of considerable debate. Theoretically it should be a central bank, and the latest *Commonwealth Year Book* cautiously says that its operations "have developed toward those of a Central Bank." The objective has yet to be reached.

Perhaps the outstanding reason for the failure is the fact that the bank is a political issue, the focus of that struggle over financial policy which vexes Commonwealth politics. The Labour party sees in the bank an institution which, properly handled, will give the people control over credit. Through that control, it is argued, it will open many doors to social beneficence that are now firmly closed. Achievement of this end requires that the bank be brought under the direct control of the Federal Treasurer and used to realize the government's political program. The conservatives, on the other hand, while hardly denying the utility of a central bank under present-day conditions, feel strongly that the bank should be independent of direct government control, inclining to the idea that the private banks should have a determining voice in all banking questions.

The most powerful private bank is the Bank of New South Wales, and it has often stood out against policies which had wide popular support. As a matter of fact, this is one of those issues in which the conservative fear of the Labour party and its real or alleged purposes reaches fever pitch. Far from being based upon any clear technical grounds, the conservative opposition to strengthening the tie between the Commonwealth Bank and the Federal Treasury is founded on political considerations. The chances of a fairly independent bank board taking a line hostile to the interests of the conservatives are reckoned slight; and it is hoped and expected that such a bank will frustrate any plan put forward by Labour which may seem hostile to those interests.

A Royal commission on the monetary and banking systems which reported in 1937 dealt with the issue in these words:

In our view, the proper relations between the two authorities are these. The Federal Parliament is ultimately responsible for monetary policy, and the Government of the day is the executive of the Parliament. The Commonwealth Bank has certain powers delegated to it by statute, and the Board's duty to the community is to exercise those powers to the best of its ability. Where there is a conflict between the Government's view of what is best in the national interest, and the Board's view, the first essential is full and frank discussion between the two authorities with a view to exploring the whole problem. In most cases this should ensure agreement on a policy to be carried out by the Bank which it can reconcile with its duty to the community, and which has the approval of the Government. In cases in which it is clear beyond doubt that the differences are irreconcilable, the Government should give the Bank an assurance that it accepts full responsibility for the proposed policy, and is in a position to take, and will take, any action necessary to implement it. It is then the duty of the Bank to accept this assurance and to carry out the policy of the Government. [The Chairman accepts this statement subject to reservation, and Mr. Pitt (a member) dissents.] This does not imply that there should at any time be interference by the Government or by any member of the Government, in the administration of the Commonwealth Bank. Once the question of authority is decided, there should be little difficulty in preserving close and cordial relations between the Commonwealth Government and the Commonwealth Bank.

Even this cautious and sensible statement was badly received in conservative quarters. It was, naturally, seized upon by Labour, for it favors the Labour case. But it is far from the position of the Reserve Bank in New Zealand, which is required by law "to give effect as far as may be to the monetary policy of the Government as communicated to it from time to time by the Minister of

Finance." Since Australia had a conservative government at the
time the report was made, nothing was done to implement this
suggestion. In fact the whole report became something of a political football. Its reception showed how hot the financial question
really is.

During the depression the bank was the center of extremely
important opposition to Labour's proposals for meeting the financial difficulties of the time. It fell in line with the proposals eventually adopted. It seems to me that the evidence is pretty clear
that the bank, in evaluating the proposals, was more concerned
with the sponsorship of them than with their character objectively considered. It opposed Labour's inflationary ideas; but in
the end it accepted and implemented the inflationary ideas of the
economists.

The increase in importance during the depression of the Loan
Council and the Commonwealth Bank, plus the rapid development of the domestic money market, are changes which had and
will continue to have vast influence on the financial position in
Australia. Obviously the Commonwealth cannot escape the consequences of its "financial nexus" with the United Kingdom, but
it can go a long way toward being more completely master of its
own financial house. Australia is a tremendous distance from
transforming herself into a creditor nation in relation to Britain.
She is not comparable to Canada. But her internal strength will
be of immense importance to her in the difficult years ahead.

Foreign private investments in Australia are largely of British
origin—from the United Kingdom. American investments run
as poor a second here as in the field of public obligations. While
they are expected to grow, there is no prospect, immediate or remote, that the United States will ever top Britain in this field in
Australia as it has in Canada. Just how large the British investments are has never been authoritatively stated in detail. An official estimate gave the figure of £175,000,000 as the total long-term
private capital invested in Australia in 1937. It has since increased.
A recent estimate of American direct investments is £35,000,000.
This leaves a heavy balance in favor of the United Kingdom, for
the holdings of other foreign nations are small.

Where the British investments are found in the structure of Australian industry is, of course, a matter of great importance. The point has not been carefully studied until very recently, and the most detailed analysis I have seen has yet to be published. Drawing upon Brian Fitzpatrick's unpublished survey, it is possible to say with reasonable certainty that United Kingdom capital is strongly represented in the key industries of the Commonwealth. I have already commented on the role it plays in steel. Mr. Fitzpatrick finds it playing an equally strategic role in gold mining, base metals, chemicals, and rubber. "The great companies of Australia, most of which are British capital undertakings," he writes, "present a history of a strengthening grip on industry over wider and wider fields, by the absorption of other concerns; and most of them show a tendency to conserve the advantages gained by eliminating competition, by confining fresh issues of capital to their shareholders, and making those issues in the form of bonus shares."

According to Mr. Fitzpatrick the thirteen richest companies operating in Australia in 1939 were, in order of size, in "steel, sugar milling and refining, tobacco manufacture, steel, brewing, metal refining, glass and allied manufacture, wool-broking, rubber manufacture, wool-broking, wool-broking, and chemicals manufacture." The thirteen great companies have stockholders' funds to a total of £A102,179,027 and, including outside funds under their control, total funds of £A111,967,375. The richest company of all is the BHP, followed by the Colonial Sugar Refining Company, Ltd. Listed in order of total funds controlled, the thirteen great companies are:

1. The Broken Hill Proprietary Company, Ltd.
2. The Colonial Sugar Refining Company, Ltd.
3. The British Tobacco Company (Australia), Ltd.
4. Australian Iron & Steel, Ltd. (A wholly owned subsidiary of BHP)
5. Tooth & Company, Ltd. (Brewers)
6. Electrolytic Zinc Company of Australia, Ltd.
7. Australian Consolidated Industries, Ltd. (Chiefly glass)
8. Adelaide Electricity Supply Company, Ltd.
9. Goldsbrough Mort, Ltd. (wool-brokers)

10. Dunlop Perdriau Rubber Company, Ltd.
11. Dalgety's, Ltd. (wool-brokers)
12. New Zealand Loan and Mercantile Agency Company, Ltd. (wool-brokers)
13. Imperial Chemical Industries of Australia & New Zealand, Ltd.

Most of the company names explain the activities in which the concerns are engaged. A wool-broking concern, it may be helpful to state, is engaged in marketing wool for station owners, selling them supplies and equipment, lending them money, and generally acting as universal service and supply agents. These concerns are also heavily involved in the actual ownership of sheep stations which they run through hired managers and, together with the banks, are generally considered to be the predominant interest in the wool-growing industry. That a brewery is high up in the list of great companies recalls that beer is the great Australian drink, and the manufacture of it is naturally an important matter.

Mr. Fitzpatrick quotes Wilfred Prest, a business economist, as stating that under the joint-stock company set-up "the ownership of property no longer implies any right to direct control over it; it may not imply any right to choose those who shall exercise control, and, even if it does, the right to vote may be ineffective or impossible to use." Berle and Means, in 1934, explored this situation in the United States. It is not unexpected, therefore, that in Australia interlocking directorates are a common phenomenon and that tremendous power is in the hands of a small group of men. There is concentration of control in industry, both on the personal and financial sides. Mr. Fitzpatrick makes it clear that some of the important company directors are also on bank boards, but he does not speculate on the extent to which the banks control the companies, if at all. It would seem a reasonable guess that the power is still in the hands of the companies. There is little development of what is called finance capitalism in Australia.

It should not be assumed from these observations that United Kingdom capital is predominant throughout Australian industry. It is almost certain that, taking the whole field of private capital investment, Australian owned and controlled capital is by far the most important element in the total. This is borne out by the fact that, as remarked before, Australian businessmen are apt to be economic nationalists, and they obviously give that slant to the official outlook of such organizations as the Chamber of Manufacturers.

With the decline in the volume of public investments due to the depression, it has been suggested by several conservative economists—for example, D. B. Copland and G. L. Wood—that the hope of the future is more and more private investment. They feel that private investment should be encouraged by political policy —as it probably should. But another school of economists, of whom Colin Clark and John G. Crawford are representatives, contends that private investment, even under the most favorable conditions, cannot hope to achieve levels which will keep the Australian economy functioning satisfactorily. It must be supplemented by heavy government investments; and these must be heaviest during slumps. They therefore suggest as a permanent policy low interest rates and easy credit conditions which will encourage public investment in such fields as housing. This is, in essence, a political issue. It is very directly related to that which circles around the use to which the Commonwealth Bank shall be put. It is highly likely that it will be one of the central issues of postwar politics.

Australia is famous as an exporter of wool and wheat. The Commonwealth runs more sheep than any other country and is the greatest grower of fine merino wool on the globe. It is also one of the Big Four wheat exporters, ranking with Canada, the United States, and Argentina. It is, moreover, an important supplier to the United Kingdom of butter, eggs, dried fruits, wine, lamb and mutton, beef, metals, sugar, and a variety of other products. Trade policy plays an important role in Australian public policy. An intricate matter taken by itself, it is tangled up with finance, Imperial economic relations, marketing schemes, the tariff, and the large problem of national development.

Some idea of how important foreign trade is to Australia can be gained by considering the percentage exported of total production of the several commodities. But first it may be stated in another fashion. Classified according to value of foreign trade per capita (1938), Australia ranked ninth among the nations. Canada was eighth, the United Kingdom tenth. The United States was well down the list. The value of Australian foreign trade per capita was *over three and a half times the comparable American figure*. Reverting to our first point, the situation is as follows:

AUSTRALIAN PRODUCTION EXPORTED

	Percentage of total production	*Percentage exported*
Agriculture	20.47	37.61
Pastoral	22.51	68.75
Dairy & Farmyard	12.08	23.30
Mining	5.27	66.53
Forestry & Fisheries	2.76	12.28
Total, Primary Produce	63.09	47.28
Manufacturing	36.91	3.58
Grand total	100.00	31.15

The second column of figures is our interest here. It clearly shows that the agricultural and pastoral industries are deeply concerned with foreign trade as exporters. Although the mining industry exports heavily, it is not, as the figures show, such a large interest as the others.

If to this picture we add an analysis of the structure of Australian exports, we will clarify our notion of the elements of Australia's foreign trade problem.

PERCENTAGE CONTRIBUTED TO TOTAL EXPORTS

Agriculture	24.71
Pastoral	49.68
Mining	11.25
Dairy & Farmyard	9.04
Forestry & Fisheries	1.08
Total, Primary Produce	95.76
Manufacturing	4.24
	100.00

It is now plain why most foreign observers think of Australia almost exclusively in terms of a source of foodstuffs and raw materials. This view does no violence to Australia the exporter. But reference to the first table given shows that manufacturing makes the biggest single contribution to the total of national production. It is, therefore, of major importance to the internal economy of the Australian nation. Since industry is tariff-protected, the tariff issue is of primary importance to any understanding of Australian trade policy.

But before dealing with the tariff let us determine the destinations of Australian exports. Using the percentages for 1938-39 we get this result:

DESTINATIONS AUSTRALIAN EXPORTS

United Kingdom		54.45
British Possessions		15.01
Four most important		
New Zealand	5.45	
Canada	1.63	
Brit. Malaya	1.56	
India	1.46	
		—
Total Exports to British Countries		69.46
Foreign countries		30.54
Four most important		
France	7.65	
Belgium	4.53	
Japan	3.97	
U. S. A.	2.95	
		—
		100.00

Thus over half of Australian exports go to Britain and almost seven-tenths to British countries. No single foreign country takes as much as 10 per cent of them. Japan is the only foreign country which has in any year taken over 10 per cent, but as a result of trade disputes and other difficulties Japanese-Australian trade has not been in a healthy condition in recent years. The United States takes very little from Australia, the basic reason being the competitive character of the production of the two nations. To a very great extent this distribution of exports is inevitable. We have already emphasized that the principal source of loan money is the United Kingdom; and in a moment we shall see that a high percentage of Australian merchandise imports come from there also. These are powerful determinants of the direction of trade. Moreover, Australia's origin as a nation and the origin of her immigrants during all her history reinforces this tie in the realm of sentiment. And Australia is a British dominion, the political aspect of this complex of influential factors. In recent years, moreover, the established concentration has had to be maintained, for it has been difficult to expand trade because of economic nationalism, especially on the continent of Europe. The Ottawa Agreement, of 1932, was a major effort to preserve the relation as a preliminary to any ventures in expanding trade outside the British community.

Yet there are powerful reasons for thinking that the basic Australian trade problem is that of breaking out of the limits here defined. The problem is to expand existing markets and find new ones, to spread Australian trade over more and more countries and areas. It is highly unlikely that Australia will ever, in our time, cease to be primarily a member of the British trading system, at least of her own choice. But it is highly likely that we shall see Australia make a valiant effort to increase the importance of her trade with foreign countries.

Turning now to Australian imports, we will find little to astonish us. In this field, too, the United Kingdom holds the premier position.

ORIGIN AUSTRALIAN IMPORTS

United Kingdom		41.64
British Possessions		17.94
Four most important		
Canada	7.96	
India	2.96	
New Zealand	1.82	
Pacific Islands	1.43	

Total imports from British	
countries	59.58
Foreign Countries	40.42
Four most important	
U. S. A.	15.09
Netherlands East	
Indies	7.33
Germany	4.52
Japan	4.22
	——
	100.00

American readers will be most interested in the high position of the United States among the foreign suppliers of Australian imports, especially when they recall how small a percentage of Australian exports this country takes. The American position is chiefly accounted for by automobiles and industrial machinery, tobacco, gasoline and oil, agricultural and electrical machinery, chemicals, and books and printed matter. These things figure largely in the life of the Australians. In fact, having regard to the small population, Australia is a heavy consumer of American goods. It has been authoritatively stated that on a per capita basis each individual Australian consumed nearly as much American production ($9.14) in recent years as the combined amount consumed by a Frenchman, a German, an Italian, and a Japanese (total, $9.29). But there are only seven million Australians.

Viewed from the American angle, this 15 per cent of Australia's imports becomes about 2 per cent of America's exports. If we arbitrarily combine the Canadian and United States figures for exports and imports, thinking of a North American trading area, we find that while North America bulks large as a supplier, it absorbs little Australian produce. This, to repeat, is because Australian exports are competitive with North American production. But when it comes to things Australia needs—machinery, motor cars, and specialized goods—North American exports are in heavy demand. This is the essence of the trade problem between these two great areas in the Pacific Basin, which in cultural terms have so much in common.

The tariff question, known to the Australians as the fiscal issue, was introduced into Australian life during the period after the gold rushes when the decline of alluvial gold mining made it necessary to provide jobs for thousands of men in more routine lines of work. One phase of this was the further development of farming, of which the first political expression was the struggle to "unlock the land." Another phase was the building of what in Australia are called the secondary, or manufacturing industries. The political phase was the struggle over the tariff. In the colony of Victoria the tariff forces were led by David Syme, proprietor of *The Age* newspaper. Mr. Syme argued for a protective tariff and won his point in the end. This was in the late eighteen-sixties. Victoria became the center of protective tariff propaganda for the whole continent. For several decades thereafter, however, the other colonies used the tariff for revenue only, allowing industries only "natural" protection beyond this. They called their position free trade. New South Wales was the center of free trade propaganda.

The fiscal issue was one of the principal difficulties faced by the men who wrote the Federal Constitution in the late eighteen-nineties. It was not only a matter of a division between the Victorians and the other colonists; it was also that the issue divided into dissident fragments the colonial parties which might have been expected to coalesce to form a united conservative front in Federal politics. In fact, New South Wales, which was reluctant to join the Federation anyway, found in the fear of having protection imposed upon her a strong reason for being wary of the whole scheme. It thus came about that in the early days of the Federal Parliament the members were split three ways, two conservative parties divided by the fiscal issue, and the Labour party.

The first Australian tariff, that of 1902, was therefore a compromise which pleased nobody. There had to be a tariff, for the new Commonwealth was dependent upon customs for most of its revenue, as it has remained. (In recent years customs have accounted for a little over two-fifths of Commonwealth revenue.) It was not until the tariff of 1907-1908 that Australia got a really protective system. This tariff pretty much settled the fiscal issue in favor of the protectionists. In 1906 the Labour party was converted by being offered guarantees as to wages and conditions in return for support of the protectionist program. Today there is no organized free trade sentiment in all Australia. Everybody in some measure supports protection.

But because there is general agreement on the policy, it should not be thought that there is agreement on how it should be applied. An excellent statement of the actual situation is the following, taken from an Australian source:

The Tariff Committee of 1929 came to the conclusion that [the policy of protection] had enabled an increase of population to take place. . . . The policy . . . was, therefore, in every sense a development policy. This method of development involved increased costs for other production, and the main burden settled upon export industry. The chief export industries, wheat and wool, had been able to bear this burden, but there was evidence at the time of the report that the burden of excess costs of the tariff was becoming oppressive . . . The policy of protection has been adopted by the people as a means to making the full use of resources of the continent. From this point of view the cost it involves must be regarded in the same light as running railways or supplying irrigation water below cost. There is little doubt that it has played its part in securing some development of the type aimed at. The fact that it has enabled Australia to increase its population is consistent with the possibility that the larger population lives at a lower standard than a smaller population might have done. It follows that, insofar as the establishment of secondary industry involves a subsidy from the community, which falls with especial severity on export industry, there is a clash of interest between secondary industry and the interests which depend upon primary industry. Moreover, the secondary industries tend to be developed in the eastern States. These are nearer the great coal fields, and have the larger populations, and, as they had an early start, the modern tendency to concentration tends to make these industries even larger. The more sparsely settled outer States could never establish these industries except at great cost to themselves. As a result, the clash between the interests of primary and secondary industries tends to grow into a conflict between the more closely populated eastern States of Victoria and New South Wales and the sparsely settled marginal States of South Australia, Western Australia and Tasmania. Queensland occupies a middle position because of her enormous pastoral wealth, the small proportion of really arid country, and the high return of the sugar industry, protected by an embargo and price agreement which is now equivalent to a duty of about 250 per cent.

Ignoring for the present the struggle between the states, let us briefly examine that between the industries and the consequences thereof.

The broad division is between the primary and manufacturing industries. The former naturally want to keep production costs as low as possible. Since many manufactured articles enter into costs, the policy of encouraging their production behind a tariff wall may result in prices higher than those for the equivalent imports. It is also likely that wages in the manufacturing industries will be higher than in the rural industries, with a strong tendency for urban wages to pull rural wages upward and also draw off the most efficient and ambitious workers. The position of the primary producers is, therefore, that the tariff should never rise to levels which will exclude direct competition between Australian and overseas manufacturers. They contend that this has often happened and that because it has happened their costs of production have risen to levels which make it impossible for them to accept the prices of their goods on the world market without disaster to themselves. If they are nevertheless forced to do so, the argument runs, either they will drift quickly into bankruptcy, causing a large-scale abandonment of farms now productive, or rural living standards will fall below the accepted Australian level. This is stating the argument as though the rural industries had taken no counter measures other than verbal to sustain their position. As a matter of fact, that is not the case. Until just the other day only the wool and wheat industries accepted the logic of the position; today only wool accepts it. The other rural industries have discovered ways and means to gain the benefits of protection for themselves.

The slogan they use is "orderly marketing"; the most popular devices used are the "home consumption price," the guaranteed price, the government subsidy, and the bounty; the objective is "stabilization." Whatever the slogan, the particular scheme, or the objective, the organization of the primary producers into associations of various kinds is involved, this quite apart from their special protective organizations. The former have regulatory powers over the industries, voluntary or statutory. They enjoy the patronage of the governments, which sometimes outline policy for them in broad terms. Taken separately, the associations, or boards, are enormously powerful forces within the particular industries; taken as a group, they form a tremendous concentration of political pressure, especially when allied to the protective societies. Perhaps in no country in the world are the owner-producers better organized than in Australia, their interests better guarded, or their numerous complaints more sympathetically listened to. From the standpoint of rationalizing the marketing system, the schemes are admirable. It is also highly desirable that farmers, who tend toward anarchy in their productive activities, should be gathered together for joint action and discussion of mutual problems. No one deliberately favors disorderly marketing, viciously low prices, or crippling instability. There can be no quarrel with the objectives, broadly speaking. But there is reason to think that the farmer-entrepreneurs in Australia have been allowed to gain too much power in the community, especially at the expense of the consumers.

The Australian farmer appears to think that he has a special and unique claim upon the community for a high degree of security. He demands protection against the ups and downs of prices, especially the downs, and from all the other factors which go to make farming, like every other kind of capitalist enterprise, a more or less hazardous occupation. In Australia the farmers have come around to this position largely by arguing from the application of the tariff for the protection of manufacturing to the application of the protective principle to primary production. There can be no very logical objection to that general line of argument. But when the Australian farmers proceed also to argue that they have a superior right to special protection because they are, as they put it, "the backbone of the country," it is time to dissent.

Surely it is obvious to the meanest intelligence that the backbone of Australia, as of any other country, is the economy in all its various divisions, the total structure of production and the services. To select one section of the economy for special and unique honor is a neat political dodge, but it confuses understanding. The farmers are important—*very!* But there is no reason why their claims for favors should be treated with special tenderness. They are, to use an Australian term, a powerful "sectional interest," and their claims should be treated in the light of that fact. They get special treatment because they are highly organized and know the ins and outs of pressure politics. Government in a democracy is, in theory, a matter of reconciling the claims of the sectional interests in the light of the larger public interest. They can't all win. When a particular interest gets far out of line the only thing to do is to "talk right back to it," or laugh at its pretensions. The Australian farmers can do with a little good-humored remonstrance. This point is underscored when it is stated that the Australian consumer is often forced to pay a higher price for farm products (e.g., butter and sugar) than his opposite number in the United Kingdom. The supplies of particular products for Australian domestic consumption are regulated carefully and priced at a level which will, when the returns from exports are added in, give an average return which comes somewhere near a "reasonable" return to the producer. A "reasonable" return is one which will enable the producer to maintain an Australian standard of living. These are very vague criteria. They are not susceptible to exact definition today. But there they are.

The flow of exports from Australia, especially to the United Kingdom, must be maintained. That has been demonstrated here already. Under the schemes to which the primary producers are devoted, the flow is maintained well enough but too often at the expense of the home consumers. It thus comes about that Australian primary producers stand for protection at home plus dumping abroad. Their dumped exports help keep Australia in a sound financial position. But that the wisest method of accomplishing this has been found, one may presume to doubt. The only occasion on which the voters of Australia have been given an opportunity to express an opinion on these schemes was in 1937 when they were asked to modify the constitution, through a referendum, in such a fashion that the last legal obstacle to Commonwealth-wide application of producer control of farm production would have been removed. The obstacle was the prohibition of Commonwealth interference with the absolute freedom of trade between states. The referendum was defeated. But the producer organizations proved strong enough to weather the blow and carry on by the power of organization and official patronage. This is in itself a dangerous amount of power to be in the hands of any group within a community, but at least it is less power than it would have had had the constitutional change been made. "Power corrupts, and absolute power corrupts absolutely." The extension of these schemes still goes on. As recently as May, 1941, the Federal government was reported to have decided "to give the wheat-growers of Australia almost complete power to organize and carry on their industry without government control under the stabilization scheme adopted last year."

The Australian producers strongly resist all efforts to place curbs on production. Abstractly viewed, this is an admirable stand. But the Australian farmers take it, not with the idea of providing abundant cheap food for the malnourished of the world, but to guarantee greater and greater national development of agriculture —to insure that there are more, and more successful, commercial farmers. This raises the problem of where to sell the stuff to the best advantage. In the Australian instance, the principal outlet— often the only significant outlet—is the United Kingdom. Since more and more stuff comes forward all the time, this means that the producers keep their eyes firmly fixed on the United Kingdom market. That is inevitable. They would be silly not to. But it is a concentration of interest which is easily twisted into odd shapes. Two of these are, first, the desire of some of the producers to have the United Kingdom authorities limit or entirely eliminate competitive supplies coming forward from non-British sources; and, second, pressure on the Australian government to grant United Kingdom exporters of manufactured articles every possible tariff concession as a *quid pro quo* for acceptance of Australian goods by Britain. Both of these efforts point directly toward a "closed Empire" system of trading, a madhouse idea which has many partisans throughout the British world. And, what is far more important here, they divert attention from the fundamental Australian trade problem—how to increase the size and number of export outlets.

That, roughly speaking, is the situation with regard to the

Australian farmers and trade policy. They have used the tariff as a reason for gaining protection themselves. To sustain their position it is necessary that the British market be kept as open to them as possible. To see to it that that is done, they are prepared to waive, not their own privileges, but those of the Australian manufacturers. Thinking of this contradiction, a Labour protectionist, Mr. J. S. Rosevear, remarked, "The farmers are for expensive food and cheap forks."

No one acquainted with the world-wide crisis in agriculture will assert that the Australian farmers lack excuse for their peculiar actions. They have simply followed their noses in a search for an elusive security—a security which, as the Australian economist, A. G. B. Fisher, has demonstrated, is incompatible with social progress. What inspires criticism, rather than irony or laughter, is, first, their blindness to any interest other than their own as farmer-businessmen bent on profit-making, and, second, their bland assumption that they have *solved* the Australian farm problem. (Criticism should also be directed against the politicians and other public figures who accept and abet the pretensions of the farmers.)

The Australian farm problem is no nearer solution than the American farm problem. In both countries it muddles trade policy. In both countries the problem is yet to be faced; indeed one may assert that it has yet to be outlined for reasonable consideration. But that is another story. A tremendous crisis in Australian agriculture, which will shake the producers' organizations to their foundations, is due after this war. Premonitions of it were to be observed in 1938.

The wool-growers usually take a broader view of international trade than their fellow producers. For one thing their product has a wider sale than most Australian primary products. While much of it goes to England, parcels of wool go to a long list of countries. In fact, aside from wheat, wool gives Commonwealth merchandise a large part of the dispersion it has achieved. In the second place, the wool-growers have not succumbed to the protectionist urge, though they do accept favors like reduced rates for the carrying of wool on the railways. There are a few small wool-growers, chiefly men who run sheep in conjunction with the growing of wheat, who have put forward the demand for government-guaranteed prices, but they have thus far been put down without diffi-culty. All in all, the wool industry is the outstanding example of an Australian exporting industry which operates on the basis of the world price for its product. Its importance to Australia cannot be exaggerated. The "wool cheque" is the largest single item in the export returns. Over nine-tenths of Australia's wool is sold abroad.

Theoretically the wool people should be free-traders. Actually they are moderate protectionists. Much more clearly than their high protectionist fellow primary producers, they see that the export trade must be spread over a great number of countries. Their eyes are not riveted on the United Kingdom. It was the wool people who, as much as any single group, encouraged the development of trade with Japan. The Japanese at one period were such heavy wool-buyers that they were regarded as an im-portant influence in keeping prices at a remunerative level. The Japanese were not regarded as dangerous competitors of the Brit-ish dealers, for they tended to buy types of wool the English did not want and to invade with their cloths the low-price Eastern markets which the English vendors had never reached. It was felt, therefore, that selling wool to Japan opened up an entirely new outlet. Disastrous competition was not being abetted. The trouble came with regard to Japanese exports to Australia to pay for the wool and other commodities. No more than any other people have the Japanese discovered how to buy without selling. What they had to sell in Australia was alleged to be cruelly com-petitive with locally produced goods and supplies from England, especially cotton and rayon piece goods. The Australian govern-ment therefore attempted, in 1936, to cut down the permissible imports of Japanese goods and to "divert" purchases to British merchants. This policy, which wrecked the growing Japanese-Australian trade, was generally unpopular in Australia, but the wool people entered an especially vigorous protest. In their eyes the government acted contrary to the larger Australian interest and to the interest of the wool industry in particular. The govern-ment acted, it would seem, in an effort to protect what it thought to be an Imperial interest, but at the expense of an Australian national interest.

Speaking broadly, it can be said that the wool people make up the strongest pressure group which favors an international trading system, opposing both the "closed Empire" idea and extreme economic nationalism. They are better prepared to accept the logic of such a position, not only in its export aspects but also in its importing phases. Nevertheless they are not so theoretical in their approach that they would allow the destruction of either Australian industries or British trade in Australia. What they seem to be driving at is a balanced outlook designed to serve Australia's interests as an exporting nation. In attempting this they collide head on with the extreme protectionists among the Australian manufacturers and farmers on the one hand and the British merchants in Australia on the other. Given their position as spokesmen for an industry absolutely dependent upon export trade, it is difficult to see what other stand they can take. (Incidentally their attitude is the reverse of that taken by the American wool-producers.)

The outlook of the Australian manufacturers needs little elaboration for an American audience. It is, in essence, the same as that of the American manufacturers whose primary concern is the domestic market. Exports of Australian manufactures have not yet risen to a level which gives them much significance, least of all in the formation of opinion. The Australian manufacturer, speaking generally, wants sufficient protection to enable him to establish and maintain any and all industries in Australia that can find an outlet in the domestic market. To do this he must have protection against two groups of competitors, the British and the foreigners. To the former the Australians have, since 1908, granted "preference." This means that British goods entering Australia do so at a lower rate of duty than foreign goods of the same description. This gives them an advantage in the market. But in practice the duties are run up to such a height that "preference" amounts merely to a little less protection than that given against foreign goods. The Australian manufacturer is well protected against his British competitors even with preference. There is no evidence that he would have it otherwise. This was shown by the reaction to the Ottawa Agreement, of 1932, which was, it may be recalled, essentially an effort to stimulate trade *within* the British Commonwealth of Nations.

Criticism of the Ottawa Agreement was mostly directed against the following provisions:

. . . protective duties shall not exceed such a level as will give United Kingdom producers full opportunity of reasonable competition on the basis of the relative cost of economical and efficient production. . . .

. . . after the receipt of the report of the Tariff Board, the Commonwealth Parliament shall be invited to vary, wherever necessary, the tariff on goods of United Kingdom origin in such a manner as to give effect to such principles.

. . . no existing duty shall be increased on United Kingdom goods to an amount in excess of the recommendation of the Tariff Tribunal.

The criticism may be summed up under three headings which are really, when closely examined, facets of the same fundamental objection: that Ottawa took away Australia's fiscal freedom; that the Tariff Board was made a legislative organ to the subversion of the powers of the Australian Parliament; and that a substantial part of the Australian market was permanently given away to the British manufacturers to the infinite hurt of local industries.

The thought obviously underlying all these criticisms is that Australia must retain its fiscal autonomy under all circumstances. Such concessions as may be made are to be made only after the hardest bargaining, with Australia's immediate interests always paramount. That the manufacturers take this line is to be expected. What is rather surprising is that the Labour party also takes it. The coalescence of the manufacturers and labor on the tariff issue is one of the extraordinary phases of Australian politics.

At the heart of the tariff issue, when manufacturing is the industry under consideration, is the question of costs. This is closely related to the question of efficiency. It is difficult to be dogmatic about the relative efficiency of nations, so I shall not attempt to strike a balance between the critics of Australian industry and its defenders. Rather I shall quote two opposed Australian views. A critical statement is that of the economist, Colin Clark, who says after a statistical analysis:

The comparatively poor showing made by Australian industry is not due to inefficiency on the part of the basic industries of this country [the primary industries]. . . . The fault lies in the profuse extension of manufacturing activity into a larger number of hitherto unexplored fields during recent years. . . . So far these extensions have proved uneconomic. If the claims of their sponsors are true, that they will eventually prove themselves efficient and economic industries, Australia has a tremendous industrial improvement to look forward to during the next few years, without any further tariff protection. . . . We should not rest content until we have raised their [the industrial workers'] productivity to the American or Canadian level, which is almost double that of present-day Australian manufacture.

The nearest thing to a reply to these strictures that I have seen is the following quotation from an article by Sir Herbert Gepp, a brilliant Australian businessman:

I am afraid that I consider this serious criticism of some of our secondary industries to be too severe and sweeping, but I am thoroughly prepared to agree that our development in the future must be more informed and better planned than it has been in the past. While efficiency becomes a most elusive and difficult concept when examined closely, and although there are all kinds of factors which make comparisons between the proved efficiency of secondary industry in one country as against another very difficult, and the conclusions to be drawn rather hazy, I think that we would be well advised to follow one suggestion which Mr. Clark has made. He says, "the next step in Australian industry can only be illumined, I suggest, by an intensive study of the industrial economics of Canada and the United States, eschewing generalizations, and concentrating on the essential technique whereby such high average output per head has been obtained in these countries." It does not follow that by carrying out this suggestion we could eventually raise the "efficiency" of our own manufacturing industries so that a direct comparison could be made with the corresponding "efficiency" of the countries mentioned, but at least we could make profitable use of the broad facts and methods, the application of which other countries have found to be advantageous. There is much loose thinking about efficiency and about comparative costs of production in different countries. . . .

It would appear that both parties agree that the productivity of the workers in Australian manufacturing industries is, in the newer sectors at least, well below that of American and Canadian workers. They disagree on the precise weight to give this discrepancy, but they both feel that the slack should be taken up if possible. Sir Herbert seems to feel that the differences between the North American countries and Australia are so great that exact comparisons will always be more or less futile. For one thing, the Australian manufacturers cater to a market one-twentieth the size of the American. It would seem that Australia will always, in many fields of manufacturing, have to bear higher costs than North America. The great task before the Australians is, therefore, to prevent the excessive development of industries of which this is particularly, and probably permanently, true. Temporarily, the whole issue is shelved, for the expansion of industry for war purposes must be carried out in defiance of any nice economic discriminations. What the situation will be when industry reverts to peace-time activities is impossible to foretell.

The critics of Australian industry appear to have a strong case. The criticism chiefly comes from the primary producers who, as we have seen, are particularly sensitive to the question of costs. They are, of course, given to oversimplification of their case, and frequently their remarks are more notable for vehemence than understanding. Perhaps the most important considerations to keep in mind in evaluating them are two: First, whereas Australian land industries are often justified on political grounds, regardless of their cost to the community as a whole, the same reasoning applies with equal force to Australian manufacturing. Second, while Australian manufacturing must accept the indictment for high costs, its leaders can reply that high costs in the primary industries, particularly those that have accepted protection, are also a burden on the community and help raise costs in manufacturing. Professor Douglas Copland was profoundly right when he wrote some years ago:

There is urgent need for a national policy that will apply the same critical review of the excess costs of protecting primary industry as is now applied to protected secondary industry. . . . Our most costly protected industries are now some of the primary industries, notably sugar and butter . . . the increasing burdens of protecting primary industry are being neglected.

The Australian Tariff Board was established in 1921 to deal with the questions which inevitably arise under the protective tariff system. It was suggested by the example of the United States Tariff Commission. In general the board has done a good job, but it has not taken the tariff out of politics. Both of the opposed political groups have persisted in dragging it into the political arena. There are some issues of politics which are too fundamental in character ever to be handed over to impartial commissions by the representatives of the people. It is one of the ironies of democratic politics that it is precisely such issues that are the principal concern of the innumerable pressure groups in a modern community.

In July, 1938, representatives of Australia negotiated an agreement with the United Kingdom, which, concealed in its formal phrases, sums up the trade problem of Australia. I shall quote verbatim three series of propositions from the agreement. They represent an official recognition of a position independent writers have been insisting for some time was really the situation Australia confronted.

The Australian Ministers recognize—

(a) the necessity for the United Kingdom to safeguard and develop her own agriculture;

(b) the position of the United Kingdom as a great international trader, investor and shipowner;

(c) the consequential necessity that the United Kingdom should maintain her position as a great overseas trader and in particular as an exporter of manufactured goods to Empire and foreign countries;

(d) that these facts impose an upward limit upon the extent to which increased opportunities can be afforded to Dominion producers in the United Kingdom market;

(e) that any diminution of total exports from the United Kingdom will tend to affect the capacity of the United Kingdom to purchase foodstuffs and raw materials from overseas suppliers, including Australia.

United Kingdom Ministers recognize—

(a) that in the interests of both countries and of the British Empire as a whole it is desirable for Australia to endeavour to bring about as soon as possible a substantial increase in her population;

(b) that it is impossible to achieve this objective solely or principally by an expansion of Australian primary industries;

(c) that there is therefore a necessity to combine with such expansion the sound and progressive development of Australian secondary industries.

The agreement goes on: "Certain immediate difficulties arise when an attempt is made to reconcile the desirability for Australia to expand her secondary industries to the maximum extent economically possible with that of the United Kingdom to maintain her exports and to secure for her exports a stable position in the Australian market." In attempting to deal with this extremely puzzling job, the Australian authorities proposed to take into account the following factors:

(a) the necessity for increased Australian population,

(b) the economics and future growth of primary production in Australia,

(c) the necessity on national and economic grounds for a continued development of Australian secondary industries,

(d) the defence needs of Australia,

(e) the maintenance of United-Kingdom-Australian trade by effective preference to United Kingdom in Australia and to Australia in the United Kingdom,

(f) the need for new markets for Australian exports and for foreign trade arrangements.

These propositions seem to me to mean: First, that the long period during which Australian primary producers could find ratification for more and more development in the constantly increasing sales of commodities that could be made in the United Kingdom is definitely coming to an end. Second, that since further development of primary industry is no longer the principal prop of Australian national development, industrial development is the principal task of the Australian nation as far as production is concerned. (During this war manufacturing is running away with the ball, and it will seek to hold its gains when the war is over, upsetting all calculations based on the position in 1938.) Lastly, the fullest Australian development can now be achieved only insofar as Australia expands old and finds new outlets for her exports outside the British Empire. I come back to the point I have been hammering at all along: that Australia's great task as a trading nation is to do just that. It opens up a very rocky avenue which cannot, within the limits of this book, be explored with profit. I do not think that Australia can move down this avenue successfully alone. What we really have here is an intricate international economic problem which can only be handled successfully by the joint action of the nations of the world.

Closely related to the conclusions to be drawn from the vitally important document I have just quoted is another set of considerations of an equally difficult character. I refer to the problem of substitutes for commodities of great importance to Australian producers. I shall not enter into this complex matter, for it would carry us far afield. I shall content myself with quoting brief passages from two articles by Australian specialists. The first is by I. A. Butler, of the economic staff of the Rural Bank of New South Wales:

. . . the discussion . . . would seem to indicate that at least three main Australian agricultural industries were on a somewhat insecure basis—wool and butter on account of substitutes and wheat on account of excessive world production capacity. The consequences of agricultural protection in one part of the world with industrial protection in another part, are gradually overtaking these industries. The war has to a certain extent given a respite, but there is every reason for believing that it will not alter the fundamental trends. If it does not, then very drastic modifications will need to be made not only in the structure of the Australian agricultural industry, but in the Australian economy as a whole.

The second is from an article by Dr. Ian Clunies Ross, Australia's leading authority on the wool industry:

At the end of the war the wool industries of Australia and the British Dominions will face the problem of (a) regaining markets confirmed to a greater or less extent in the use of substitutes greatly superior to those employed in the last war, and of (b) marketing, in the face of this competition and the impoverishment and financial difficulties of both victors and vanquished, wool clips nearly a third larger than those to be disposed of at the end of the last war, together with an accumulated surplus at least as great as that of 1919.

Add these two quotations to the propositions from the official statement (which minimize rather than maximize the difficulties ahead) and you have full warrant for predicting a crisis in Australia after the present war, a crisis which will fall most heavily upon the primary industries and with especial weight upon the *protected* primary industries. It will take Australia's best efforts to surmount the crisis successfully.

7. THE STANDARD OF LIVING

TRADE-UNIONISM has reached a high stage of development in Australia. The unions are more thoroughly accepted as a right and necessary part of the machinery of social life than is customary in North America. That bald statement, which has been made over and over again by Australians, requires a good deal of clarification and annotation before it is really understandable. Americans who accept it, either with pleasure or pain, and evaluate its significance in the light of what they know of trade unions and the reactions to them in the United States, will be far astray from the facts. As I have so many times implied, analogies drawn between Australia and the United States are only useful as tools of thought, to open up and illuminate a subject, but hardly at all as conclusions. Even the point that the unions are accepted in Australia should not be taken as meaning that all Australians are enthusiastic about them and the attitudes of their leaders. It is nearer the truth to say that the unions have, to a marked degree, been incorporated into the governmental machinery of social control. They are, therefore, accepted about to the extent that they bow to that control, which cannot continue to exist without their co-operation, and are criticized in proportion as they seek to evade or override it. How the unions got into this position is a very important chapter in the story of Australia.

The first Australian labor force was the convict group. The earliest labor legislation was concerned with regulating the relations of the free masters and the convict servants assigned to them. These relations were far nearer to those of the slave system than the free labor system. As a class of free laborers slowly developed by emigration from England and by the rise of a native-born population, the outstanding labor problem was the competition between convict and free servants in the labor market. The wages of the convicts were very low, being merely maintenance plus a small bonus of luxuries usually paid in "truck" from the master's own store. The cost of convict servants, however, tended to determine the scale of wages for the free workers. The relations of the masters and their free workers were deeply colored by the master-convict relations. The free laborers were therefore confronted with two very difficult problems—how to gain higher wages in the face of devastating competition, and how to free themselves from legal restrictions more appropriate to convicts. While there are records of strikes by free workers in the early days, of pressure on the authorities to liberalize the laws relating to masters and servants, and for special consideration in times of depression, the condition of the free workers in Australia was bad until the gold rushes. The decade which elapsed between the cessation of convict transportation into eastern Australia and the rushes hardly afforded time for any very fundamental change in this field.

The gold rushes revolutionized the situation in at least three important respects. They created an immediate labor shortage and wages rose accordingly. They so vastly increased the population that the bad conditions which existed in the convict period were wiped out in fact if not in law. And they thus created the conditions which made it possible to build successful protective organizations for the workers. Moreover, it was at this time that many men arrived in Australia who, while mostly bent on gaining wealth quickly on the gold fields, were not prepared to accept quietly either English or Australian social injustices if their "luck was out," and they had to take ordinary work at ordinary wages. It is sometimes said that these men brought into Australia the ideas of the English Chartists and trade-union pioneers and gave them general circulation there. Too much should not be made of this, especially in the matter of details. But it is a fact that the new-comers did bring with them a strong feeling that in the new land old injustices should not be perpetuated. They found the native-born Australians quite ready to take the same line. To accomplish their ends the working people had, as it happened, to realize Chartist ideals. To say that they were simply English Chartists in a new world is stretching a point beyond the facts of the case.

Being above all pragmatic in their approach, as they have ever since remained, the Australian workers quickly developed their own ideas about what should be done, although English suggestions were never to be scorned.

In 1854 a rebellion took place on the gold field near Ballarat, Victoria, which has been given symbolic significance by Australian labor. As can be imagined, the sudden appearance of thousands of miners in the young colony of Victoria (in 1854 but three years old as a separate government) brought charges on the administration it found difficulty in meeting. In attempting to deal with the problem the authorities increased the license fee demanded of the prospectors for the right to dig for gold. Eventually it was raised to a height which provoked criticism and evasion. Though in 1854 the miners on the Ballarat field numbered twenty thousand, they had no representation in the government. They considered the large fee demanded to be taxation without representation. The police, recruited in part from ex-convicts from Tasmania, were instructed to raid the camps and demand that the miners produce certificates of payment of the license. Their methods were extremely provocative and brutal, and late in 1854 the miners were driven to armed resistance. Their Reform League formulated their demands as the right to full parliamentary representation; manhood suffrage; no property qualifications for Parliament; payment of members; short parliaments; and abolition of miners' and storekeepers' licenses.

In defending their cause, the men erected a fortification which they dubbed Eureka Stockade. Early in the morning of December 3, 1854, the stockade was surprised by armed military forces brought up from Melbourne, and in the melee which followed several men on both sides were killed and others wounded. This broke up the rebellion. What leaders could be found were seized and sent to Melbourne for trial, but no jury would convict any of them. The rewards offered for the capture of fugitives were withdrawn. One of the leaders of the rebellion, Peter Lalor, who lost an arm in the affray, later rose to a distinguished place in Victorian politics.

Both because of the nature of the political demands of the miners and because of the spirit of rebellion which their action expressed, labor has glorified the episode. "The Eureka Stockade," wrote Dr. H. V. Evatt in 1940, "was of crucial importance in the making of Australian democracy." In a more rhetorical vein, Robert Ross wrote in *Eureka! Freedom's Fight of '54* (1914), the book which best expresses labor's conception of the rebellion, as follows:

Of the few epochal industrial upheavals of our land the Eureka Stockade was the first and foremost—the forerunner of the Labor Movement, the miracle of our Commonwealth. The Rebellion did sow the seed which in due season germinated and fructified in separate, distinctive, and independent working-class political parties. . . . the rough-and-ready miners . . . builded greater and stronger than they ever knew, the beginnings of a working-class democratic thought and action sweeping ever towards economic emancipation for a people and a continent.

The first enduring trade union was the Operative Masons' Society, established in Melbourne on November 16, 1850. It was followed by others, either local growths or offshoots of English unions founded by immigrant members, but it was not until the eighteen-seventies and eighties that the trade-union idea swept the country. The progression was from the building trades to the mines (beginning in the gold mines when they became company operated) to the pastoral industry (beginning with the shearers) and then to the waterside workers and water transport people generally. The earliest general demand was for the eight-hour day, achieved in certain trades in Victoria as early as 1856. As time passed, however, the central issue between unions and employers became the "closed shop," in which all union demands could be easily enforced.

But from very early days the unions were concerned with wider issues than the strictly industrial. The working people were confronted not only with the task of bettering their position as employees; they were also compelled to deal with such political issues as a campaign for manhood suffrage, payment of members of legislative bodies, land legislation, and control of Chinese competition in trades like furniture-making. Dr. Victor Clark, an astute American observer, wrote in 1906:

"The difference in the history of social movements in the United States and Australasia is partly due to the fact that industrial and political problems that presented themselves in succession in the United States have come up for solution simultaneously in the colonies. . . . Because we realized so many phases of social and political equality before the great labor questions of the present became prominent, the latter are with us a distinct and purely industrial issue, and therefore less directly the concern of the government. If the working people of the United States were fighting for equal suffrage, free schools, immigration restriction, and liberal land laws at the same time as for higher wages, shorter hours, and generally better conditions of employment, trade union methods would appear to them as inadequate as they do to colonial workmen."

This gets us a bit ahead of our story, but it serves to emphasize an important point which is too frequently forgotten in comparing Australian and American labor. It certainly rules out of court all dogmatic opinion on which group is the more "advanced," an exercise in the invidious of which Australians are unduly fond. Today we might not put the distinction precisely as Clark put it a quarter-century ago, but we should nevertheless be forced to emphasize the differing social contexts of Australia and America in order to arrive at a sensible judgment.

Australian labor was, from the beginning, unmistakably and inescapably, confronted with industrial *and also* political problems. Except in the very first years of their existence, the union workers always paid some attention to current politics. Thus they established a range of interests which has always continued. Occasionally union-supported laboring men were actually elected to Parliament. But in the first phase of labor history the emphasis fell upon industrial aspects.

During the seventies and eighties the unions went from success to success, largely I think because it was a time when the employers were prosperous and felt that they could afford to grant concessions without fundamentally jeopardizing their interests. It probably seemed to them cheaper to give in than to fight. Public opinion was also made more favorable to the unions than otherwise might have been the case when Royal Commissions revealed terrible "sweating" of women workers in certain urban trades.

One aspect of the story requires emphasis and explanation. It may surprise American readers to learn that one of the key unions was that of the shearers in the pastoral industry. This was made possible because the Australian "frontier" has always been a frontier of "big men" rather than "little men." The great sheep stations were the typical frontier enterprises. They represented very considerable capital investments, and they were run by hired hands. The owner, if he resided on his station at all, performed the functions of a manager. In such a situation there was little difference between the relations of employer and employees on the stations in the outback and those existing in the urban industries, or in mining.

Shearers were, moreover, not permanent employees and hence were scattered over wide areas the year around. They either had homes in the towns or they were, at this period, struggling farmers who went shearing each year to get cash. They traveled in groups or working gangs and met together on the track between jobs at traditional camping places. For these reasons they were accessible to union propaganda. The shearers' union was originally organized under the direction of William Guthrie Spence, who made his reputation by organizing the gold-miners of Victoria and who started his campaign among the shearers in their home towns. It thus came about that this important group of migratory workers was organized in Australia years before migratory workers in America formed unions at all, and at a far earlier stage in the economic evolution of the country. For when the unions became strong in such occupations as mining, shearing, coastal water transport, and waterside, they had footholds in the basic activities of the nation. Manufacturing was not then important in Australia. The farmers had not yet become so firmly established that they were ready to take a position hostile to co-operation with the labor unions. Indeed the farmers were then in sharp economic and political conflict with the pastoralists, a fact which the union people seized upon and exploited, as the labor political leaders did a little later.

It was not in the stars that the unions should go from triumph to triumph without being challenged. The challenge came in the eighteen-nineties, a period of falling prices, drought, and general depression in most lines. The great employers had reached a temporary end to their capacity to accede to the demands of the unions

We, the undersigned duly accredited Representatives of The Pastoralists' Federal Council of Australia, on behalf of New South Wales and having direct interest in pastoral properties in the Colony of New South Wales, on the one hand, **And We** the undersigned, duly accredited Representatives of The Amalgamated Shearers' Union of Australasia on behalf of New South Wales, on the other hand hereby agree and declare on behalf of our respective Associations and as a preliminary to a Conference to be held — between us, that employers shall be free to employ and shearers shall be free to accept employment, whether belonging to Shearers' or other Unions, or not, without favour, molestation or intimidation on either side; this being in accordance with the admission made in the Memorandum of the 23rd July, addressed by the Secretary of the Young Branch of The Amalgamated Shearers' Union to the Pastoralists Union of New South Wales, which says:— "I concede that members of this Union may work with non-members," which admission was ratified by the Secretary of The Amalgamated — Shearers' Union in his letter dated from Creswick on 30th July 1891 and by him expressly confirmed in his telegram dated from — Creswick on 3rd August 1891; and it is also agreed on behalf of The Pastoralists' Federal Council, that the Council will use its influence to prevent the employment of Chinese or Kanakas as Shearers or shearers cooks.

Dated at Sydney the Seventh day of August, 1891.

For the Pastoralists' Federal Council of Australia on behalf of New South Wales.

W. E. Abbott President
J. A. Campbell
Alex Wilson
David Elder
W. Cossey

For the Amalgamated Shearers' Union of Australasia on behalf of New South Wales.

W. G. Spence President
David Temple Secretary
Thomas Williams
Hugh Langwell Vice President
J. H. Tormey

THE SHEARERS ACCEPT "OPEN SHOP," 1891
(Signatures more reduced than text)

and began to resist them with all the power they could command. The battle was fought out in a series of strikes which involved coastal shipping and waterside workers, shearers, and metal and coal miners. The workers tried to maintain their wages, hours, and conditions under the comprehensive demand for the union or closed shop. The employers sought to gain complete control over their industries by demanding "freedom of contract" which meant, in practice, the right to determine wages, hours, and conditions, by direct negotiations with workers of their own choosing, union or nonunion alike. This Americans would call the "open shop." The Australian employers of that period rarely claimed that they wanted to smash the unions entirely, though if they won, that would be a logical consequence of their victory. In fact they did win, and the unions were reduced to a very low and precarious state.

The great strikes of the eighteen-nineties were genuinely epical and epochal affairs. In shearing they were fought out over vast areas. They were not fought with delicacy on either side, especially in their later phases. Employers were able to enlist the power of the state, the police, the military, and the courts. Occasionally the workers would burn down a woolshed. The strikers were not broken in the end, I think it fair to say, by the power of the employers as employers or by the power of the police and military, but rather by the courts. Ancient English laws, already repealed in England, were invoked against them. In the colonial courts, incredibly prejudiced judges, one of whom stated from the bench that to shoot strikers would have been entirely in order, pressed home the charges to cowed juries. Union members were carted off to jail under severe sentences for conspiracy, inducing men to leave their lawful employment, and so on. Elected state officials openly sided with the employers. In one celebrated instance a colonial premier refused a union request for an unconditional conference with employers, saying that he spoke as "a member of the Government and the Australian Pastoralists' Association." Confronted with this situation, plus depression, the wonder is not that the workers lost; the wonder is that they had the resiliency to rise and fight again. Labor turned to politics because it had been roundly defeated on the industrial front. It was because they were beaten by the use of the state power against them, that the Australian workingmen began to organize political parties. They hoped to win a position in the colonial legislatures which would allow them to use the state power to achieve some of their objectives.

Unionism arrived at Broken Hill with the first workers. In 1884 the miners working around Silverton formed the Barrier Ranges Miners' Association and demanded $2.50 an eight-hour day. The following year the group joined the Amalgamated Miners' Association, an inclusive organization which had grown up on the Victorian gold fields after the shift from alluvial to deep mining. In 1886 the Barrier union followed the drift of population and established its headquarters at Broken Hill. Within two years conditions had transformed the organization from what was practically a mutual benefit society into an industrial union. Under this impetus a drive for 100 per cent unionization was made, and in November 1889, after an eight-day strike, the closed shop was won. The early strikes of the nineties tied up operations at Broken Hill, but the stoppage was involuntary, and when work was resumed the union asked a forty-four hour week and got a forty-six hour week. It was also agreed that future disputes were to be handled by arbitration.

The turn of the Broken Hill miners to feel the iron hand of the employers came in 1892. The BHP chose in the beginning to fight from behind a smoke screen of evasions, but the issue is clear in perspective. Success elsewhere encouraged the mine-owners to declare war on the unions. Ignoring the arbitration clause in the 1890 agreement, they put forward the demand that days' work in the mines give way to "stoping by contract." The blow fell suddenly after repeated denials of rumors of its imminence, and the men were given no chance to negotiate. It was a clear case of either accepting the company's terms or striking. The men struck. Patrick McMahon Glynn, a liberal South Australian lawyer who visited Broken Hill during the strike, wrote that the miners were suspicious of the contract system because "They have been taught by general experience that the ultimate result of free competition in the contract system would bring wages gradually down to a minimum. My opinion is that there is a good deal of force in the contention." When the die was cast, the *Silver Age* newspaper (which, before the strike was over, was to turn savagely on the men, who replied by boycotting it out of existence), said:

The surprise sprung upon the town yesterday by the manager of the Pty. Co. is one of the most discreditable episodes connected with the recent history of the latter concern. Naturally assuming that a gentleman in the position of manager of the Pty. Co. would feel bound to place the fullest and most reliable information before the public, we kept ourselves in constant communication with him on this contract system, and to the very last were assured that no alteration in the mode of working the mines was contemplated, and that no difficulty with the men need be anticipated.

The strike was intensely bitter. The owners showed no quarter to the workers, to truth, or to fair dealing, and they successfully enlisted the New South Wales government on their side, as well as most of the newspapers. The government spent about $65,000 in sending 385 police and five law officers to Broken Hill. The leader of the men, Richard Sleath, appeared at the Ordinary General Meeting of the BHP in Melbourne in the guise of a stock-holder. The treatment he received is as fine an example of upper-class muckerism as has ever been recorded in print. Sleath said in part:

The question between the Board and the men is not a question of stoping by contract at all. The men have never refused stoping by contract. . . . When it was the intention of the Board to introduce stoping by contract, that was never refused by the employees of the Company; but when the employees simply asked for an explanation as to what sort of contract that it was intended to introduce, they were met with the answer that it was intended to annul the agreement and introduce freedom of contract. (Loud applause.) I am glad you thoroughly understand the action of the Board. ("Yes, we do.") . . . The shareholders and the Board have been the aggressive party. (Laughter.)

John Darling spoke for the Company:

We are now told that the shareholders and their Directors are the men who made the first aggressive movement. I say that is false in toto. (Hear, hear.) . . . How absurd to say we are the aggressive party at this stage, when the liberties of our officers, of our workmen, and of the townspeople of Broken Hill are taken away by the establishment of a system of pickets.

He then continued in a vein which revealed the real intent behind the Company's move:

After what has happened we feel it is imperative that if those mines are to be reopened, they can only be opened under freedom of contract (Hear, hear, and loud applause). I may say, gentlemen, that, unfortunately, I have had some little experience in the maritime strikes. After we had for a considerable time suffered and endured persecution from what are called the leaders of the labor organizations, we were compelled, in our own self-defence, to act aggressively, and in defending ourselves, to say—"The banner we must have in future must be freedom of contract." (Cheers.)

The shareholders then voted down—howled down—a motion put by a decent spirit among them asking that negotiations with the men be opened up. This kind of situation, especially when set in a similar atmosphere created by sheep station, shipping, and coalmine owners, lets one understand the origin of that bitterness toward the boss which is still characteristic in labor circles. (As late as 1937 when I visited Broken Hill the men were muttering against an unpopular mine manager, "We'll 'dump' him, we'll comb his hair for him.") The government of New South Wales finished off the dirty business of 1892 by arresting eight of the strike leaders and sending them for trial away from Broken Hill. They were tried for conspiracy by a jury of farmers, not exactly their peers. Five leaders, including Richard Sleath, were sentenced for from nine months to two years. The strike collapsed. The drive against unionism continued, the strikers were "victimized," their places being taken by scabs. Wages were reduced and hours increased. The union was reduced to a shadow.

At first glance it may seem odd that labor, unable to win on the industrial front, felt itself able to win on the political front. The explanation is simple. There was no question about the cohesiveness of the laboring group, for if the unions suffered heavily as organizations after the unsuccessful strikes, no one really doubted the fundamental solidarity of labor. The conservatives tried to put labor on the defensive by emphasizing in season and out that its real program was unionism plus socialism. But labor's alleged socialism was not of the tough ideological variety based on Marxism, but a peculiar amalgam of Edward Bellamy, Henry George, Robert Blatchford, and a wide variety of writers of the literature of protest, including Carlyle, Ruskin, Disraeli, Kingsley, and Dickens. One of the most powerful unions gave away hundreds of copies of *Looking Backward* and *Merrie England*. A figure of immense importance in formulating the outlook was William Lane. Dr. Lloyd Ross points out that Lane was notably weak in the realm of ideas and notably strong in agitational journalism. One gets the impression that most of the early leaders could be similarly described. If they could not write, like Lane, they could talk. And some of them had an additional quality which was of crucial importance—they knew how to organize. There was nothing in the labor outlook which prevented it from formulating a political program of wide appeal. It is therefore logical that the pioneer labor party should have as its objective, "To bring all electors who are in favour of democratic and progressive legislation under one common banner, and to thoroughly organize such voters with a view to concerted and effective action at all Parliamentary elections in the future."

The political situation of the moment offered labor extremely important allies. The victorious employers were a relatively small group of "big men." They held enormous social power in the relatively primitive Australian economy of the eighteen-nineties, but they held it on suffrance. The reigning conservative parties, which served their interests, were bankrupt politically. The real political arbiters were labor, the nascent middle class, and the farmers. The middle class was deeply disturbed by the catch-as-catch-can tactics of open social warfare and showed small disposition to rejoice in the crudely won victory of the "big men." It did not at all like the horrid vision of an Australia dominated by the reactionary big owners. The farmers, for their part, were anti-grazier in attitude. The big graziers held much land required for agriculture and, in dominating the government, controlled the power of granting agricultural credit and building the required railways for opening up new country and transportation to the seaboard.

The presence of *Progress and Poverty* among the books that formed labor's outlook, and of an active and vocal group of single-taxers in the community, insured that little trouble would arise with regard to formulating a program appealing to the farmers. The position was equally fortunate with regard to the middle class. The conservatives had long neglected political reform in their effort to preserve their economic power. By formulating a program of political demands, indispensable to its own advance, of course, labor could hope to capture a large segment of the middle-class vote. Nationalism was closely associated with social rebellion in those days. Any program labor formulated was bound to concentrate on local issues and so to draw to its support the nationalists who felt that they had nothing in common with the Imperialist conservatives. Finally, labor could command two strong "opposition" interests, the Roman Catholic church and the liquor trade. Indeed if labor could formulate a well-rounded program, it could tap sources of strength in politics which were not available to it on a strictly trade-union basis. This it proceeded to do, and hence it could aspire to political power at the very moment that it was weak on the industrial side. In the very first campaign it entered in New South Wales—that of 1891—the Labour party won 28 per cent of the seats in the House. This gave it the balance of power between the two conservative parties.

An important consequence of the strikes was a rapid rise of a belief in arbitration courts, or conciliation committees, as a means of settling industrial disputes. The general idea was taken up most vigorously, not by the employers, but by middle-class liberals with the support of working-class spokesmen. The employers were inclined to oppose the proposals. At an earlier stage the unions had been skeptical of formal governmental participation in the handling of industrial disputes, but now the leaders thought they saw in the suggested courts a way of reconstructing the wrecked unions. Just who should be given the credit for introducing the idea into Australia is difficult to say, for it seems to have been "in the air" of the times. Charles Cameron Kingston, a liberal South Australian politician, introduced a bill into the parliament of that colony in 1890 which embodied the essential ideas. It failed. But it attracted the attention of William Pember Reeves in New Zealand, and he succeeded in getting his version adopted by the parliament of that country. From New Zealand the scheme was brought back to Australia. The New South Wales Royal Commission on the strikes was especially taken with the idea and investigated as best it could all efforts made in the field, including some experiments in the United States. By so writing the law that to appear before the court the workers must be organized into unions, the labor leaders foresaw a rapid rise in membership of the established organizations and the more or less automatic formation of new unions. Cameron Kingston's law had as its defined purpose "to encourage the formation of industrial unions and associations, and to facilitate the settlement of industrial disputes." On this basis, the formation of unions was the indispensable prerequisite to negotiations before the courts. Though the courts in Australia have gone through a complicated evolution and even today have not arrived at a final form, this essential principle has never been abandoned.

The reasoning of the union leaders of fifty years ago has proved correct, and when, after the turn of the century, the courts were firmly established, the unions grew quite rapidly. Australia today has a very high ratio of union members per thousand workers. The unions obviously lean heavily on the courts. What percentage of the membership would remain if they stood on their own feet is anybody's guess, though it is true that the pro-union spirit among the workers is very strong. Moreover, it is also a nice question how far reliance on the courts has sapped union militancy. Middle-class people in Australia seem to think it has not done so at all, but left-wing union leaders are not so sure. Certainly union militancy is not absent. But because the unions are so deeply involved with the courts, the position of Australian labor is *sui generis*, not readily assessed in relation to overseas standards.

Insofar as the left-wing people in Australia are not "intellectuals" operating in a vacuum of their own devising, they find their social base in the trade unions. This has always been the case.

From the early days there has periodically been dissension in the labor movement, not only between the left and right wings of the unions, but also between the unions and the Labour party parliamentarians. The unionists as a total group always stand a little to the left of the majority of the parliamentarians. In the eyes of the unionists, most of the parliamentarians rightly enjoy the odium of being politicians.

The issues which have divided the unionists from one another and from the politicians have differed widely in importance and character from time to time. From about 1907 until 1916 the chief disturbing influence was that of the I.W.W. This organization, oddly enough, was exported from "laggard" United States to "advanced" Australia. It brought into the unions a militant movement for direct action as opposed to reliance upon the arbitration courts and the politicians. Its notion of "one big union" organized on an industrial basis was also stirring to many Australian unionists. The labor politicians early took fright at this infiltration, and none of them lifted a finger when, in 1916, the Commonwealth government proclaimed the I.W.W. an illegal organization.

Between the two world wars the chief radical influence was that exerted by the Communist party. How extensive the influence was (and is today) is impossible to say. As in the United States, the party built an impressive structure of organizations around and about itself and engaged in an elaborate publication program, periodicals, pamphlets, and books. It probably influenced both the Australian "intellectuals" and the unions about to the extent that it influenced their American counterparts. Only a few Labour party men ever gave it aid and comfort, even in its peripheral activities, like the League Against War and Fascism. In the trade unions it appears to have gained its important influence in those unions which have always been on the radical side of the fence. While many conspicuous executive officers of such unions were accused of being Communists, only one seems to have confessed membership openly, the Secretary of the Miners' Federation. Under Australian conditions Communist influence would chiefly show itself by supporting direct action and bringing the socialist objective to the fore. The party was outlawed in 1940.

Subject to qualifications which will immediately be made, one might phrase the position of the left unionists as direct action plus socialism. The position of the left politicians would, on the same reasoning, be liberal parliamentarianism plus socialism. The trade-unionists of the right would stand, therefore, for the use of the arbitration courts plus support for liberal parliamentarianism, while the right-wing politicians would come out with liberal parliamentarianism plus private enterprise! The whole situation is muddled by the fact that many trade unions which hold to the ultimate objective of socialism are today bound up with the courts. In fact, the Australasian Council of Trade Unions has a socialist objective, but it is not anti-court. The Labour party has declared, since 1921, that its ultimate objective is socialism also. But the party has never, in all its long career, been really seriously socialist in outlook, not even during the turbulent years after the First World War. It has never gone beyond a mild Fabianism which, demonstrably, has not transformed the Australian social order.

The fundamental divisions in the Australian labor movement appear to be determined, first, by the seriousness with which the socialist objective is entertained and, second, by the willingness to use direct action when the court system of settling industrial disputes has failed. The true socialists and direct-actionists are chiefly found in the trade unions, and they, as their influence waxes or wanes, determine the degree of harmony or uproar in the labor movement as a whole. Experience thus far has shown, however, that the left-wing unionists are unable to win a majority position within the unions as a whole, let alone the Labour party. Nevertheless, as a pressure group they have caused tremendous upheavals in both at various times in the past and may well do so again in the difficult years ahead. If Australia ever goes all-out for socialism, the reason will be that the ideal was kept alive by the left-wingers in the trade unions. This may be what Henry Boote, the veteran labor editor, had in mind when he declared in 1940:

I feel certain, after a lifelong experience as a labor propagandist, that the psychological development of the working class, not in Australia alone, but in all countries, will be greater in the next ten years than it has been in the whole of the half-century we are so proudly celebrating.

In discussing the Australian unions it is necessary always to keep the courts in mind. Americans should not, therefore, wrench the figures and facts from the context here established and try to draw broad conclusions from them by reference to American criteria. That would lead one into absurdities.

Trade-union membership fluctuates in Australia as elsewhere, the figures reflecting political and economic conditions. The situation in 1938 was that of the total employees (excluding workers under twenty years of age) 50 per cent of the males and 33 per cent of the females were organized in unions, or 46 per cent of all adult workers. There is in Australia the division of the unions into the two familiar forms, craft and industrial. The unions are not yet organized into an all-inclusive federation. In 1938 there were 366 distinct unions and interstate groups of unions in the Commonwealth, not counting branches. Only forty-three of these unions operated in all six states and only 113 in more than one state, this leaving a host of local unions. But the 113 having interstate affiliations to some degree included over four-fifths (83 per cent) of all union members.

Within the states there is a tendency for the unions to join in central organizations on a city or town basis, though some unions always stand aside. The central organizations are called, variously, the Labour Council, Trades Hall Council, or the Labour Federation. In many instances some of the individual unions and the central council occupy offices in a building, called, usually, the Trades Hall, built on land granted free by the government. The degree to which the city and town central organizations are tied together on a state-wide basis varies, the most complete unity having been achieved in Western Australia. Usually the local central organizations are autonomous in the areas they cover. The unions making up the city or town council are, in most cases, local branches of a state-wide union and hence owe allegiance to a head office which is usually located in the capital city. Since these head offices are represented on the central council of the capital city, this council has the greatest prestige, and it gives the unions a degree of unity otherwise difficult to achieve. However, if the head office of a union is in disagreement with the dominant faction in the capital city council, that war is apt to be reflected through the branches in the provincial councils. Australian unions run the gamut from intense conservatism to extreme radicalism. Therefore it is usual to find them disagreeing on general outlook and short-term tactics.

Congresses of trade-union leaders from several or all of the states have taken place at intervals since 1879. Many efforts have been made to form a permanent, all-inclusive, Commonwealth-wide central organization. Although thus far the objective has not been reached, there has been since 1927 an Australasian Council of Trade Unions, with headquarters in Melbourne. This council is built upon the Trades Hall councils of the capital cities, which are theoretically branches of it. But as the local councils are not themselves all-inclusive in their respective areas, so the A.C.T.U. does not achieve complete unification. It is nevertheless a very powerful and influential body, and its decisions and policies are widely interpreted as reflecting the sentiments of all trade-unionists. It is wise to be cautious about this, for even unions affiliated with the A.C.T.U. are apt to take a contrary line on extremely important issues. It is far from being in a position to dictate to the constituent unions. However the A.C.T.U. has no rival in the national sphere.

Although a high degree of unionization has been achieved, there is always room for improvement. Constant attention is given to conducting pro-union propaganda among nonunion workers and to keeping the union members on their toes, industrially and politically. Under the laws of Australia, unions are permitted to publish union papers carrying political propaganda as well as union news. The form and tendency of the propaganda is dictated by the general outlook of the union conducting the paper. A leaflet distributed by the New South Wales branch of the Australian Railways Union, makes the following appeal to nonunion railway workers:

Every worker should be a member of a bona-fide Union because the Unions are your strength, your bulwark against the attacks of the employer—in your case, the Commissioner—and the governments in particular.

The Arbitration Court is still recognized by Trade Unions and so the case for the worker is in the hands of the Unions, who have always put up a strenuous fight against the employers when they have applied for a new award or a variation of the old one.

If we had no Unions the employers would be able to give us the bare basic wage, margins would disappear, passes would be taken away and conditions in general worsened. This in itself should make every worker realize the necessity of becoming a member of a Union.

In propagandizing its members this union also emphasizes solidarity among the workers and pays particular attention to its program for the future. In 1938 the union was making seven demands: a shorter working week; higher real wages; increased holidays; sick pay; extended passes; weekly payment of wages; and the right to hold union meetings on the job. While some of these obviously relate to the railways alone, several of them are demands all Australian unions have been making for years past and with particular vehemence in the immediate prewar period. A conservative union would probably have such immediate demands only. But the radical Railways Union adds to its pamphlet this warning: "Do not regard this campaign as an alternative to social reconstruction, but as a step in building up activity and confidence for a change in the social system." This union would, therefore, always be conscious of the fact that its ultimate objective could not possibly be realized within the arbitration court system. No judge is ever going to change the social system! Under these circumstances, a radical union is "accepted" only as long as it stays within the court system. Efforts on its part to reach its ultimate objective will bring down criticism on its head whose vehemence will be in exact ratio to the conservatism of the particular observer.

The system of arbitration courts is most complicated. Agreements between employers and workers can be arrived at by direct negotiations and then registered with the appropriate court, this giving them binding effect. If direct negotiations fail, then the matter goes to court. Both employers and workers usually initiate discussions with the understanding that such a move will follow any breakdown, rather than a strike. (Nevertheless, most strikes occur at this stage.) Or either the employers or the workers can appeal to the proper court for an award, thus automatically bring-

ing the other party before the court for discussions. But there is
no single court, or unified system of courts, for all Australia.

The most important and influential court is the Commonwealth
Court of Conciliation and Arbitration which makes and interprets
awards in industries with interstate ramifications. About 80 per
cent of all the trade-unionists are members of unions registered
with this court. Registration is not compulsory, but only when
the union is formally registered does it have the right to appear
before the court. Once registered the union must accept extensive
interference with its internal affairs. As an Australian writer
summarizes it:

> . . . the Arbitration Court supervises the work of the unions. It can
> order the unions to take a secret ballot upon matters before the Court;
> it can refuse to register the rules of a union, and the rules of a union
> do not become operative until registered by the Court. The Court may
> disallow those rules; it can hear appeals from members of the union
> and decide as to who is right. It may issue orders to do what the Court
> thinks necessary to carry out the rules of a union that is registered
> in the Arbitration Court, or under the supervision of the Common-
> wealth Arbitration Court—and that is not very far from making the
> union really an agency of the Government. The conception of a trade
> union as a body of people with power to make its own rules and en-
> force them is gone.

Just as the court system encourages the organization of unions,
so it also encourages the organization of employers for the purpose
of dealing with the courts. (These employer organizations are often
quite separate from the usual trade associations.) In the courts,
therefore, it is a case of organized employers vs. organized workers.
The unions, to underline the point, do not face one employer;
they face all, or a large number, of the employers in the line of
business involved in the case.

The states are also concerned in this all-important matter. The
people are not prepared to transfer exclusive control to the Commonwealth. A constitutional amendment designed to achieve this
was decisively defeated in 1929, and the government which proposed it was turned out of office. Therefore, in addition to the
Commonwealth Court, there are arbitration courts with state-wide
jurisdiction in four states: New South Wales, Queensland, South

Australia, and Western Australia; and all these states, excepting Queensland, have wages boards which deal with wage questions within industries. In Victoria and Tasmania the wages boards alone operate, these two states never having established arbitration courts. Under this complicated set-up numerous conflicts between the awards of the Commonwealth Court and the state tribunals are bound to occur, and it was with the objective of eliminating them that it was proposed to transfer the whole business to the Commonwealth. (As a war-time measure, the Commonwealth Court has been given increased powers under the National Security Act, which make it supreme, leaving the state courts in a subordinate, but still active, position. This results in a situation which is *ultra vires* the Constitution. The permanent supremacy of the Commonwealth Court can only be assured by a constitutional amendment. As uniformity of rule and practice in the field of labor relations is desirable, I hope that the needed amendment will eventually be made. But "government by regulation" is unpopular in Australia, and when peace comes good and bad regulations alike will probably be thrown out. So what the court does with its new powers during the war is of great importance, for on its record will depend the public's willingness to vote for the necessary constitutional change in the postwar period.) Unions are accused of selecting the particular award, Commonwealth or state, which at the moment seems best, to the utter confusion of all concerned, especially since awards cover unions or trades and not industries as a whole. The employers therefore complain that if they employ members of several unions, some working under Commonwealth and some under state awards, they never know where they are and have to employ experts to untangle their relations with employees. (It is indicative of the situation that *The Pastoral Employment Guide,* issued by the graziers' associations of New South Wales for the use of their members runs to 312 closely printed pages.)

The awards of the courts are concerned with wages, hours, and working conditions and often enter minutely into the complexities of particular industries in fixing the wage to be paid for one type of work as against another. Employers and union leaders alike complain that the judges are without expert knowledge in such matters and often make errors in their awards. Since the awards are not concerned with the broader issues only, the opportunities for wrangling are multiplied. Both sides are often dissatisfied with the award when it is handed down, starting off a new train of disagreements.

The awards are generally well observed, but more in the letter than in the spirit. My own judgment is that some employers have, in sticking to the letter of the awards and making everything turn upon whether or not the unions have succeeded in establishing a particular point in the courts, made labor relations about as difficult and unfriendly as they well can be. The unions also are prone to take the same line, giving the employers no edge whatever. Then "the letter killeth."

Middle-class writers in Australia in recent years have usually evaluated the courts by reference to the idea of "industrial peace" or the avoidance of strikes. Strikes have not been eliminated, nor are they always illegal, but they have probably been reduced in number. (Who can tell exactly how many strikes would have occurred in any given year if the courts had not existed?) The incidence of strikes in Australia seems to bear about the same relation to general economic conditions as in America. Australian strikes are usually of short duration. In 1938 out of a total of 376 strikes 196 lasted but one day or less and only eighteen for four weeks or more. The principal causes are wage disputes, disagreements over working conditions, and the discharge of workers under circumstances considered unfair or discriminatory. Two-thirds of the strikes are settled by direct negotiations between employers and union officials. The most strike-ridden industry is coal mining, which in Australia as elsewere is in a state of chronic disorder.

What percentage of the strikes are actually illegal in the technical sense is not specified in the records. Under Australian conditions a strike can be illegal for various technical reasons, such as a strike called without a secret ballot of the union membership, or before an award in force has run a specified number of months. Little effort is ever made to enforce these provisions. The mere declaration that a strike is illegal would, ordinarily, make very little difference. But if penalties are invoked, then the situation becomes serious indeed. This is only done when the strike is protracted and the dislocation is causing serious trouble in industry. A disastrous and peculiarly Australian penalty is the "deregistration" of the offending union. Once "deregistered" the union is unable to defend its case in the courts, and it is possible that the court will register a new union for that trade, thus driving the old one out of existence. (Usually the offending union succeeds in getting reregistered before this happens.) Strikes which involve trade and commerce can be dealt with under the Crimes Act which is a direct descendant of the War Precautions Act of the First World War and deals chiefly with sedition. It is also possible to deal with such strikes under a Transport Workers' Act in such a fashion that the workers are forced to obtain licenses or abandon their occupation entirely. (The unionists call this the "dog collar" act.) A government invoking either of these acts is, naturally, in for a political fight as well as a straight strike fight. But even under war-time conditions it has not proved possible to make strikes completely illegal, for when it was proposed to take such action, the Labour party leaders persuaded the conservatives to shelve the measure indefinitely.

The decisions of the courts with regard to wages are by far the most important. Wages are the first concern of the unions, but beyond that the wage awards determine the Australian standard of living. If there is any single subject about which Australians are more concerned than any other, it is the standard of living. For this reason it is hazardous to write about it at all, let alone critically. International comparisons of standards are excessively difficult to make, except where the variations are extremely wide. But I have never seen one made by persons of competence which grants the common Australian claim to the highest standard of living in the world.

What is true is that Australia is one of the high standard countries, ranking along with, but nevertheless below, its neighbor New Zealand, the United States, and Canada. Often when driven from their position by obviously true calculations about real wages, Australians will take refuge in the allegation that the social services warrant their claim. This is not true either. Here again Australia is an advanced country, but it is not the most advanced country in the world today. The horrid fact is that the uncritical Australian boosters have become the principal obstacles to the realization of the claim they so vociferously make.

The foundation wage is the "basic wage." It can be defined as the lowest wage which can be paid to an unskilled worker in full employment. It is supposed to bear a direct relation to "the normal needs of an average employee regarded as a human being in a civilized community." Like so many Australian ideas about the labor question, this one also was "in the air" before it was given specific application. In 1890, Sir Samuel Griffith, later Chief Justice of the High Court of Australia, introduced into the Queensland parliament a law which was not passed but which declared that:

> The natural and proper measure of wages is such a sum as is a fair immediate recompense for the labor for which they are paid, having regard to its character and duration; but it can never be taken at a less sum than such as is sufficient to maintain the laborer and his family in a state of health and reasonable comfort.

Not until 1907 was this idea elaborated in relation to the practical job of wage determination and it is not at all certain that Sir Samuel's idea was in the mind of the judge who undertook the task. He probably arrived at his philosophy of wages quite independently. The judge was Henry Bournes Higgins. Justice Higgins has the best claim to being a philosopher of labor relations of any of the justices who have sat in the arbitration courts of Australia. His little book, *A New Province for Law and Order,* is a classic statement not only of his personal position, but also of the whole question as it appeared to a man not committed to any more drastic social philosophy than Victorian liberalism. In 1907, Justice Higgins was confronted with the task of determining a wage scale which could be called fair and reasonable. He took the opportunity to make both a pragmatic and theoretical investigation of the subject. He it was who formulated the definition of the basic wage quoted above. The standards determined in this case became the foundation on which Australian wages rested for many years, for the Commonwealth Court awards influence, and even determine in New South Wales and Victoria, the basic wages of the other courts and boards.

Other than the exact sum of money which is to be taken at any particular moment as the basic wage, there are other important issues involved in wage fixation. What is a family unit? The Commonwealth Court takes a man, wife, and three children. Of the four states in which a basic wage is declared, New South Wales, Queensland, South Australia, and Western Australia, only two agree on the family unit. Queensland and South Australia take a man, wife, and three children. New South Wales takes a man, wife, and one child, Western Australia a man, wife, and two children. In all cases the bachelor is at a decided advantage, but no move has ever been made to penalize him in terms of wages. On the other hand, only New South Wales, before 1941, ever made an effort to assist by special allowance a man on low wages with a large family. From 1927, New South Wales used a family endowment scheme to assist such cases. In 1941 the endowment scheme was put on a Commonwealth-wide basis by the Federal government. But if the single man has had an advantage, and the married man with many children has been disadvantaged until the other day, women workers have been and still are in a very poor position indeed. The basic wage for women has always been a fraction of the male basic wage, usually about 54 per cent. Only where women take work ordinarily reserved for men is there equal pay for equal work and then the award is made to *discourage* the employment of women.

Of a different character is the problem of adjusting the basic wage to variations in the cost of living. For a considerable time this has been accomplished by the use of index numbers, the components of them having been changed from time to time. Thus, once the basic wage is determined, it is moved up (or down) in accordance with the cost of living, the changes involving as little as a shilling on the weekly wage. The scheme is chiefly useful in stabilizing the established standard. It does not assist in raising living standards. It is rather remarkable, then, that the determination of Justice Higgins in 1907 was not thoroughly reviewed until 1934, although Higgins himself urged the need for review on several occasions. It is even more remarkable that the review was so long delayed when it is known that in 1920 a Royal Commission on the basic wage went thoroughly into the matter and found that to realize the theoretical objective of the basic wage it would have to be materially higher than it actually was in that year on the basis of the automatic cost of living adjustments. This discrepancy has never been eliminated, even by the 1934 revision. Thus the basic wage of Australia is not in practice a wage which will enable family men to secure the ideal set out by Justice Higgins. It is not related to "needs." Rather it has become what Americans would call a "floor," below which wages are not allowed to sink—at least the wages of men in full employment. It is still possible for men irregularly employed to average less than the basic wage, dividing their yearly income by the fifty-two weeks in the year.

While the basic wage is a "floor," there is no fixed ceiling on Australian wages. The ceiling is whatever figure the unions or the individual employees can reach. In the courts these variations upward are known as "margins." They are allowed for skill or responsibility and vary accordingly, being very considerable in the case of highly specialized workmen. (The differentiation between wages for unskilled and skilled workmen has never reached the American proportions.) The "margins" are determined by the value which can be attached to the work in question and are taken as fixed until the matter is debated again. They do not vary with the cost of living. In recent years the unions have placed great emphasis on "margins" with two objectives in view—to raise the standard of living of skilled workers and, by minutely analyzing job requirements, to get as many workmen off the basic wage onto "margins" as possible. Various "allowances" are also awarded for dangerous, disagreeable, or especially exhausting work. In some instances, a "climatic allowance" is made for work in parts of the country where conditions are far from salubrious.

The courts are concerned only with determining *minimum rates*. If the unions or individual employees can obtain rates above the minimum, that is their good luck. Such additional rewards are called "merit money" or "bonuses." The leading Australian authority says that "the payment of merit money to workers who are above the average is exceedingly common. . . ." But not all unions favor the practice. The employer, says a union leaflet, "has always done his best to keep the workers divided. This he does in many ways, such as merit money, bonuses, and various sorts of preference. . . ." The union rejects such favors as hostile to labor solidarity.

With all the marching and counter-marching that has gone on around the wage question in Australia one might suspect that important advances in living standards had been registered. The official figures do not bear out such a conclusion, especially if allowance is made for unemployment. Taking the *real wage* for the year 1911 as one thousand, real wages for men in full work declined in the years following until a low point was reached in 1919 when the figure was 808. Thereafter there was a fluctuating but steady rise, until in 1938 the figure stood at 1207. (The average weekly hours of labor in Australia declined from 48.9 in 1914 to 44.8 in 1938.) A correction for unemployment would seriously change this showing and reveal that the apparent gain is partly illusory. Unemployment in Australia has never been exactly measured, the figure customarily quoted being the percentage of trade-unionists reported out of work. At the outbreak of war it appeared to be stabilizing somewhere between 8 and 10 per cent, after having reached 29 per cent at the bottom of the Great Depression. As the Australasian Council of Trade Unions has pointed out, this is the position of "a section, consisting, roughly, of half the best-placed Australian workers." It tells nothing about unemployment among nonunion workers. The facts upon which an inference can be based indicate that the nonunion rate is high.

It seems to me a fair conclusion that the Australians have made the best effort of which I have knowledge to put a "floor" under the wages of men in full work which will, by automatic adjustments to cost of living changes, remain fairly stable over long periods. Beyond that it is hardly safe to go. The Australians have not, with all their experiments, succeeded in causing any essential modification of the distribution of the national income among the claimant groups and classes. The Australian distribution is that characteristic in other capitalist countries, including the United States. This was demonstrated by J. T. Sutcliffe in 1926 and again by Clark and Crawford in 1938. It remains true when the social service benefits are also included.

Social services have given Australia world-wide fame, especially among liberals. This reputation was justified in full measure for many years, but in recent times Australia has ceased to be a leader in the field. Only lately has there been any evidence of a revival of interest in the matter. As is always the case with such revivals under democracy, it has been preceded by an outburst of severe criticism by the Australians themselves.

There was a time when the world regarded Australia as affording an interesting field for the testing of advanced and progressive legislation. . . . Untrammeled by traditions of the past, and obliged by circumstance to fashion the legislation in this last important outpost of British settlement, the laws which early Parliaments enacted had a strong democratic flavor. . . . Pioneers themselves, they carried the pioneering spirit into their Acts of Parliament. Not every experiment was successful, but they were undaunted and unafraid. . . . Times have changed. There are acknowledged existent evils curable by legislative remedies . . . the means of amelioration, though they lie ready to our hand, have not been applied. The way has been shown but we do not follow.

—Federal Labour Senator R. V. Keane, of Victoria.

While Australia led the world before the [First World] war in better hours and working conditions, she has fallen from grace, lagging behind other nations, all bent on reducing hours and improving social legislation generally.

—Statement by the A.C.T.U.

Measured against the scope and content of social services in older countries, such as Sweden or Great Britain, ours in Australia are rudimentary. Once famed as pioneer workers in the social laboratory, we have fallen far behind, smugly satisfied with our achievements. . . .

—Professor F. A. Bland, University of Sydney.

This country has not gone as far as Great Britain in the provision of social services.

—Professor G. V. Portus, University of Adelaide.

What are the social services? Ideas on the subject differ. Only ameliorative measures may be included, or one may range as far afield as police protection. The Commonwealth Grants Commission, in an analysis made incidental to determining the allowances of claimant states, classified Australian services under three headings—education; health, hospitals, and charities; and law, order, and public safety. In this fashion the commission included such various matters as libraries and museums, recreation facilities, care of aborigines, and the police forces, as well as the familiar relief for the aged, indigent, and infirm. If this extremely broad conception had been applied to the United States at any time in the last quarter-century no liberal cheek need have blushed too red. But the ordinary person in America rarely uses the term in this fashion. The American meaning is far more circumscribed, including, usually, what are called the ameliorative services which involve payments of public funds to individuals who fall into specified categories because of measurable disabilities. Such services may be either contributory and hence of the nature of insurance or noncontributory and hence free grants from public tax funds. Here I shall deal with Australian services largely in the light of this conception, liberalizing it only slightly. Education will be touched on later, but I am afraid we shall have to satisfy ourselves with regard to law, order, and public safety with the simple statement that they are entirely adequate, or at least rarely subjected to public criticism.

What, then, is the situation with regard to public health, hospitals, care of mothers and children, recreational facilities, relief of the aged, indigent, and infirm, child welfare, and family endowment?

Public health is a matter reserved to the states, although the Commonwealth has made some tentative moves in the field, starting from the few health matters directly in its province, like the quarantine service, and branching out into various laboratory and research activities, like the provision of serums, vaccines, and prophylactics, and the investigation of the problem of malnutrition. There is a Federal health council which offers general advice and promotes interstate co-operation. The states are finding it difficult to maintain and advance their services because of financial troubles. This applies to the health services and, says an expert, "There is little uniformity among the various state health acts, except, perhaps, that of obsolescence. . . ." Yet, within the financial and legal limitations, the public health services are said to be at about the average American level. Perhaps the outstanding difference is that whereas in America we have high peaks and low hollows, in Australia, in public health as in so many other matters, a fair uniformity in practice and achievements (if not in law) has been reached. Hospitals are usually supported partially or wholly by private funds. Mental hospitals, however, are chiefly a charge on the states. In some instances the hospitals receive a share of the profits of the state-operated lotteries as a contribution to their support! It is significant, however, that the expert just quoted is of the opinion that the findings of the American Technical Committee on Medical Care to Co-ordinate Health and Welfare Activities apply equally well in Australia: (1) Preventive health services for the nation as a whole insufficient. (2) Hospital and institutional facilities inadequate in many communities—especially rural, and for people unable to bear the cost of the care they need. (3) One-third of the population, including persons with and without income, receives inadequate or no medical service. (4) An even larger fraction of the population suffers economic burdens created by illness. The case for national health insurance is, therefore, very strong.

Public recreational facilities have not been as elaborately developed as in America for the simple reason that there is no real cause for doing so. Even the largest Australian city is not so large that many people are deprived of recreational facilities by the location of their dwellings. In the season, practically every resident of Sydney can, at little cost, get to one of the several remarkable beaches, or to bush "reserves," not to mention the fine parks, public gardens, and excellent zoo. The great harbor itself is a recreational area for those who can support a sailboat. The "eighteen-footers" make the harbor gay with their sails every week end. The other capital cities are also well provided, Adelaide being especially rich in green spaces within the city area, and Melbourne famous for its public gardens. No city lacks bathing beaches. Perhaps in all cities there is need for more playgrounds with modern equipment in certain thickly settled districts, especially those of a slum character where juvenile delinquency has become a problem. (Yes, the Australian cities do have what, by Australian standards, are definitely slums.) In the country towns the outstanding need is for swimming pools, but these have become very common in recent years. There seems little cause for alarm in the small expenditures on public recreational facilities. Australians could never have acquired their reputation for being sports-loving sun-worshipers if they really lacked opportunity to indulge their fancy.

We come now to what most Americans think of as the real social services. It is necessary to emphasize that it is always unwise to say that such and such a service is established "in Australia," for it may be established in only one state. It is also unwise to conclude from information from one state that the existing services "in Australia" are organized on such and such lines, or derive their funds from such and such sources. There is no uniformity in these matters, and full information on the Australian services has never, to my knowledge, been correlated and analyzed. It is buried in the year books of the several states and the Commonwealth. For that reason I should say candidly that the remarks which follow are designed only to suggest the general position. The observations made are, moreover, confined to services which derive all, or the major portion, of their funds from government sources. There are many admirable private services maintained, either by "friendly societies" which go in for medical care and make provision for funeral expenses on an insurance basis, or by other specially organized groups as, for example, the "flying doctors" who bring medical care to isolated settlers in the outback.

The Commonwealth government provides old-age pensions (since 1909), invalid pensions (1910), maternity allowances (1912), and child (or family) endowment (1941). It is also promoting kindergartens as an offshoot of its public health activities.

The states deal with child welfare, especially with deserted and ill-treated children whose care becomes a state problem, baby health through clinics, and the maintenance of deserted wives and children. The states also deal with child health through the schools, offering medical and dental services. New South Wales has a widow's pension scheme. Almost every state has a scheme whereby people on wages can borrow money to finance the purchase or building of homes. Usually these schemes operate through the state banks. Interest rates are low and the provision for repayment of principal liberal. Slum clearance, a closely related problem, is also chiefly in the hands of the states, but progress has been slow, though some remarkable studies of the slum problem have been made.

On the states falls the burden of dealing with unemployment. When the Great Depression came, the Australian states lacked even the "poor laws" familiar to Americans as part of their British heritage. Relief was customarily granted to the destitute either by private charities or by the state authorities, but no fixed standards or machinery had been built up. When unemployment became acute, schemes for dealing with it had to be improvised, as in the United States. The only exception to these generalizations is Queensland, which has had an unemployment insurance scheme in operation since 1923. The states evolved schemes which differed from one another, but all forms of relief familiar to Americans were used singly or in combination—direct or sustenance relief, work relief, and allowances for transients. Huge sums were expended. The money was usually derived in part from special wage and salary taxes, but these had to be supplemented by grants from the Commonwealth and borrowings. This experience has not yet resulted in the establishment of unemployment insurance in any other state than Queensland or on a Commonwealth-wide basis, although the latter possibility has been discussed. The New South Wales Labour party has announced that it will introduce unemployment insurance in that state if the Commonwealth does not act shortly.

Unless we take an inclusive definition of social services, like that of the Grants Commission, or the even broader conception which includes the arbitration courts and war pensions, the picture is not as impressive as it might be. But there is danger of belittling what has been done because "many of the Australian dreams . . . may still be little more than dreams." One can do a grave injustice to a nation by paying so much attention to its collective dream that the reality seems pitiful. Australia has a firm foundation of basic ameliorative services on which to build and a tradition of thought and action which justifies the building of a far more comprehensive and better structure of services than it now possesses. It must be emphasized, too, that while Australia is no longer the most advanced country in the world, it is nevertheless one of the truly advanced countries and should always be thought of in that light.

But it cannot be denied that the union leaders are quite right in rejecting the thesis that the Australian workingman has the "highest standard of living in the world" because of the benefits accruing from the social services. The union leaders have maintained that the social services really influence the standard of the low income groups only. Once a worker's wage has passed a certain point, which is not in their view very high, he is automatically excluded from receiving benefits under some of the laws. From this angle, the social services are important only insofar as they reinforce the wage "floor." These considerations apply only to the strictly ameliorative services. There can be no question that the standard of living of all workers, no matter what their wages, is influenced by the quality of the educational facilities, the availability of libraries, art museums, and other amenities of civilized life. But that is another story.

8. GOVERNING THE COUNTRY

THE Australian political system combines English and American elements. The country is governed under a written constitution, patterned in important particulars after that of the United States, which was devised by Australians in Australia and brought into force by an act of the Imperial Parliament. It came into operation on January 1, 1901, and federated the six Australian colonies. The Constitution is interpreted by the High Court, but leave can be granted in some instances for appeals to the Privy Council in London.

In spite of an effort to make use of the best that had been thought and said in the world about federal systems, especially in the United States and Canada, the fathers of the Australian Constitution failed to find any final answers to the problems of federalism. The familiar issue of the states versus the Federal government is very alive in the land, both politically and as a problem in constitutional interpretation. The political drift is toward increased Federal power. While the control of the Federal government does not determine the complexion of Australian affairs in all particulars, it is nevertheless very important, both politically and economically. The Federal power can only be extended within the limitations imposed by the constitution which, under Article 51, grants the Commonwealth thirty-nine specific powers. It is difficult to put through a constitutional amendment, for each change must be approved by the people in a somewhat complicated referendum. On only two occasions out of ten attempts has the Commonwealth won increased power in this fashion. Significantly enough, both had to do with finance.

The government consists of the House of Representatives, the Senate, and the Cabinet, presided over by the Prime Minister. The King's representative is the Governor-General who has always been, with the exception of one Australian whose appointment was recommended by a Labour government, a Britisher. The Governer-General is not, as is often thought by Americans, the representative of the United Kingdom government. That government is represented in Australia by the High Commissioner, who is, in a sense, a diplomatic officer, an "Intra-Empire Ambassador." The Governor-General stands in the place of the King, who is, in one of his phases, King of Australia as well as of the United Kingdom. His powers are, like those of the King, mostly nominal and in some respects vague, and under ordinary circumstances he does not interfere in Australian affairs. The Governor-General is appointed by the King on the advice of his *Australian* ministers, the United Kingdom government taking no part in the affair. (Each Australian state also has a governor who comes out from England and performs for the state functions comparable to the Governor-General's. Unlike the Canadians, the Australians did not abolish this office on federating.) All Australian Cabinet members, including the Prime Minister, must have been elected to seats in the House or the Senate. Before the present war broke out the Cabinet was limited by law to twelve ministers of state. The following ministers handled most of the public business. Frequently a single person held two ministerships (or portfolios, as they are called) and also took on special tasks, like dealing with the territories. In June, 1941, the legal limit was increased to nineteen ministers of state.

> Prime Minister
> Minister for Commerce
> Minister for Health
> Attorney-General
> Minister for Industry
> Minister for External Affairs
> Postmaster-General
> Minister for Trade and Customs
> Treasurer
> Minister for Defence
> Minister for the Interior

In addition, each cabinet has several ministers without portfolio, also called Assistant Ministers, who are assigned to aiding ministers with especially heavy duties.

Real political power is in the House, the Senate never having assumed even the position in the government the framers of the Constitution envisaged. But though it lacks prestige, the Senate has the important power of obstruction, and a government with control of the House can be frustrated by a hostile Senate. The constitutional provisions under which a government can deal with a hostile Senate have proved too cumbersome to be of practical political use. Each state has six senators, who retire in relays of three and are elected for six years; therefore the political complexion of the Senate changes more slowly than that of the House and is a factor in bringing an obstructive Senate into existence. The leader of the majority party in the House, who is elected by party caucus, automatically becomes Prime Minister. Since in recent years the Commonwealth has been mostly ruled by a conservative coalition, the usual custom is that the prime-ministership shall go to the party in the coalition holding the greater number of seats in the House. The leader of the Official Opposition, which is always the largest party standing outside the government, is also elected by party caucus. Minor opposition parties also arrange their leadership in caucus, but such leaders have no special recognition beyond that granted by the courtesy of the House. Ordinarily, too, the House has a few independent members. On occasion a secondary opposition party controls enough votes to hold what is in effect the balance of power in the House. That is to say that under the coalition system it holds the balance between the government and the Official Opposition. More rarely the independent members are in this position. At present, the House has seventy-five members. The government party supplies the speaker.

The legal life of a parliament is three years, when it must "go to the country by the effluxion of time," but an election can be precipitated at any moment if a bill "brought down" by the government fails, causing the government's resignation; or if a "no confidence" vote passes on an issue the government chooses to regard as important. The Prime Minister can then advise the Governor-General to dissolve Parliament and an election takes place. If the government loses, it resigns and the leader of the opposition (as he was) is "sent for" and asked to form a government. Or a change of government can take place without an election, as when Labour replaced a conservative coalition in October 1941. These are the usual courses, but there are variations from them, some of which are likely to cause hot constitutional disputes. All in all, however, this machinery works very well in Australia.

Though they are the agents of Parliament, the Prime Minister and his Cabinet have large powers once they are in office. In recent years there have been complaints in Australia that Parliament is not in session often enough or long enough. The Cabinet decides when Parliament shall meet. From 1932 through 1937 the House was in session an average of only fifty-five days each year. The fear is that if Parliament is not on the job, the autocratic tendencies of the ministers will be given too free play. Some bad ministerial regulations have intensified this feeling. Australia suffers from, and is hostile to, what Walt Whitman called "the eternal audacity of elected persons."

There are three important parties in the Federal sphere, two of which are of major significance because of their size and the third important because it usually holds the balance of power. These are the United Australia party, the Labour party, and the Country party. The principal conservative party has changed its name several times, the current version, United Australia, not coming into use until 1932. Before that it was known as the Nationalist party. The Country party first came into Federal politics in 1919 as a regrouping of conservatives. It is a loosely organized party, the strength of which is in the eastern continental states. The Labour party has a continuous Federal history since 1901.

What these parties represent in terms of economic interest is rather difficult to say. Certainly no very fruitful analogies with American parties can be drawn.

The UAP seems to be based upon the urban banking, merchant, manufacturing, and mining interests, but it also enlists farmers and wealthy graziers, as well as professional and academic people. Its candidates reflect this general background occupationally speaking.

The Country party ostensibly represents farmers and graziers, but it is also openly accused of representing the great wool-broking concerns. A review of its candidates in a typical election shows that farmers do not monopolize the chances at office. Of the three leaders it has had in its lifetime, the one holding the office longest was a surgeon, the second a farmer and military man, and the third what Americans would call a C. P. A.

The power of the Labour party is founded on the trade-union membership, but it is not identical with the trade unions by any manner of means. While among its candidates at elections are machinists, clerks, miners, drapers, and electricians, the list also includes lawyers, journalists, merchants, schoolteachers, farmers, graziers, and doctors.

These facts are confusing. The confusion is more confounded the more details one assembles. But it is clear that the UAP and the Country party represent Australian conservatism, even though that conservatism may, abstracted from its social context, seem like liberalism to some Americans! Above all, these two parties constitute what the newspapers call "the anti-Labour forces" (not anti-labour, note). Whatever they are for, permanently or transiently, they are consistently against the Labour party. To hold their power they must, however, make concessions to the Labour party, labor, and the masses of the people generally, so they often enact liberal measures, usually when the Labour party, the spearhead of the opposition forces in the nation, is strongest. It thus comes about that in Australian politics the position of the Labour party, both as to program and actual strength in Parliament, is a determining factor from which the politicians calculate their course, right or left. It is no exaggeration to say that the Labour party determines the complexion of Australian political life by its strength or weakness at the moment. To do this it does not necessarily have to hold office. In the Federal sphere, indeed, it has usually been kept out of office in recent years by the standing alliance of the UAP and the Country party, the latter bringing to the former the votes required to overwhelm the Labour party. To gain office, Labour must be able to outvote both conservative parties. The Country party therefore has an exaggerated importance in politics, of which it has always taken full advantage. It is always more heavily represented in conservative cabinets than its number of seats in the House warrants. It has no hope whatever of ruling alone. In the forty years of the Federal Parliament, the Labour party has held office for but seven years and two months (speaking as of August, 1941); and since the First World War for but two years and two months.

A "policy speech" takes the place of a party platform in Australian elections. Usually it is delivered by the party leader in the principal town of his home electorate. But as no leader can hope to win power for his party by basing his campaign on his own state, all leaders direct their attention primarily to New South Wales and Victoria. Of the fourteen men who have been Prime Minister once or several times, six have come from New South Wales and four from Victoria. Queensland has contributed two, Tasmania one, and Western Australia one. Just as the leaders must appeal to all states if possible, so must they also appeal to as wide an audience as possible within each state. No party can hope to win Federal power by appealing exclusively to any one economic group or interest, not even the Labour party. All parties try to appeal to all interests, the narrowest line being taken by the Country party, which, therefore, only wins country seats. This necessity of making a wide appeal has been an important factor in making the Labour party less a radical than a liberal party as the years have passed. The Australian left, nevertheless, supports the Labour party in elections, always nominally, sometimes actively.

What the parties are doing when they make these wide appeals is attempting to draw the "floating voters" to their side. All parties have a solid phalanx of loyal supporters, who are, however, insufficiently numerous to carry them to office; to succeed they must capture the floating vote.

Since voting has been compulsory in Commonwealth elections since 1924, the American problem of getting the voters to the polls does not exist. There is a fine for failing to vote without adequate excuse, and the check-up is extraordinarily good. When I was living in Australia I was sent a form asking me why I hadn't voted in the general election of 1937. My reason was fairly obvious. Disinterested voters, however, can either spoil their ballot papers, in which case the vote is recorded as "informal," or lazily vote for the "ins" and let it go at that. In American elections such people simply don't bother to vote. Voting is on officially prepared, carefully guarded ballot papers, and is secret, a system which originated in Australia and spread from there to many parts of the world, including forty-five American states. The problem of the parties is to get the floating voters really to make firm decisions and mark their ballots properly. Since Australia uses the preferential system of voting, this is more complicated than one might think. It is not merely a matter of switching parties by observing the party symbols, for these are not used, but of knowing the names of the candidates and marking with a figure 1 the name of the man standing for the party you favor. Since Australians, like most democrats, tend to vote *against* men and proposals, it is not surprising that frequently voters act like the blind man in the story. He asked the officer assisting him if a certain famous politician was standing for office. On being told that he was, the blind voter said, "Put the bugger last." Often the results seem to show that more care has been taken to get "the bugger" last than the best man first.

If the necessity for appealing to a wide audience has taken the edge off political labor's radicalism, it has also taken the edge off the conservatives' conservatism, at least the verbal edge. For if they are safely in the office—that is, if Labour is decidedly the minority party—the conservatives are conservative enough, in all conscience. And though some of them are always fairly liberal, a sufficient number in the Cabinet will be conservative enough to obstruct and delay really liberal legislation, and even impose downright reactionary measures. Only a few years ago the conservatives within a cabinet which included liberal members forced the abandonment of a highly desirable legislative measure after the people had expressed approval of it in an election, after the bill had passed the House, and after a considerable amount of money had been spent preparing the administrative machinery. Indeed, one important reason why the principal Australian conservative party must periodically be reconstructed to do business at the old stand at all is the fact that as time passes and the arrogance of office overtakes it, the party loses contact with the masses of the voters. When that happens, the party usually crashes and not only loses office but becomes a mere hectoring minority which must be liquidated before the conservatives can gain office once more. Only by taking on a protective coloration of liberalism can they win office; and their liberalism is sometimes symbolized by making an ex-Labour man leader of the "new" party, as was done in 1932.

It is therefore no longer entirely mysterious why all Australian parties tend to converge as to program. With the Labour party trying to be liberal and the conservatives trying to be liberal, everybody at least appears to be liberal. The differences between them are matters of emphasis rather than of fundamental character. This may seem to contradict what I have said earlier about the conservative fear of Labour in certain connections like the use it might make of the Commonwealth Bank. But here we are thinking analytically, seeking to judge the party programs objectively, rather than politically. To make politics go at all, perfectly horrific accusations are exchanged by the parties. The Labour party rarely, during elections, is judged by the predominantly moderate character of its members and candidates, but rather efforts are made by non-Labourites to convince the people that the extremists of every variety really represent the party, even extremists who are outside it but who are, or profess to be, spokesmen for labor. Thus in the 1937 general election the Labour party was alleged to be under the sinister influence of "Jack" Lang and also of the Communists, whom Lang disliked. In the 1941 state election in New South Wales, Labour was allegedly an aggregation of madmen who listened to three leaders who offered contradictory programs—the official leader of the party, "Jack" Lang, the perennial bogeyman, and the leader of a splinter group called the New South Wales Labour party, which was probably supported by the Communists since their organizations were by then illegal. On their part, the Labour party people make equally hair-raising allegations about the conservatives, denouncing them as vicious exploiters, toadies to the rich, minions of Collins House (headquarters of financial and mining interests in Melbourne), and mere servants of the "drapery Knights" (i.e., department-store owners) of Sydney, as the situation seems to require. Most of this stuff, which probably assays for truth at about an ounce to the ton, seems to go right over the heads of the voters. For if the Labour party lost the 1937 Federal election, it won the 1941 New South Wales election; and the accusations against it were equally appalling on both occasions. No doubt some people swallow the allegations holus-bolus, in season and out, for all countries have gullible people.

I have met some Australian conservatives who are so conservative that they make Herbert Hoover seem like a Red firebrand; and I have also met some thoroughgoing Australian Communists who would stick at nothing to achieve their ends. But I never became convinced that the first type dominated in conservative politics, or that the second dominated the Labour party. This is not to say that the moderates of the two parties cannot dislike one another's measures. That also would be a silly conclusion. They do, and with reason, for they stand for different economic interests at bottom. Contrary to the impression of some people, who take a romantic view of politics, this is not disgraceful. Politics is not an eleemosynary activity. But discounting the froth and bubble of political campaigning, the conditions of winning office in Australia are such that the two great political groups tend to approach one another in their programs, disagreeing—and strongly disagreeing—on methods. In politics "deviations" from the proper line cause as much bitterness as fundamental disagreements.

One further point must be made. You cannot get much idea about Australian political battles from the newspapers, least of all from the "leaders" or editorials. The Australian press is predominantly committed to the conservative side. Only three or four daily papers in the Commonwealth ever give the Labour party a break during campaigns for office. It is possible for a stranger in the country to gain from some papers the conviction that all Labour candidates are about to be roundly defeated right up until the returns announcing a Labour party victory are printed. Labor entirely lacks a press which reaches the general public. There is, at present, no labor daily newspaper in any Australian capital city, no weekly of general circulation, and no monthly. Labor's papers are trade-union organs or propaganda sheets of one kind or another going chiefly to the converted and only rarely falling into the hands of middle-class people who can be induced to vote Labour on occasion. During a campaign the Labour party reaches the people by speechmaking, the speeches being fragmentarily reported in the big press, by paid advertisements in the papers, and by talks over the radio. The government is obliged by law to grant time on the radio to all parties. Most of Labour's propaganda passes about by word of mouth. I have come to the conclusion that the floating voters in Australia change to the Labour party not because they have become radicals all of a sudden, but because they instinctively know that Labour is not really radical and also and most important because a vote for Labour is the only worth-while protest vote that can be cast. I strongly feel that the Australian conservatives tip themselves out of office on their own records, which are public property, when those records become so bad that the voters feel they must "turn the rascals out." Labour, on its part, loses office for much the same reasons, plus its inability to put its case to the people through a well-edited, intelligent press of general circulation.

The Labour party first gained political office in the colony of Queensland in 1899. While its record for office-holding in the Commonwealth is poor, it has a good record in most of the states. The Labour party has a fundamental strength which no political misadventures seem to destroy. Unlike the conservative parties, it keeps rolling along under the same name. The degree of industrialization of the states does not appear to influence the Labour party's political history to any marked degree. Labour's position in the states seems to me roughly analogous to the position the Democratic party of the United States held for many years. It too had little success in national politics but won many state elections during the same period. While the Commonwealth has a conservative government, several states may have Labour party governments.

Why the Labour parties in the states should have greater strength than the Federal party is far from clear. It has been suggested to me that the Australian voters are willing enough to have their state affairs handled by Labour but feel it wiser to put Federal business in conservative hands. I doubt this. Rather it seems to me that state Labour parties win office because the problems of the states touch the people closely and Labour can more successfully dramatize the issues than in the case of Federal problems and policies.

The conservative United Australia party in state politics is closely associated with the corresponding party in the Federal arena. The

Country party, however, has managed to get itself into some very odd tangles. In Victoria it calls itself the Liberal Country party and is at war with the Federal party, while in South Australia there is an organization called the Liberal Country League. The Victorian LCP has struck up an alliance with the state Labour party, under which it holds office with Labour support, thus reducing the UAP to a pathetic minority. Apparently Victorian Labour finds this a more profitable arrangement politically than holding office itself. In South Australia the political situation reached such a degree of confusion a few years ago that at one moment the Lower House was actually dominated by so-called independent members. A group of these formed the Liberal Country League, which now rules the state, the Labour party being the official opposition. Where Labour rules in 1941, as in Queensland, New South Wales, Tasmania, and Western Australia, the UAP is the official opposition. In outlook and policy the conservative state parties do not differ markedly from their Federal counterparts. Apparently what makes the Victorian LCP liberal is its alliance with Labour; and the South Australian LCL is perhaps more interested in a state industrialization program than one might offhand expect.

For the population it supports, Australia has a tremendous amount of governmental machinery, and the states make a heavy contribution to it. For that reason it is widely felt that the states should be reorganized or, as some extremists argue, entirely abolished. Five of the six states have both upper and lower houses. The Labour party entered politics fifty years ago with the abolition of the upper houses as one of its objectives. The upper houses are usually undemocratically elected. Either the indirect system of elections is used, the vote being taken in the lower house, or a property franchise is employed. Designed in the original instance to frustrate what used to be called "democratical tendencies," they still serve that purpose, to a degree, and few others. Only in Queensland has the Labour party succeeded in abolishing the upper house, and today the question is discussed only occasionally. Unicameralism seems to interest the Australian voters as little as the American. State cabinets are formed much as in the Federal government. Occasionally the name of a ministry will directly recall the colonial period, as in New South Wales where the treasurer is called the

Colonial Treasurer. The chief executive officer is called the Premier. He corresponds to a state governor under the American system. He is not a prime minister, a title reserved for use in Commonwealth affairs. It is incorrect, on the other hand, to call the Federal Prime Minister a Premier as is sometimes done in American newspapers. And, of course, the governor of an Australian state is the King's representative, not a man dependent upon the people's votes. Each Australian state maintains an official representative in London.

Local government in Australia is astoundingly underdeveloped and is, to political experts and interested citizens, a perennial problem. Within the states the important political power is concentrated in the capital, leaving very little to the local communities. The reasons for this are complex, involving political traditions and the distribution of population. The Australian states evolved from autocratic forms in which power was in the hands of a governor, whose seat was the principal city. As the government was liberalized the changes chiefly affected the franchise and the location of responsibility, the distribution of powers between the central government and the local units being untouched. Population within the states is so distributed, moreover, that aside from the capital city and a few minor provincial centers, there is no local unit with a sufficiently numerous population to undertake more than elementary governmental tasks. The local governments are often scornfully called "curb and gutter" authorities.

A result is that the residents in the country districts suspect and believe that their interests are neglected in favor of the metropolis. If sufficiently roused, they set up claims for more power. On occasion large country districts have demanded that they be made into separate states. The new-states issue seems to me to be rather academic. The very character of the country requires large states, and while the existing units might be better designed and run, I don't think it would be profitable to create new ones, at least at this time. Thus far the new-states movements seem to have been chiefly important as campaigns of political pressure against unpopular state governments. When their backers achieved office, the movements died. There is, however, a very strong case for giving the local governments more responsibility and taxing power, if only to stimulate

Labour Political Leader—
Prime Minister John Curtin.

Conservative Political Leader—
Arthur W. Fadden.

Novelist—Katherine Susannah Prichard. Journalist—Brian Penton.

Wool Expert—Dr. Ian Clunies Ross.

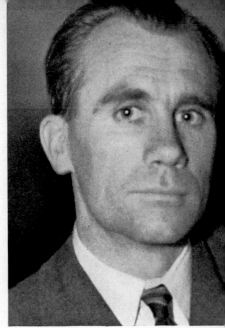

Union Leader—Dr. Lloyd Ross.

Commander of Soldiers—
Vernon A. Sturdee, Chief of General Staff.

Diplomat—Richard Gardiner Casey,
Minister to U.S.A.

civic pride, which is deplorably lacking in many communities.

In the metropolitan areas the problem is different. There the difficulty is not lack of population; it is that the population has made old boundary lines of little importance except as political obstructions. How to create a framework of government better suited to the new conditions is a vexing problem. As matters now stand, what appears to a traveler to be a closely integrated city is, in governmental terms, a group of independent municipalities with very limited powers. Exceptions are Newcastle (N.S.W.) and Brisbane (Q'land). In the view of Professor F. A. Bland, the outstanding expert on these problems and the only professor of public administration in all Australia, the essential task is to develop a system of city government which will allow the central authorities to plan on a comprehensive basis and employ experts to run the technical services, while leaving primary responsibility for carrying out the master plan to the minor units. It is a matter of a proper distribution of powers, but first the powers themselves must be wrested from the state government.

The relations between the Commonwealth and the states are rather uneasy. Here the distribution of powers has proved unsatisfactory within forty years after the Constitution was written. The fundamental complaint of the states is that while they have been left responsibility for many expensive services, they lack the tax revenues required to support them in first-class fashion. Until 1901 the states could use all sources of tax money and, being independent colonies, they built up their services accordingly. When the Commonwealth was established it took over customs revenue and excise; and as time has passed it has invaded other fields, often duplicating state taxes, as on income and land. Under the Constitution provision was made for the states to receive compensation from the Commonwealth for the lost revenue. We have seen how this obligation played a part in the evolution of the Federal Loan Council. But three states—Tasmania, South Australia, and Western Australia—strongly feel that they suffer special disabilities under federation, especially from the tariff. To satisfy them a Commonwealth Grants Commission was set up in 1933. The Commission deals with the claims for subsidies put forward in formal fashion each year by the "claimant states." In an attempt to make the matter as little hit-or-miss as possible, the Grants Commission has delved deeply into the economics of the situation, and its reports contain some of the best writing on Australian economic problems found anywhere. The long quotation on page 101 is from one of its reports.

But even if we add to these sums of money which reach several or all of the states such Federal grants as those for roads, the fact remains that the states are dissatisfied. There is a strong feeling that unless the tax system is redesigned, Commonwealth subsidies are the only way out. The trend seems to be for the Commonwealth to take more and more responsibility for certain matters, gaining control through the power of the purse until, if the evolution reaches its logical conclusion, the heft of the burden will rest with the Commonwealth. The votes in constitutional referenda show the people to be disposed to transfer financial powers, if no others, to the Commonwealth.

To an outsider it would appear that this is desirable in some cases, though not all. For example, if I were an Australian I should support the growth of Commonwealth responsibility for agricultural policy. But I should at the same time want the states to continue to play a large role in agricultural research and technical assistance to the farmers. I see no logical reason why the Commonwealth should not gradually take over and extend the ameliorative social services to make their application uniform throughout Australia. Recently this was done with regard to child endowment, a service which only one state, New South Wales, had developed. I should advocate the same course with regard to unemployment insurance, in force today only in Queensland. I can see plenty of reasons for a Commonwealth-wide railway policy, toward which important moves have already been made, but I should want to retain state responsibility for actual operations. With regard to education, however, I should view Commonwealth control with profound misgiving. I should hope that as financial responsibility for other matters passed to the Commonwealth, the states would be able to find the money adequately to support education. There is, however, a field in which Commonwealth law should, it seems

to me, run to the entire Commonwealth. That is industrial legislation in all its phases. Uniformity here is highly desirable if only to
avoid competitive lowering of standards by the states. One of the
desirable features of the Australian situation today is the measure
of uniformity that has been achieved. But even here I should want
decentralization of administration, for bureaucratic centralization
should be avoided at all cost.

In short, faced with the Australian difficulties, I should advocate
a constitutional convention to redistribute the powers between the
Commonwealth and the states, followed by a Royal Commission to
work out an acceptable compromise of the problem of taxation. I
should reject the suggestion sometimes made that the states be
abolished and federalism abandoned in favor of a unitary government. Any analogy between Australia and the United Kingdom or
New Zealand, leading to the conclusion that a unitary government
is what is required, seems to me false. The true analogy is with
Canada and the United States. Harold Laski to the contrary, I am
not convinced that federalism is obsolete in these countries and
hence do not feel it is obsolete in Australia. What all three countries have on their hands is a crisis induced by a failure of governmental forms to adapt themselves to a changing material base of
society. The remedy is not to abolish the federal system, but to
modify it to conform to the new requirements. In Australia, as
elsewhere, the people who want to abolish the states and aggran-
dize the central government are insufficiently suspicious of the ty-
rannical propensities of centralized bureaucracies. Australia will
never cease to have regional problems, any more than the United
States and Canada. This is in itself a sufficient reason for retaining
the states, even though in Australia they do not exactly conform to
the regions into which the continent naturally divides itself. (The
situation is, however, infinitely better than in the United States.)
But an equally powerful consideration in favor of the states is the
perpetual need of keeping government in a democracy as close to
the people as possible. Uniformity of law and practice, yes; but
also decentralization of responsibility and administration with as
intimate a participation of the people in the making of the broad
decisions on policy as it is possible to arrange.

Government employees are naturally numerous in a country like Australia. It is not only a matter of civil servants within the limits familiar to Americans. It is also, and most importantly, a matter of workers on the railways and other publicly owned utilities. Not all Australians who draw their incomes from government sources are under the Public Service Acts, and an exhaustive study of the proportion of the working population which actually is employed by the governments has never been made. However, I have an unpublished but authoritative estimate of the situation in 1933-34. At that time, "expressed in percentages, public servants were about 11.5 per cent of the total voting population . . . 16.6 per cent . . . of those seeking employment, and 21.8 per cent . . . of those actually in full employment at June 30, 1933." In addition, it is observed that "the position of pensioners is anomalous. They are not working for the government yet draw their income from government funds. Considerable political capital is made of them and their voting power is considerable." If you had visited Australia in 1933 or 1934, every ninth voter you met would have been a government servant. And of the people actually working at the time— it was a period of depression—one out of five would have been employed by the government.

Is this a good or a bad situation? I am sure I don't know, but I do know that Australia has far outrun the United States in this respect. It is something like the condition we can expect under the bureaucratic state which, it is widely believed, is in the making throughout the world. As governments give more and more attention to regulating, controlling, and conducting economic activities, more and more people will become dependent upon governments for their incomes. Australia is well advanced on this road. The number of civil servants has been growing for years, both those who have been brought under the Public Service Acts (i.e., civil service) and those who have not. There is no indication that the maximum figure has been reached, or that the rate of growth is slackening. On the contrary. The multiplication of the number of government servants goes merrily on in Australia as elsewhere in the world.

9. CULTURAL LIFE

WHEN asked about their literature and art Australians divide themselves into three groups—(1) those who feel that little of worth has been done in either field, (2) those who feel that everything that has been done is precious and to be protected against the assaults of the critical, and (3) those who are sure that there is an Australian tradition of good work if only it can be discriminated from the rubbish and *faux bon* stuff in which it is now embedded.

It has always seemed to me that the latter group has the right of the matter, and I have on several occasions in the past fourteen years done battle for their point of view against both the others. There are many Australian writers and artists whose work seems to me to be important as an expression of the Australian ethos, or *weltanschauung,* or whatever it should be called. There are many more books and pictures which are important in relation to the development of Australian writing and painting but which cannot stand up to exacting critical standards. Nevertheless they should never be neglected. The great trouble is that in neither field has a canon been established. Australian cultural criticism has not been consistently vigorous. Here I shall merely try to suggest the gist of the matter without introducing details of fact or the intimate discussion which would be expected were I addressing the Australian audience alone.

First, literature. During the first eighty years of Australian history little work of aesthetic import was produced, and less survives to win the suffrage of readers in more critical times. It was entirely natural that a pioneering society should be an unsympathetic environment for literary people. But from G. B. Barton's valuable evidence, presented in two surveys printed in 1866, it is clear that, relatively speaking, a great deal of reading was done in New South

Wales from early times. The same seems to have been true in the other colonies. Early South Australia had a very high percentage of cultured colonists, and Victoria established a notable record for pioneering in the establishment of cultural institutions. It was rather against the origin of the reading matter that Barton raised complaints. It is amusing that the objections he formulated are still voiced in Australia today, frequently by people who show no knowledge of their antiquity.

Reading material from England was avidly sought after. Barton estimated that in 1865 New South Wales imported English reviews, magazines, miscellanies, and newspapers to the value of about $50,000 and books to the value of $250,000. The population was then about 400,000. He complained that this material, almost exclusively contemporary in character, provided the bulk of the reading matter available. But while English publications were prized, local productions were pretty completely ignored, and this Barton deplored.

Rising out of the wreckage which strews the first eight decades of Australian literary history are a few names, and fewer books, that should be known. Among the names that of W. C. Wentworth, far more famous as a political leader, should be recalled and his poem "Australasia" (1824) remembered. In spite of the labored character of the verses, it does convey to the reader a sense of nascent Australian patriotism, of enthusiasm for the continent and its destiny, which insures it a quiet immortality. In 1854 a novel was published by a young South Australian, Catherine Helen Spence. This was called *Clara Morrison*. It is just now being revived. Miss Spence wrote other novels later, but her energies were, for most of her long and interesting life (she did not die until 1910), deflected into social reform. In a way Catherine Spence's career is a forecast of the basic pattern of the Australian literary tradition. Like so much American literature, Australian writing has a rich vein of social criticism, and many of the very best Australian writers have directly associated themselves with the rebellious social movements of their day.

In this period, also, the earliest of the many novels about Australia by visitors was produced, *Geoffry Hamlyn* (1859) by Henry Kingsley. Kingsley thus initiated a tradition which is still alive and to which William Howitt, Anthony Trollope, Havelock Ellis, and D. H. Lawrence have, in one way or another, made contributions. Lawrence's *Kangaroo* (1923) is today the best-known novel of its kind. To my mind it takes considerable knowledge of Australia to disentangle the truly Australian and the peculiarly Laurentian elements.

Just as Barton was closing his review in 1866 a new vigor was apparent. Henry Kendall published his first volume of poetry in 1862 at the age of twenty-three. He was Australian-born like Wentworth. Kendall continued to write and publish verse until his death in 1882. Two facets of it are of particular importance, and while as a poet he is "minor," as a precursor he has a perennial interest. The two facets are, first, the valiant effort to assimilate the Australian environment to poetry and, second, his dream of a utopia in Australia—in Kendall's term, Hy-Brazil. Almost all the important poets in Australia since Kendall's day have, in some measure, been concerned with both problems.

In the seventies and eighties the cultivation of literature was much more active in Melbourne than in Sydney. The Melbourne group—it was not a "school"—produced two novels that will always be read—Marcus Clarke's *For the Term of His Natural Life* (1870) and Rolf Boldrewood's *Robbery Under Arms* (1882). Both men wrote a great deal more, and they established for all time the point that the Australian scene is rich in the materials for fiction. Clarke's novel is an exciting melodrama of the convict days in Tasmania, while Boldrewood's is a bushranging story almost equally stirring. (Bushranging, chiefly in the form of highway robbery, was common in Australia during and immediately after the gold rushes.) Neither of these novels is first-rate according to exacting standards, but both are excellent yarns and, in the absence of better works, should always be read. They are classics by default. Also associated with the Melbourne group was Adam Lindsay Gordon, a romantic poet fascinated by horses and horsemanship, who wrote many ballads and laments. His work has little intrinsic worth, but it is still alive among people who know nothing of better Australian poets. In fact, Adam Lindsay Gordon is an old man of the sea to contemporary Australians of literary taste; but the English with a persistence worthy of a better cause, still insist that he is the great Australian poet. Gordon committed suicide seventy years ago. His ghost still gallops along.

It was not until the eighteen-nineties that things literary really began to move in Australia. The nineties brought the first literary generation in which the majority of the first-rate writers were Australian-born. By great good fortune a vehicle existed which desired to focus the literary energy of the nation—*The Bulletin*. It had an astute editor, J. F. Archibald, and an equally astute literary editor, A. G. Stephens. Finally, there was the influence which I regard as the most important of all—social rebellion was in the air. Many of the very best writers were closely associated with the labor movement, and all had in some measure the bias characterized by one of them as "offensively Australian."

All these elements can be found in the lives and writings of the men and women who must be regarded as the finest literary representatives of the time—Henry Lawson, Tom Collins, Bernard O'Dowd, and Miles Franklin. Whether one picks up *While the Billy Boils* (1896), *Such is Life* (1903), *Poetry Militant* (1909) and *The Bush* (1912), or *My Brilliant Career* (1901), makes little difference. Pride of country, revolt against the *status quo,* glorification of the common man, high hope for the future, run through all of them. These writers were critical of the world in which they found themselves, but they believed in the possibility of fruitful change—change, moreover, that was to be directed by and for the benefit of the Australian common man. It was the common man's renaissance they forecasted, and an Australian renaissance. The greatest book yet produced in Australia, Tom Collins's *Such is Life,* is a glorious compound of these elements. Henry Lawson's stories and his rough and ready poems have carried them into thousands of Australian hearts and minds. Bernard O'Dowd made powerful poetry of them. And Miles Franklin expressed them in an excellent novel.

The minor writers of the period also shared, in some measure, the general outlook, but their chief contribution was the production of slices of Australian life. A. G. Stephens himself took this view of them. Most of them failed to fly very high. But among the lesser writers who did far better than average work are Louis Stone, with his novel of Sydney slum life *Jonah* (1911), Randolph

Bedford, with his excellent book of European travel, *Explorations in Civilization* (1916), Barbara Baynton, with her terrifying sketches, which were admired by Havelock Ellis, *Bush Studies* (1902), Dowell O'Reilly with his imaginative short stories, and C. E. W. Bean with his classic of the wool industry, *On the Wool Track* (1910). Nor should one neglect the popular poetry of the period by Lawson, A. B. Paterson, and C. J. Dennis. The literary ballad became the rage, and some swinging verses were written. Moreover Paterson performed the signal service of making a collection of real ballads in a book called *Old Bush Songs* (1905). He also wrote the words of "the unofficial national anthem of Australia," "Waltzing Matilda." C. J. Dennis got the Australian "mug" into verse in *The Songs of a Sentimental Bloke* (1915). It was a rich period.

In recent years there has been a reassessment of the nature and purpose of poetry. In this task the ideas of two men have been especially influential, Bernard O'Dowd and Furnley Maurice. They have insisted upon the necessity of producing a poetry that deals with the central issues of life, and Maurice has been especially active in the advocacy of the use of new forms, as well as the continued assimilation of the Australian environment (including the urban environment) to poetry. To these names should be added those of Christopher Brennan, William Baylebridge, Shaw Neilson, and Robert Fitzgerald. These represent all the kinds of poetry produced with success in Australia, except the purely decorative variety. The most highly regarded exponent of the latter is Hugh McCrae, whose best work is collected in *Poems* (1939).

It is certainly to the credit of Australia that it has produced five, possibly six, poets in about thirty years who have something to say and can say it effectively. The place of O'Dowd has been indicated. William Baylebridge defines his central "issue" thus:

> *True earth am I, of earth I'm knit—*
> *O, let me be at peace with it!*

In form and language Baylebridge is traditional, but in content he deals with most of the matters to which O'Dowd so vehemently directed attention in *Poetry Militant*. In making his peace with earth, he has been especially concerned with the relations of the sexes and with national regeneration—the adaptation of the Australians to their environment. This attaches him to the great Australian tradition of "utopianism." Baylebridge's most important book to date is *The Vital Flesh* (1939).

Christopher Brennan's case is very special. It is not only that he was a scholar and a character (in the old English sense) but it is also that he wrote a kind of poetry which will always remain difficult for the casual reader. What makes his poetry unique not only in Australian literature but also a poetry of the first interest to all concerned with the art is the fact that he attempted to assimilate French Symbolism to English verse. In doing so he necessarily concentrated his attention on the internal mental and emotional life of man as contrasted to his external and active life, the usual concern of Australian poets. Brennan gives notice that Australia is not, as those who are behind the times would have it, exclusively a matter of swaggies, bullockies, and billy-cans. He is far more personal than O'Dowd and even Baylebridge, who, after all, are more traditional writers. For complete appreciation in Australia Brennan awaits the appearance of readers of greater sensibility than are now common. It is perhaps indicative of his peculiar position that while his greatness is recognized there is no inclusive collection of his poetry. The reader must chiefly rely upon *Poems* (1913).

Shaw Neilson stands in this company because when he is at his best he writes a direct, unaffected lyric. His ideas are few and simple, as befits a man of the people. And, as is rare among Australian lyricists, he is not burdened with absurd and theatrical poetical notions. Neilson's *Collected Poems* appeared in 1934.

Furnley Maurice, a keen critic as well as excellent poet, is the most experimental of the Australian poets in subject matter if not in form. He is also, among those still active, perhaps the most radical in social outlook. His *Melbourne Odes* (1934) is one of the most interesting books of poetry recently published in Australia. The preface contains an admirable statement of his credo "In these verses," he begins, ". . . I have followed a natural tendency to draw imaginative significance from everyday things. One result is that objection has been taken to the use of 'unpoetic' words and material. . . . Australians have always been backward in ideas about verse." And so he wades into them! And he presents poems —titled "Upon a Row of Old Boots and Shoes in a Pawnbroker's Window" and "The Victoria Markets Recollected in Tranquillity"!

Robert Fitzgerald, the youngest of the important poets, is chiefly known for his book *Moonlight Acre* (1938), which contains "Essay on Memory," the prize-winning poem in the sesquicentennial celebrations of that year. It is distinguished work, showing that Mr. Fitzgerald has a sensibility and a capacity for discipline which should carry him to the front rank of the poets of Australia.

Among the prose writers of the day who are very important to Australia's literary standing and development are Brent of Bin Bin, Katherine Susannah Prichard, and Henry Handel Richardson.

Of these, the first, who writes under an impenetrable pseudonym, has given at last a classic expression to the novel of the squattocracy, a class which has appeared time and again in Australian fiction since the days of Henry Kingsley. The roots of Brent's three novels—*Up the Country* (1928), *Ten Creeks Run* (1930), and *Back to Bool Bool* (1931)—are to be found in the riches of the reminiscences of the squatters.

Katherine Susannah Prichard is the strongest of all the writers of fiction in Australia today. She has vigor, insight, and a distinctive literary character, and while she may lack "finish," more important characteristics outweigh this fault. In her successive novels since 1915, she has presented many different aspects of Australian life in a fashion which should be taken as a reassessment of the Australian world of the first importance. Her best novels are *Working Bullocks* (1926), *Coonardoo* (1929), and *Fay's Circus* (1930). Miss Prichard also writes excellent short stories, some of which are collected in *Kiss on the Lips* (1933).

Henry Handel Richardson stands as the greatest of the Australian literary expatriates, of whom there are a considerable number in England, and while she does not justify expatriation, she has proved that it need not dry up the creative powers. There is general misunderstanding of the relation of her great Australian novel, *The Fortunes of Richard Mahony,* to the Australian scene. This remarkable novel was published in three parts in 1917, 1925, and 1929 and then in one volume in 1930. H. H. Richardson is not a reportorial realist, nor is she of the company of the ideological

rebels of the nineties. She is one of the greatest literary psychol-
ogists of our day. What she had in mind in her Mahony series was
to study the effect of emigration to a raw, new country on a highly
strung man of considerable cultivation provided with a profession
of immediate utility, medicine—a man, moreover, who was con-
genitally a "life-fighter" and obviously doomed to defeat in whatever society he chose to make his career. Mahony's stiff-necked
sense of right and wrong, his devotion to the principles, social and
moral, to which he had been bred, were carried without adjustment into the judgment of life in a new country—Australia at the
time of the gold rushes. His egoism, which slowly corrupted his
precariously balanced sense of his true worth as man and doctor,
his morbid sensitivity to the attitude toward him of his associates
and patients drove him inexorably to his destiny, a pilgrim who
achieved oblivion short of the grave. Naturally the Australian environment comes off badly in a study of a man of this type, for
it is seen through the eyes of, and in relation to, a deeply malad-
justed person. Nor is it Australia as such to which he objects, for
he similarly fights the English environment when he temporarily
returns to it. To fail to perceive that the value of the book is in
the psychological analysis, to demand of it that it give a favorable
report of Australia, is to misread and misjudge the book.

Associated with these outstanding writers are figures of less distinctive power. Miles Franklin returned to Australian fiction with
All That Swagger (1936), an historical novel dealing with the
squatters, which associates her with Brent of Bin Bin. Three
years later she wrote, in collaboration with Dymphna Cusack, a
witty, rakish, debunking novel, around the sesquicentennial celebrations, called *Pioneers on Parade* (1939), which thoroughly
roasted the Australian snobs and was a *succès de scandale*. Around
Katherine Susannah Prichard may be grouped several writers,
mostly young, who, however much they may differ in outlook and
manner, do have in common the desire realistically to assess the
Australian scene. These are Kylie Tennant, Dymphna Cusack,
Leonard Mann, Brian Penton, Norman Lindsay, Dal Stivens,
Godfrey Blunden and Xavier Herbert. In many instances, these
writers would rather hang separately than unite to live. Kylie Tennant has produced three fine novels, *Tiburon* (1935), a story of

small-town life, *Foveaux* (1939), a story of Sydney slum life, and *The Battlers* (1941), which deals with life on the track among the wandering workers of both sexes. Miss Cusack's *Jungfrau* (1936) is an intense and slightly overwrought story of life among the young people of Sydney. *Murder in Sydney* (1937) by Leonard Mann is more than a murder story; it is also an excellent study of *déclassé* life in Sydney. In *Landtakers* (1934) and *Inheritors* (1936), Brian Penton provides a scarifying portrait of the "smash and grab" pioneer and his children. Norman Lindsay's *Saturdee* (1933) seems to me the best of his fiction, for it is an amusing study of small boys, whereas in his other books he is chiefly concerned with adult adolescents. Mr. Lindsay has also written a charming story for children, *The Magic Pudding* (1920). Dal Stivens has contributed a well-done book of short stories in the modern manner, *The Tramp and Other Stories* (1936), while Godfrey Blunden has written one first-class novel, *No More Reality* (1935). Both have a fine sense for life in its quieter and less violent moments. Herbert's *Capricornia* (1938) captures a new region for Australian fiction, the Northern Territory, and does it with an unwincing realism and fine gusto. (Back in 1908 Mrs. Aeneas Gunn brought the Territory into Australian literature with *We of the Never Never,* and in 1905 she had contributed *The Little Black Princess.* Both of these are now classics, the first being in the line of squatting reminiscenes, the second being notable for its sympathetic understanding of aboriginals.)

A group of writers, not absolutely different from the foregoing but more concerned with psychological problems, consists of Vance Palmer, Barnard Eldershaw, Frank Dalby Davison, and Eleanor Dark. Vance Palmer is the senior member of this group and, with his wife Nettie, has been for many years a leader in Australian literary affairs. Frank Davison recently dedicated a book of short stories to the Palmers, concluding with these words, "to Vance Palmer and to Nettie Palmer, whose lamps have burned with a clear and steady flame." The Palmers, particularly Vance, have used many forms, including the essay, the critical review, the short story, and the novel. Mr. Palmer's first book of fiction appeared in 1915, but of the long line I think he is best represented by *Sea and Spinifex* (1934) for short stories, and by *The Passage*

(1930) for the novel. M. Barnard Eldershaw (the pen name of two women) is prolific, having produced several novels, including the staid and competent *A House is Built* (1929) and the witty but light *Plaque Without Laurel* (1937), as well as historical studies and literary criticism. Dalby Davison has written a brilliantly successful animal story *Man Shy* (1931), many excellent short stories, and other material. Eleanor Dark has contributed one of the strongest books produced by this general group, *Prelude to Christopher* (1933), an extremely acute psychological study of marriage, and also a long line of well-done novels, which usually turn on psychological analysis, including *The Timeless Land* (1941), a profound study of the clash of the white and aboriginal cultures.

Even with all these writers named and characterized, we are far from having exhausted the list of Australian writers who have produced interesting and, in some instances, important books. But the range is sufficiently wide to suggest that, whatever else may be at fault, the Australians cannot be accused of failing to write!

If it is ever possible to learn from the past by disentangling essential principles from the accidents of circumstance in which they are always embedded, I should say that the inspiration for a sound Australian literary culture today and tomorrow is to be found in the writings of Tom Collins, Henry Lawson, Bernard O'Dowd, and those who stand in the relation of allies, heirs, and assigns to them down the years. The basic Australian literary tradition is a compound of sound learning, rebelliousness, ardent faith in the common man, and an even more ardent faith in the Australian future. What better tradition could any nation want?

Many Australians are of the opinion that Australian painting is far better and far more important than Australian literature. I think the situation is the reverse. The artists are extremely active and well organized. They have, to an extent surpassing the writers, captured the patronage of the well-to-do. Australian painting has long since received the cachet of respectability. But we have in Australia a fairly familiar situation. A rebellion which succeeded is now exhausted, though it remains in firm possession of the institutions of art—the schools, galleries, publications, and public taste—and stridently denies that any further change is desirable. This is not to say that there is no interesting Australian painting, for there is a good deal of work which is of perennial interest. But it is to put forward the view that this work represents a "period" or "school" and cannot (I hope) be taken as the final expression of art in Australia.

Australian art, like the literature, is oriented toward England. Even the rebellion that succeeded did not take its inspiration directly from the source, the impressionist movement in France, but indirectly, largely through London. It has been suggested that Constable, excellently represented in the Melbourne gallery, has had a profound influence on Australian painting. The Mecca of Australian artists has always been London, and more rarely Paris, especially after student days. They are chiefly impressionists whose work has been "stiffened" by orthodox drawing. Their pictures strike an American as oddly old-fashioned. After all, American painting has for many years been oriented toward France, and Americans interested in painting at all are familiar with the work of Cézanne and his successors. But in Australia it is different, and tradition, not rebellion, is the important factor.

The so-called "modernists" are still an issue in Australia, and wordy battles are fought about them in the press. Even in 1940 most of the established artists and gallery directors were opposed to the modernists, Cézanne and his successors, to the point of being vituperative about them. A quotation from an article printed in that year by James S. MacDonald of the National Gallery of Victoria, the most important museum in Australia, will be a sufficient sample of their point of view:

The art that Australian "modernists" profess is imported and is foreign to this relatively happiest of countries. The importers body-snatched the corpse abroad, smuggled it in, and warmed it up. For it is dead, even if it has not yet lain down. European insecurity begat this yelling, shocking art which at any cost was out to attract notice; terror of what unknown calamity might instantly rain from the air kept it alive. The distraction this leprous art furnished was pounced upon by overseas picture dealers and newspaper writers on art matters. They saw in it, respectively, profit and notoriety, and by their actions encouraged a section of the community to supply them with more and yet more degenerate productions—outdoing the work of men who had first been made mad and then sending them to their graves by the pallid but victorious spirochaete or lepra bacillus, or both. However, let us leave the work of perverts, feeling sure that in Australia it is not to remain for long. Its influence is the last of the importations.

As it happens, other than the artists and patrons who traveled abroad, few Australians had any opportunity to see the work of the modernists, except in color reproductions, until 1939. In that year the *Melbourne Herald* arranged a traveling show, which toured the capital cities. The moving spirits behind this important effort to educate public taste were Sir Keith Murdoch, one of the most intelligent Australian collectors, and Basil Burdett, advisor to Sir Keith and art critic for the *Herald*. This show is described in *Australian Art Annual, 1939* as "the first comprehensive view of modern art the Australian public has so far been given." It included works by Cézanne, van Gogh, Gauguin, Seurat, Picasso, Matisse, Derain, Utrillo, Braque, Modigliani, Vlaminck, and Bonnard among the French, and Steer, Tonks, John, Nash, and Wadsworth among the English. There was also a small sculpture section which included works by Maillol, Epstein, and Lambert, the latter the expatriate son of an Australian painter. What ultimate effect this show will have on Australian art is, of course, impossible to say. In Sydney the exhibition of continental art was a failure, but a memorial exhibition of the work of a highly regarded Australian painter drew an attendance of 53,000. It is notable that even after the tour the conservatives were still pursuing the moderns with ghoulish figures of speech and contumely, even alleging that they were, in some obscure way, responsible for the present condition of Europe.

But the fact that the conservatives are provoked to such self-revealing anger and anguish is an indication that there are Australian painters, and writers about painting, who are aware of the work of the moderns and are trying to assimilate it. These people, however, are still outside the Australian temple of art. They either form small societies of their own or exist in a somewhat envenomed isolation. I know of but one *book* -which states their

Wallace Kirkland, courtesy *Life*

Bondi Beach, Sydney.

Snow—at 6,000 feet.

Hume Reservoir, Murray River, key to irrigation.

point of view, although the literature of art in Australia is very extensive. It is a very personal and highly amusing book, *Arquebus* by Adrian Lawlor. Mr. Lawlor, an inspired controversialist, collected his forays against "the enemy" and enlivened them with a running commentary. The book makes delightful reading and is an oasis in the desert of Australian art criticism. It is the most vigorous onslaught on the "look and put" school yet produced. As if confronted with Director MacDonald, Mr. Lawlor roars at one point:

Let us quit this dismal howling. We've *got* to go on. Australia, if you wish to know, is due for a kick in the pants. Australia, in less impolite terms, is due for cultural, as well as industrial, development. And Australia is not going to like it.

But the skirmishes of the artists today give one little conception of what the Australian artists have accomplished in times past. Iconographically speaking, Australia is very rich. From the very earliest days the pictorial record is almost as varied and extensive as the written record. Several fascinating and valuable books could readily be compiled which would progressively unfold the history of Australia from various angles, all in contemporaneous pictures. If few of them would have aesthetic worth, that would not disturb the passionate iconographer. It is when aesthetic considerations come in at the door that the trouble begins.

Sir Lionel Lindsay, conservative critic and one of Australia's most distinguished etchers has observed:

The main problem in Australian art was the conquest of the landscape. Until that was resolved the actual appearance of the country as seen by the eyes of the native-born, could never be satisfactorily established. The early artists painted from drawings and notes, sophisticating form and generalizing color, so that they missed the essential character of the Australian landscape, its light and atmospheric color, only to be attained by direct painting.

The gum tree puzzled and dismayed them. Accustomed to the lateral disposition of deciduous foliage, this strange protean tree with its pendant leathern leaves and metallic reflections, refused to conform to any recognized formula—it lay out of bounds. So they produced a sort of hybrid. The graft of a northern specimen on to a hostile stock. This bastard elm-gum is common to all the early Australian landscape painting, about which, until the arrival of Louis Buvelot, there is no unmistakable "look of Australia." Though Buvelot did not quite succeed, he was the bridge that led to Roberts and Streeton.

With Roberts and Streeton we arrive at contemporary Australian art in its respectable phase. Those who succeeded these two men never swung entirely clear of their influence, of the standards they and their fellows established. On this showing, a truly Australian art began in the eighteen-eighties and is thus but sixty years old. It first began to conquer public taste in the eighteen-nineties—this once again underlining the vast importance of the nineties in Australian history—and it has held it in a tight grip ever since.

The precursors of contemporary Australian art were Conrad Martens (1801-1878, in Australia from 1835), who sums up the best in the very early period, and Louis Buvelot (1814-1888, in Australia from 1865), who, as Sir Lionel pointed out, is the "bridge" between the early period and the present. The actual founders of the Australian school were Tom Roberts (1856-1931), above all, and Sir Arthur Streeton (1867-   ). The most influential teacher is Julian Ashton (1851-   ). Great figures are Sir John Longstaff (1862-1941), George Washington Lambert (1873-1930), the most bravura personality—he was half American —and the most versatile artist of them all, Hans Heysen (1877-   ), Elioth Gruner (1882-1939), and the *trompe-l'oeil* painter Max Meldrum, who stands a bit off side and hence is considered "radical." All selections from a long list are invidious. Here I have tried, since I am confessedly a not too sympathetic witness, to mention those names which a conservative would probably select from the host. Such a man might well add Charles Condor (1868-1909) for his early Australian associations, Walter Withers (1857-1914), David Davies (1863-1939), Fred McCubbin (1855-1917), George Coates (1869-1930), Rupert Bunny (1864-   ), Margaret Preston (1883-   ), and John Moore (1888-   ). He would also want to say something about two sculptors, Web Gilbert (1867-1925) and Rayner Hoff (1894-1937). And perhaps he would claim some of the Australian expatriates in addition to George Coates, who spent most of his life in London, and Rupert Bunny, who spent many years in Paris but is now once more in Australia.

Since Sir Lionel Lindsay has defined the problem of the Australian artist as "the conquest of the landscape" and indicated the nature of the problem, it is to be taken for granted that the Australians are proudest of their landscape painters, or of the landscapes produced by men and women who also did portraits, still-lifes, and decorative work of various kinds. Flower pieces run a strong second, followed at a distance by portraits which, however, tend as in all countries to be chiefly more or less striking "likenesses." Given the Australian landscape characteristics of subdued colors bathed in vivid light, it was almost inevitable that painters, hitherto only acquainted with the traditional "dark" work of European artists, should have joyfully seized upon impressionism, founded as it was on the study of light and its effects. Far better than any style of painting to that time it gave the "answers" which they were, consciously or unconsciously, seeking. By the same token, it still to a high degree gives the "answers." But it is not, as many conservatives seem to feel, a choice between impressionism and academic drawing and no art at all when it is suggested that the impressionist influence has exhausted itself. It is rather that if art is not to become entirely unrewarding as a branch of living human experience, it cannot go on repeating its formulae with minute variations to the end of time. There is no reason to suppose that art can come to a dead level in Australia and survive, any more than it can in any other country on the globe.

The great pictures of the Australian impressionist school are hardly known at all in America, which is a misfortune. As opportunities offer to see them, Americans interested in Australia should certainly seize them, for whatever else may be said about the pictures, they do get Australia on canvas.* It would be a sorry curmudgeon who would fail to grant to such pictures as the following the laurels they unquestionably command: "The Purple Noon's Transparent Light" and "Australia Felix" by Streeton, "The Golden Fleece" by Tom Roberts, "A Solitary Ramble" by Julian Ashton, "The Murrumbidgee Ranges" and "The Valley of the Tweed" by Gruner, "White Gums" by Heysen and "Charred Stumps" by John D. Moore. These canvases justify the Australian

* An astutely selected show of Australian art which was to tour the country opened at the National Gallery, Washington, D.C., October 1, 1941.

impressionists in full measure. These artists and their fellows have made a great and important contribution to the development of art in Australia. But they do not justify the ridiculous "stone-walling" in which the conservatives are today engaged.

Australia has produced a considerable number of highly talented black and white artists or cartoonists, some of whom have done superior work in other ranges of art. The best known, and also the best, are Livingston Hopkins, Phil May, Norman Lindsay, Will Dyson, David Low, and George Finey. By a curious accident of circumstances, only two of them are Australians by birth, Norman Lindsay and Will Dyson. Low and Finey are New Zealanders. Phil May was an Englishman and Livingston Hopkins an American.

What gives these men their distinction is their ability in drawing, an art cultivated in Australia, and their unusual humor or wit, for if weak in one phase, they made it up in another. Of them all, I suppose, Will Dyson had the most highly cultivated and "literate" wit. In his later days he produced a series of satirical etchings of a rare quality indeed, most of which have been seen in America. Low, of course, excels in political understanding. It is indicative of something or other that Low's work has not, since he migrated to London, been reproduced as often in Australian papers as in American. Phil May, now almost forgotten by all except historians and sentimental oldsters, had a happy humor, especially in the depiction of guttersnipes, which made him a London favorite in his post-Australian days. He slowly achieved a remarkable economy of line. It is worth noting that Low, too, has progressively simplified his style. May once said that the fewer lines he was forced to draw to get his effects, the higher the fees he would expect. George Finey, the youngest member of the group, strikes a powerful sardonic note, being especially adept at bone-crushing political comment. Norman Lindsay has always cultivated a decorative art which has lent itself to infinite elaboration. He fills his paper with an incredible profusion of detail. Of the group he is, I think, the least witty, though he has considerable humor. He has long cultivated an inverted "wowserism" which I find tiresome if taken in large doses. (For "wowserism" read "Puritanism.") Livingston Hopkins, the American, was doyen of the *Bulletin* cartoonists, and most of the men famous for black and white work have worked for that paper at one time or another. After successfully beginning a career as cartoonist and illustrator in New York, Hopkins was induced to go to Australia to be staff-cartoonist for the *Bulletin* in 1882. Until his death in 1927 he was a kindly critic of life and politics in Australia. I have never met an American who knew anything about Hopkins, though he is passingly mentioned in Weitenkampf's *American Graphic Art* and before going to Australia was sufficiently advanced to have illustrated one of Josh Billings's books and to have written and illustrated *A Comic History of the United States* that is still amusing.

With regard to music it is my misfortune to be a complete philistine. (I only know what I like.) I have no real understanding of it. I cannot, therefore, do more than report that the Australians are a musical people. Public performances have been popular since early times, and today the larger newspapers maintain music critics on their staffs. Not only are performances by local artists common, but a high proportion of the great artists seen on the American concert stage are also seen, sooner or later, in Australia. The development of the government radio has increased the country's capacity to offer fees attractive to the great artists of the day. And the fact that Australian seasons are the reverse of those of the Northern Hemisphere makes it possible for the artists to visit the Commonwealth without missing a single concert in Europe or America.

Professors of music are found in the universities, and several states maintain conservatoria. The state schools also cultivate the talents of the scholars, and regular examinations are held, the examiner coming out from England. Australia has thus produced many talented performers, both instrumental and vocal, including the celebrated Nellie Melba. There are Australians attached to the staff of the Metropolitan Opera Company and others who are conspicuous elsewhere in the musical life of the United States. Ernest Hutcheson, President of the Julliard School of Music, is an Australian. So are Percy Grainger, the pianist and composer, and Marjorie Lawrence and John Brownlee, the operatic stars. Australia also exports musical talent to London.

The quality of the work of Australian composers is a closed book to me. Among the names frequently mentioned, in addition to Grainger, are Alfred Hill and Henry Tate. Tate is regarded as the most original "theorist" about music. His *Australian Musical Possibilities* (1924) makes interesting reading, for Tate argues from the accomplishments in the other arts, that Australia can and will produce distinctive creative work in music.

The first theatrical performance in Australia was given on June 4, 1789, by a company of convicts, eighteen months after settlement was first made at Sydney. Since that date the theater has had an extraordinary career, but in its commercial phases it is now jeopardized by the movies. At various times, usually in periods of great prosperity, it has flourished like the green bay tree. Many of the greatest of the theatrical performers of the world have, in their time, played an Australian season. The record shows such names as Laura Keene, Edwin Booth, Charles Kean, Dion Boucicault, Sarah Bernhardt, H. B. Irving, Oscar Asche, Guy Bates Post, Seymour Hicks, and many others. The most famous and best-loved Australian actress of all times was Nellie Stewart (1858-1931). It was my privilege in 1927 to see her perform her favorite role, the lead in *Sweet Nell of Old Drury*.

At the present time the future of the stage is chiefly in the hands of the "little theater" groups, which are exceedingly active. They have lately begun to encourage the writing of plays on Australian themes, a hitherto neglected field of literary activity. The Australian radio is also encouraging the writing of radio plays from native material. Several volumes of plays have been printed, notably *Best Australian One-Act Plays* (1937). Full-length dramas are also finding their way into print, among the interesting examples being *Brumby Innes* (1927) by Katherine Susannah Prichard and *Men Without Wives* (1938) by Henrietta Drake-Brockman. The pioneer of Australian drama of literary significance is Louis Esson, who in 1920 published a little volume entitled *Dead Timber and Other Plays,* which is today regarded as a landmark in its field.

Australia has exported actors and actresses as it has musicians. The American stage has claimed many of them, and the movies are now absorbing them, too. The late O. P. Heggie was an Australian. So was Frank Tinney. Judith Anderson was born in South Australia, Erroll Flynn and Merle Oberon (Merle O'Brien Thompson) in Tasmania.

Institutional culture in Australia—libraries, museums, state schools and universities—is today in such a ferment that only experts in the several fields are entitled to hold dogmatic opinions. The fact that the volume of discussion is great and the temper of much of it sharply critical is an indication that all is not well, or at least not sufficiently well to warrant complacence. Much of the ferment has been focused by, and now circles around, a series of reports financed by the Carnegie Corporation of New York and made by English, Australian, and American experts. Notable among them are the reports on museums and art galleries, 1933, and libraries, 1936, and the numerous studies issued by the Australian Council for Educational Research, an institution subsidized by the Carnegie Corporation for ten years from 1930. Speaking generally, these reports, and also the informal observations of visiting experts on related matters, have been well received, though a minority has vigorously attacked them for one reason or another, including the fact that those who made them were, in most instances, outsiders. But since the critical remarks are usually supported by the Australians intimately concerned with the various matters, as well as by private citizens who have knowledge of developments overseas, it is widely assumed that there is warrant for them. The total effect has been to stimulate the resolution to make sweeping changes to bring the institutions into line with their English and American counterparts. Movements are started with this end in view, of which the Free Library Movement of New South Wales is a notable example.

The table below shows approximately when the principal institutions were founded. Approximately, for should one select the date when private citizens first launched a particular venture or the date when the government took charge? Sooner or later the institutions became charges on the several state governments. Even the libraries, art museums, and schools are state-supported, the local communities taking practically no responsibility for them. This underlines the point that "local government" is underdeveloped in Australia. To be sure, there are a few municipal art museums in Victoria and still fewer in New South Wales, as well as a scattering of rather poor municipal libraries, but these are the exceptions. There are, of course, no municipally supported schools in any Australian state, other than a few kindergartens. Outside the state systems, administered by state government departments, there are the private schools, chiefly run by religious bodies. The Catholics maintain parochial schools throughout the Commonwealth. The most fashionable private preparatory schools are associated with the Church of England. As I am not an educationalist I shall say little about the state schools, merely remarking that they are under fire these days, both in technical journals and the newspapers. The Australian state system is "free, compulsory, and secular." The leaving age is thus far uniformly fourteen years, or at the level of the five American states of Georgia, Louisiana, North Carolina, South Carolina, and Texas.

No Australian state has developed a satisfactory system of free public libraries, either as a state or municipal enterprise. The libraries in the table below are in the nature of state reference libraries and are in the capital cities, although some of them have schemes for circulating books in the country districts. The Carnegie report on libraries opens with these words, "In the widespread establishment of free public libraries as an essential part of the nation's educational plan, Australia ranks below most of the other English-speaking countries."

	STATE SCHOOLS	UNIVER- SITY	LIBRARY	ART MUSEUM	TECHNO- LOGICAL MUSEUM	GEOLOGICAL & NATURAL HISTORY MUSEUM
Q'land	1875	1909	1896	1895		1855
N.S.W.	1880	1851	1869	1875	1881	1827
Vic.	1872	1854	1856	1861	1870	1854
So. A.	1878	1874	1884	1881		1861
Tas.	1885	1890	1870			1845
West. A.	1893	1913	1887	1895		1860
Federal.			1902			1924

In the Carnegie report on museums and art galleries it is observed that " . . . in general it may be said that where the later decades of the nineteenth century witnessed the establishment of museums . . . the first fifteen years of the twentieth century saw them enriched and expanded in a most remarkable manner. Governments, scientists, men of wealth, and even artists, combined in this remarkable development. . . . The knell of this period sounded in August, 1914." With proper reservations to take account of the varying character of the institutions, these remarks can be applied to all. After the initial impulse had exhausted itself, the institutions tended slowly to relapse into a debilitating routine, out of which they were only occasionally jolted until comparatively recent years. There are, of course, brilliant exceptions. I should hazard the inference that between the outbreak of the First World War and the sharp increase in self-criticism provoked by the Great Depression, institutional culture in Australia was not in a progressive condition.

Reading the recent expert assessments, whether foreign or domestic, one is constantly struck by two recurring points, both of which are of basic importance—that the institutions have been starved for funds, and that private benefactions have been uncommon. While Australian governments have found millions for economic development, they have found meager thousands for cultural development outside the state schools.

Each Australian state now maintains its own university. I am not in a position to assess the worth of them, and my work in Australia has never brought me into particularly close contact with them. But in all the universities I have found men who struck me as being absolutely first-rate in their specialties. No Australian university in 1937 had a yearly revenue of as much as one million dollars, taking the pound at $4.00. The range was from $95,000 for the University of Tasmania, the smallest, to $885,000 for the University of Sydney, the largest. All the universities, excepting those in Tasmania and Western Australia, rely heavily on lecture and examination fees for income. The required balance is made up of government grants and income from private foundations, or what we would call endowments, the former being uniformly the larger sum. Sydney, which has the largest endowment income, derives about 30 per cent of its total income from that source, but in the revenue of the University of Western Australia this item accounts for only 4 per cent of the total. The latter university gets four-fifths of its income from the government, while Tasmania gets about three-fifths. Sydney has the largest student body, in 1937, 3,378, but Melbourne was close behind with 3,325. Adelaide had 2,113. Tasmania had the smallest student body, 270.

The largest collections of books in public reference libraries are found in Sydney (in 1933, 460,000) and Melbourne (in 1933, 517,-000). While the Melbourne institution has the larger collection in point of numbers, and had, until the other day, by far the best building, Sydney has two very important special libraries, which make it the library center of Australia. These are the Mitchell Library, which contains the world's greatest collection of Australiana, and the Fisher Library of the University of Sydney, by far the largest university library in the Commonwealth, containing about a quarter of a million volumes. Both of these special libraries exist because of private benefactions, the former representing the generosity of David Scott Mitchell (1836-1907), who presented the basic collection in 1907 together with an endowment equal to a third of a million dollars, while the latter is a monument to the public spirit of Thomas Fisher, who in 1885 left approximately $150,000 to the university library. South Australia and Western Australia maintain good public reference libraries, but those in Tasmania and Queensland are of a very indifferent order. A National Library is in process of development in Canberra. It is being planned along the lines of the United States Library of Congress, but today it is still small.

The National Gallery of Victoria in Melbourne is the richest art museum, in all senses, in Australia. This gallery benefits from the Alfred Felton bequest of 1904, which has enabled it to escape the prevailing limitations of Australian galleries, poverty and excessive concentration on English and especially Australian pictures. By accumulating more and more Australian pictures, to the neglect of the artists of other countries, the museums confirm that isolation and inbreeding by which Director MacDonald sets such store. The Carnegie report of 1933 stated that "Modern German, Italian, or American art is practically unrepresented" in Australian museums.

That is still true, and it is painful for an American to notice in this field, as in so many others, how completely uninformed the public is about the accomplishments of his countrymen. At Melbourne, however, one can see "Old Masters" other than English "Old Masters." One can see pictures by Goya, Van Eyck, Corot, Rembrandt, Titian, Tiepolo, Van Dyck, Pissarro, and even, since 1938, one Cézanne, "La Route Montante." (For obvious reasons both Sargent and Whistler, who are represented in this gallery, are classified as "British," thus effectively eliminating any American representation!)

In the postwar period we may expect Australia to make great forward strides in institutional culture, not the least important objective being to bring her into contact with the currents of *world* culture. The right note has been struck by Dr. R. E. Priestly, formerly Vice-Chancellor of Melbourne University, now of the University of Birmingham, England:

. . . Australia stands once more at the crossroads. The period when she was preoccupied almost entirely with primary industry, with which may be correlated the development of her primary and secondary educational system, the pioneer period, is long past. The period of development of the secondary industries, with which may be coupled in the educational world the perfection of her training for the professions, is well advanced. She is now due, if her progress is to be maintained, to move into a tertiary period. Culture and the development of the lighter industries which deal rather with the refinements of life will need to be her principal aim. In a book I have recently read, *The Clash of Progress and Security,* by Professor Fisher . . . the same idea is adumbrated and worked out in the purely economic sphere. With this tertiary development should naturally go greater attention to, concentration upon, and support for, education of the highest and fullest kind. Universities, museums, and art galleries should all be used up to the full to convey to the people at large, and to the leaders of the next generation in particular, the achievements of the past, the special needs of today, and the promise and possibilities of the days to come.

THE Australian Outlook. When celebrating their peculiar virtues, the British people almost invariably refer to the British "race." In Australia it is the Australian "race." No doubt this is only annoying to those who remember their university courses in anthropology, but it is well to recall there is no such thing as a British, or an Australian, "race." There are people of British nationality and people of Australian nationality. Yet in a publication of 1940 we find Mr. William Morris Hughes saying in the foreword, "we have a race, hardy, virile, resourceful, courageous." And a few pages beyond we find an article, written by an emeritus professor of physiology entitled *Factors in the Development of an Australian Race.*

But the point I want to make here is not that the Australians misuse the word race. Rather I should like to establish that it is on the conception implied by the word race that they found their national unity. The unifying principle in Australian life is the fact that the people are of a common "race," or "blood." Because the adjective British is usually tied to these two ideas, the Australians customarily made their point by emphasizing that they are 98 per cent British, "race" and "blood" being unexpressed but clearly understood. The Australian approach to other nationalities is, therefore, utterly different from the American. When we use the expression "the race problem," nine times out of ten we mean the problem of white-negro relations, and the tenth time we probably refer to the relations of whites and orientals. When we refer to difficulties between people of different national origins in America, we refer to the "conflicts of nationality." But the Australians, who have inherited the British conception that race and nationality are almost interchangeable words, unconsciously think of people of non-British nationality as members of another race. And from this fact comes the extreme reluctance of Australians to face the possibility that the immigrants to their country in the future may be other than of British nationality, although not black, brown, or yellow by skin pigmentation.

Many Australians will indignantly deny the truth of these observations, except insofar as they concern the "White Australia" policy designed to exclude black, brown, and yellow peoples as permanent settlers. But in defense of my observations I can do no better than refer here to one aspect of the Australian view of the United States. I use a warning given the Australian people in recent months—the warning would never have been written if the notion discussed did not exist. It is by R. J. F. Boyer. Speaking of the United States, he said (his italics):

To be sure she is nationalistic, perhaps as keenly so as any people in Europe, but the content of her nationalism is fundamentally different. *She is a nation and not a race.* She is inter-racial without being international. Now this involves an enormous difference in the emotional factors which actuate her people and her policy. When, with the Declaration of Independence, America began her independent existence and opened her doors to all the races of Europe [Mr. Boyer really means all the *nationals* of Europe], her people suffered a major emotional operation. . . . A new cement had to replace the old, and it was found in an idea, voiced in the Declaration itself . . . 'that all men are created equal; that they are endowed by the Creator with certain inalienable rights, that among these are Life, Liberty, and the Pursuit of Happiness.' . . . America still remains non-racial, with all the dynamism elsewhere centered in race concentrated in the common allegiance to an idea.

Mr. Boyer shows a keen understanding of the American situation, but he nevertheless retains the characteristic Australian conception of race and recognizes that, while America is different, "race" is the principle of unity in his land. He thus gives a firm foundation to my description of the outlook of the Australian people. The Australians are not, therefore, unified after the American fashion by faith in an *idea*. But on different foundations the Australians and the Americans erect a body of political and social ideals which they may be said to hold in common. It is nevertheless the ideals, not the preconceptions upon which they are based, that they have in common.

The question is not whether the Australians are a race in the anthropological sense, for they are not, but rather the question is, is there a distinctive Australian nationality? That, at least, is how the question poses itself to an American observer. The answer is "Yes." (But not in law, for in that realm there is no such thing as Australian citizenship apart from British. There is only the Australian "species" of British nationality.) Here and there in this book I have stopped to indicate the nature of the Australian outlook, especially in the discussion of literature. It is not necessary to recapitulate the points here. Rather I should like to make one additional observation. Australians have a much stronger tendency to be independent in small things than in the larger things of life. With regard to these, they are often timid. In the shallows of life they are unquestionably Australian, but when they venture into the deeps they often flounder about and grasp at inherited "straws" which will rescue them from the necessity of thinking out standards of their own. Professor E. A. Ross of the University of Wisconsin remarked when he was in Australia in 1938 that the Australians had never learned as the Americans had *when* to say "be damned to you." He attributed this to the fact that the Australians have hugged the coast, whereas the Americans were soon well away from the seaboard into the interior where old-world influences were weak. I do not know that Professor Ross has hit upon the correct explanation, but I do know that until the Australians acquire less diffidence in the face of old-world standards and modes of thought about the deeper things of life, they will continue to be plagued by the emotional ambivalence which characterizes them today. They cannot long remain half Australian and half European. They must integrate themselves. The Australian attitude was excellently expressed by A. G. Stephens in one of his critical essays collected in *The Red Pagan* (1904):

It is the duty, and should be the pride, of every father and mother and teacher of Australian children to intensify the natural love of Australia, and to point out in how many ways Australia is eminently worthy to be loved—both the actual land and the national ideal. Good and evil are mingled everywhere; but there is no land with more beautiful aspects than Australia, no ideal with greater potentialities of human achievement and human happiness. Australia may never be a great country; yet it will be the fault of the people, not of the land, if it is not one of the best countries in the world to live in and die in—given that we are free from foreign aggression until we are able to resist foreign aggression.

What do Australians Look Like? A favorite idea of Americans is that all Australians are tall, lanky fellows, roughly similar in type to the mythical American cowboy. This is not true. Australians, like every other people, are of various types. They are, like the Nova Scotia farmer's foot, long and short, broad and narrow, and wide. A glance at the photographs of Australian leaders in this book will convince the sceptic that Australians do not look alike, and he may deduce also that they are not all alike in other physical characteristics.

Australian Speech. Another myth which should be laid is that Australians speak cockney. The so-called Australian accent is world-famous. In recent years some excellent technical studies of Australian speech have been made, and there is now general agreement among experts that it is not cockney. One of the best studies is *The Pronunciation of English in Australia* (1940) by A. G. Mitchell of the University of Sydney. Professor Mitchell begins his study by collecting an amusing assortment of contradictory observations on Australian speech habits and equally contradictory explanations of their origin. He then remarks that there are "two forms of the spoken language—an educated, cultivated, or professional form, and a popular, uncultivated, unprofessional form. There are no local dialects. . . ." He refuses to praise or condemn either, simply taking them as data. His analysis is technical, but his conclusion is simple: "The educated form of Australian speech will pass anywhere in the English-speaking world as a clear, unmannered, pleasant form of English. . . . The Australian popular form has a right to be considered as a legitimate, useful local variation of speech, not as a low and perverse corruption of good English." Anyone who has been in Australia will agree.

The cockney myth originated from the fact that in Australian popular speech, words containing "a" and "ai" are apt to be pronounced as though they contained a long "i." The classic illustration is the sentence, "The train is late today," which becomes "The trine is lite todi." But I like better the story of the teacher who was asking the class for French equivalents. She turned to a small boy and said, "To die." The reply came, "Aujourd'hui." Whether this peculiarity of speech is increasing or declining I cannot presume to say with certainty. But unless I have become habituated to it, I am quite sure that it is less common today than when I first visited Australia in 1927.

I am not one of those fellows who prides himself on his ability to detect subtle variations in speech. I cannot tell precisely which American state is the native state of a particular speaker. But my ear does register the broader differences. I can usually identify an Australian from his speech. My indicators are intonation and rhythm. As I know little about phonetics, I cannot indicate on paper just exactly what I mean. A shrewd Australian observer has written, "A general observation on the difference between American and Australian speech types and conversation types might be that the American is rhetorical (thus richer and more formal), and the Australian commentative (drier, more bare, the frequent oaths being an unconscious recognition of the sparseness of vocabulary)."

Australian slang is, next to the American, the most vivid, vigorous, and comprehensive in the world. A study of the Australian section of a good slang dictionary, or the reading of an Australian novel like Kylie Tennant's *The Battlers,* will convince anyone of the truth of this observation. Like all slang, the Australian variety picks up and discards words all the time. Australians make a good deal of use of American slang, but often subtly change the meaning of the familiar words. Then again, in genuinely Australian slang one encounters familiar words used in a radically different sense. Grafter in Australian is not a purloiner of public funds. A grafter is a hard worker!

When it comes to Australian swearing, it is best for an American to be modest. When I was visiting Darwin, a lady at the hotel told me that she had once overheard some Australians and an American engaged in a contest designed to discover whose swearing sounded worst. Her verdict was that the American lost, but she may have been biased in favor of her countrymen. In *Lars Porsena, Or the Future of Swearing and Improper Language* Robert Graves quotes, what he calls "The Australian Poem." The author of this notable contribution to world literature was W. T. Goodge, who in 1904 included it in a volume entitled *Hits, Skits, and Jingles.* It begins:

> The sunburnt bloody stockman stood
> And, in a dismal bloody mood,
>   Apostrophised his bloody cuddy;
> The bloody nag's no bloody good,
> He couldn't earn his bloody food—
>   A regular bloody brumby,
>   Bloody!

The number of times a really talented Australian swearer can use bloody in a conversation is incredible. When I asked an old "cove" when he first arrived in Darwin, he replied, "Young man, in nineteen bloody eight!"

After bloody, the most frequently used swear words are bugger and bastard, the latter pronounced "barstud." Both of these words have completely lost the horrid associations they once had. In clubs you will hear a man greet a good friend, "How are you, you old barstud?" The word bugger is used in numerous forms and contexts. "Oh, bugger it all." "I'll be buggered." "Buggered if I will." "Bugger him." "Oh go to buggery." "The silly bugger." "I'm all buggered up." And, triumphantly combining all the favorite words, "bugger the bloody barstud." English people profess to find Australian men foul-mouthed.

C. J. Dennis is the author of *A Real Austra-bloody-laise:*

> *Fellers of Australier,*
> *   Blokes an' coves an' coots,*
> * Shift yer bloody caraceses,*
> *Move yer bloody boots.*
> *Gird yer bloody loins up,*
> *   Get yer bloody gun,*
> *Set the bloody enermy*
> *   An' watch the bugger run.*

Chorus:
> *Get a bloody move on,*
> > *Have some bloody sense.*
> *Learn the bloody art of*
> > *Self debloodyfence.*

———

> *Fellers of Australier,*
> > *Cobbers, chaps, an' mates,*
> *Hear the bloody enermy*
> *Kickin' at the gates!*
> *Blow the bloody bugle,*
> > *Beat the bloody drum,*
> *Upper-cut and out the cow*
> *To kingdom bloody come!*

And so on.

Mr. Dennis has also made some amusing rhymes out of the native place-names common in Australia, as for example:

> *Booleroo, Billeroo,*
> *Parneroo, Pineroo,*
> *Mutooroo, Morudoo,*
> > *Garra.*
> *Orroroo, Beetaloo,*
> *Waukaloo, Warnamboo,*
> *Ninkerloo, Yednaloo,*
> > *Parra.*

Footnote to Bartlett. I have run across only two sets of quotations from Australian writers in Bartlett's *Familiar Quotations.* One is from Adam Lindsay Gordon whose egregious merits I have specified. Gordon's dates are correctly given. The other set is from Henry Lawson who is represented by two short passages from his touching poem, "When Your Pants Begin to Go." That's all right, for Lawson did write it. But what irks me is that when it comes to dates, the notation is "Floruit 1896." Fie on you, Christopher Morley! Henry Lawson is the greatest writer of sketches Australia has ever produced and particularly prized by labor as a poet who sympathized with their point of view. His dates are 1867-1922. There is an annual pilgrimage to his grave, and he is the only

Australian writer whose memory is kept green by a monument in a public park.

Food. In a curious book called *The Art of Living in Australia* (1894) by Philip E. Muskett, I find these remarks:

. . . the consumption of butcher's meat and of tea is enormously in excess of any common-sense requirements, and is paralleled nowhere else in the world. . . . I hazard the opinion that the real development of Australia will never actually begin till this willful violation of her people's food-life ceases . . . the type of the Australian dwelling-house, the clothing of the Australian people . . . prove incontestably that they have never recognized the semi-tropical character of their climate.

It is now almost half a century since Dr. Muskett set down these words, and there have been marked and decided changes for the better, but it is still true that when it comes to food, clothing, and shelter, Australians are a conservative lot. They still have a long way to go before achieving Dr. Muskett's ideal. They still resist the climate, though less and less each decade.

A rough idea of Australian eating habits can be obtained from a comparison of Australian and American annual per capita consumption of certain items of diet.

		AUSTRALIA	U. S. A.
Wheaten flour	lbs.	203	160
Sugar	"	109	105
Butter	"	30.5	16.7
Cheese	"	3.8	5.4
Beef	"	112	63
Mutton & Lamb	"	81	7
Pig Meat	"	19	55
Total Meat	"	212	125
Tea	"	6.8	.7
Coffee	"	.6	13.3

From this table it is apparent that the Australians are still great meat-eaters and drinkers of tea. Where great progress has been made in recent years is in the consumption of green vegetables, salads, and fresh fruit, especially in the capital cities and principal towns. But the Australians have a long way to go before they reach the American level in the making of salads and especially of salad dressings; and they are simply nowhere at all in competition with the Americans in the variety of salads served. With regard to fruit, the great difficulty is to get it into the meal. Following tradition, it is served in a big bowl after desert, each person selecting his apple or pear or what not and peeling it himself—if he wants it. Usually you are too full to eat fruit. While orange juice can be obtained at the big hotels, it is not in universal demand by Australians, in spite of the fact that there are plenty of oranges. Fruit-growers told me that they despair of ever getting fruit consumption up to American levels. Vegetables are plentiful, except in the outback, but they are usually overcooked. Outback your two vegetables in a hotel meal are two potatoes, one boiled and one roasted.

Clothing. The great surprise with regard to clothing is the almost complete absence of light-weight and light-colored suits for men, even in summertime. White is confined almost entirely to sports wear. The great sartorial event in my time has been the decline and fall of the bat-wing collar and string tie as standard equipment for businessmen. I find the following in the *Pacific Islands Year Book,* "All men in Sydney and the majority in Brisbane wear practically the same clothes in summer as they wear in London in winter—and look correspondingly ridiculous. They make Australia's colossal laundry charges their excuse." That is true. The Australian men favor grays and gray-blues in suits and shirts, and black shoes. A few blossom out in symphonies in brown. To American notions, they wear incredibly ridiculous underwear, even sticking to the old-fashioned, long-sleeved, long-legged heavy shirts and drawers for cold weather. This is because Australian houses and business establishments are usually imperfectly heated in the cooler months. The women dress infinitely better. They keep abreast of overseas developments in England, America, and Paris.

Shelter. Domestic architecture has improved decidedly in recent years. The standard Australian house is of the bungalow type. Even in the great cities, the majority of families occupy single-family houses. Only Sydney has any considerable number of flats, or apartments. They are not very highly esteemed. Every so often an alderman will raise the cry, "The flats of today are the slums of tomorrow." True enough. But the bungalows of yesterday are the slums of today! Nevertheless there is a good deal to be said for the single-family dwelling, and its survival in Australia is all to the good. Since central heating is uncommon, few Australian dwellings have cellars. Usually the houses are built with vents in the walls to insure a circulation of air in the hot months, but they serve equally well to let cold air in during the cool months. The commonest roofing material is corrugated galvanized iron painted red, though in some cities colored tiles are the vogue today. The red roofs give the residential areas a gay appearance when seen from a height. I suppose that the principal fault of the houses, from the standpoint of housekeeping efficiency, particularly the older ones, is that the rooms are not well arranged in relation to one another. Kitchen and dining room are often separated by a long hall. Australian house furnishings are what the taste of the householder makes them, but if his or her taste is bad, ample scope for satisfying it is provided by the local shops.

Life in Australia can be very pleasant, and if I were condemned to spend the rest of my natural life there, I should not repine for an instant.

Taxes. The Commonwealth, under normal prewar conditions, as in 1938-39, derived just short of four-fifths of its income (77.9 per cent) from taxation and most of the other fifth (18.8 per cent) from its business undertakings. Over nine-tenths of the taxes (93 per cent) came from four sources, of which customs revenue was overwhelmingly the most important (42.1 per cent), the others being excise (22.3 per cent), income tax (16 per cent) and sales tax (12.6 per cent). The states differ as to the sources of tax revenue they have tapped. The wealthy state of New South Wales derived most of its revenue in 1938-39 from the income and dividend tax (31.2 per cent), the special income and wages tax (31.4 per cent), the automobile tax (13.6 per cent), probate and succession duties (11.6 per cent), and stamp duties (6.3 per cent). All states, of course, derive considerable sums from their business undertakings, especially the railways. Local government "rates" are low. It is apparent that the Australian governments have not discovered any unique sources of revenue and are not exploiting some familiar to Americans. Speaking by and large, the Australian taxpayer comes as near to getting his money's-worth as the taxpayer of any other nation. The governmental expenditures which are local and peculiar can be justified if one looks into the matter with sufficient care and judges the activities by criteria which are relevant in the Australian context. Too much of the criticism leveled against Australian taxation is *ad hoc* criticism dictated by an anti-taxation complex. Nevertheless Australia has long since ceased to be a "low tax" country.

Landholding. One result of the character of the country and the land legislation in force is that much less land is alienated from the state than is characteristic in the United States. Victoria shows the highest percentage alienated (about 48 per cent) and Western Australia the lowest (about 2 per cent). No land has been alienated in Northern Territory. Large proportions of the *occupied* areas in all states except Victoria are held on lease. All states and the Territory have considerable areas unoccupied (and presumably not worth occupying). About two-fifths of the land alienated is held in blocks from one thousand to five thousand acres in area, another reflection of the character of the country, for the figures about equal the average size of Australian farms. Especially in the areas where wheat is grown, extensive dry-farming methods are employed, American methods having had considerable influence on Australian practices.

Religion. In the last Australian census (1933) one-eighth of the people failed to state any religious affiliation. Of the remainder, 99 per cent professed the Christian faith. The largest single church is the Church of England, with two and a half million adherents, followed by the Roman Catholic church, with about a million and a quarter. If to the Anglicans we add the adherents to other Protestant churches, it is clear that Australia is predominantly a Protestant country. Among the Protestant churches which have one hundred thousand adherents or more are the Presbyterian

(713,000), Methodist (684,000), and Baptist (105,000). The Roman Catholics are about one-fifth of the population.

Sport. The great Australian game is cricket. As much energy is put into cricket as Americans put into baseball. And baseball is as minor a sport in Australia as cricket is here. Instead of a "world series" to close each season, there are periodical matches between Australian and English cricket teams, played alternately in the two countries. The games in Australia attract their thousands; and when they are played in England, people sit up far into the night to listen to the reports on the radio. It is winter in Australia at this time, so the consumption of firewood rises, as the newspapers report. These matches are called "tests," and the object is to win "the ashes." Australia has a notable record for victories in the "tests," and her great cricketers are public heroes.

Cricket rarely impinges upon the American consciousness, though the results of the test matches are reported in New York papers, but in 1939 this generation of Americans realized that the Australians are also first-rate tennis players. In that year the Australian team captured the Davis Cup, for the first time since 1914.

Practically every sport ever heard of has its followers in Australia, and at least one remarkable game is peculiar to the country, Australian-rules football. Golf is popular with businessmen. The elderly men take up bowls, a game which requires carefully kept greens. The most attractively situated bowling green I ever saw was that on the banks of the Murray River at Renmark. Professional boxing has its followers. The most famous boxer associated with Australia was Bob Fitzsimmons, who once held the heavyweight and light-heavyweight championships of the world. Many famous American fighters have visited Australia, including Jack Johnson and Tommy Burns. Australia does not at present have a heavyweight capable of handling Joe Louis.

Australians are "crazy about horses." Although plenty of racing is done in this country, the general interest is by no manner of means as great as it is in Australia. I recall that in 1927 when I landed in Sydney the first mystery I encountered was a man shouting, "Rice! Rice! Get yer book for the rice!" I had to ask what it was all about. In all the time I have spent in Australia I have attended but two race meetings, one in Charleville, Queensland, the other the night trotting under lights at Perth, Western Australia. I do know, however, that the race horse on which greatest affection has been lavished is Phar Lap, whose bones are in a public museum. Like the Indian rajah, I have always known that one horse can run faster than another.

Sport suggests gambling, the Great Australian Vice. Not only do some of the states maintain public lotteries, but Tasmania has a lottery that does business all over Australia, Tattersall's. Thousands buy a "ticket in Tatt's." The Tasmanian government actually derives a quarter of its revenue from lottery taxes! Good Australians will bet on anything whatever. The story is told of men laying shillings on which of two flies would first rise from a sticky bar. The national gambling game is two-up, played with two pennies and a wooden paddle in a two-up "school." The pennies are tossed in the air, and the game turns on whether they fall "odds" or "evens." For some obscure reason, this game is illegal. I saw it played one Sunday morning before a large crowd in the bush outside Kalgoorlie, Western Australia. The "pot" fluctuated, but usually it contained a sizable pile of pound notes. In the old days bets at the race courses were laid with licensed bookmakers, and while these gentlemen still practice their profession most bets are placed on the totalizator, a mechanical contrivance now being introduced on American tracks. This ingenious calculator registers the bets against the odds, and pays out for winner and horses that "place." It was invented by Sir George Julius, a distinguished engineer who is not, as it happens, a racing enthusiast. His father was an Anglican Bishop. Betting is periodically the subject of Royal Commission investigations, the particular phase which has lately caused trouble being the so-called "S.P.," or starting price, betting on races. (As is well known, the odds are subject to change right up until the race starts.) This form of betting has been handled so that even as little as sixpence can be wagered, thus pulling in thousands of very poor people. The objection to it in Australia is not the fact that it is gambling as much as the fact that it is "off the course" betting conducted in disreputable betting shops or by canvassers like those employed in the New York "numbers racket." The sacred right of an Australian to lay a bet is something with which governments do not lightly interfere.

Movies. The overwhelming majority of the movies shown are of American origin. They are all reviewed by an official film-censorship board before being licensed for exhibition. Probably because American films dominate the field, it is popularly believed that the Hollywood product is the worst carrier of "dirt" of one kind or another. The censor's records do not bear this out. The percentage of eliminations from feature films in 1937 was United States films 15.4 and British films 28.1. This relation has been maintained for several years. What influence the films have on the popular conceptions of the United States is impossible to say. Once when I was visiting a farm home in a remote part of Western Australia the small boy of the household obviously wanted to ask me a question, but was too bashful. Finally his mother said that he wanted to know—did I carry a gun? *He* had been seeing too many gangster films.

Export of Talent. There is a heavy export of talent of all kinds. Finding themselves unable to make headway at home, Australians of ability go away to London or New York and are lost to their homeland thereafter. Writing in *Some Australians Take Stock* (1939), J. V. Connolly reports that of the Australian Rhodes Scholars to 1927, ". . . more than a third of the total have not been persuaded to place their training at the disposal of the country from which they were selected." While this conclusion is drawn from the record of a special group, it confirms the impression that Australia is constantly losing men and women of brains.

No single explanation of this will cover the ground, for the personal equation enters. Mr. Connolly states that there is an intolerance of exceptional persons in Australia, "a certain impatience with nonconformity and a notable tendency toward materialism. . . . Even Australians who are normally cultivated in the sense of being well informed are apt to regard any tendency toward marked neatness of attire or accuracy in speech with some slight suspicion. . . ." An Australian businessman of international experience once told me that in no country in the world is there a stronger disposition to "pull the exceptional man down." Australians sometimes describe their country contemptuously as "a paradise for the mediocre."

I am not in complete agreement with this. I see three facts which help to explain the flight of talent. One is the absence of opportunity to earn even bread and butter by the practice of many of the specialized professions, or the cultivation of non-utilitarian branches of learning, inevitable consequences of the stage of development of the country as a whole. People who get interested in such matters naturally go abroad. Why should they stay in Australia if they are going to become frustrated and embittered mediocrities, earning a poor living in fashions which go against the grain? Another point is that the nostalgia for England, reflected in the persistent use of the word "home" to mean England, sets up in sensitive minds the conviction that really to be somebody, you must become somebody at "home." A third point is related to the last. Australia has yet to evolve a center to which the talent of the nation tends to gravitate, comparable to London in England, Paris in France, and New York in the United States. The mecca of Australian talent is London. Therefore, London calls the Australian man of talent the way New York attracts talented Americans. The Australian may not like London after he gets there; he may find himself more of a nobody in London than ever he was in Australia and therefore return to Australia really to make his career; but the urge to get to London must be satisfied. As Australia grows more mature, fewer men and women of brains will make their careers abroad. Opportunities will open up, Australia will insensibly become home, and centers in which like can associate with like will develop. One can see the forces tending toward this at work already, and it will be a disastrous day for Australia if they are blocked by the "colonial minded" gentry. The export of talent is a phase in the history of Australia, not at all a necessary and permanent feature of the national life.

The reverse of this is the import of talent. Most of the imports come from England, though one finds stray Americans tucked away here and there, especially in mining and manufacturing. (I exclude the representatives of American firms temporarily resident in the country.) In the cultural field the outstanding American import is still Livingston Hopkins. Hugh Ward in the theater is another example. To my knowledge no American has ever made a career in an Australian university, and none is to be found in Australian journalism.

C.S.I.R. During the First World War the Federal government set up what it called the Commonwealth Institute of Science and Industry in an effort to bring the technical knowledge and brains of Australia to the service of a very harassed community. In 1920 the Institute was reorganized and its functions redefined, the result being the firm establishment of the Council for Scientific and Industrial Research, one of the most important and valuable institutions in Australia. Until recent years the Council has been chiefly concerned with the scientific study of the problems of primary industry, but in 1938 the government strengthened its activities on the secondary industry side by making provision for a National Standards Laboratory at Sydney and an Aeronautical Research Laboratory at Melbourne.

The work of the council is under the highly competent direction of Sir David Rivett. Its information is freely available to all persons interested, and it publishes numerous reports for general circulation. Its workers deal with plant, soil, and entomological problems, animal health and nutrition, forest products, food preservation and transport, radio research, ore dressing and mineragraphic investigations, fisheries studies, and have had successes in all these fields.

From early in 1939 the C.S.I.R. has carried an important share of the burden arising from the rapid expansion of Australian industry for war purposes and from the Australian effort to draw from her own resources goods previously imported from overseas. In the postwar period it is also bound to play a very strategic role.

This organization, it has been strongly suggested several times, should be supplemented, or complemented, by another devoted to economic and sociological research, but thus far with no results. At present, however, the Federal government is planning work of this character as a preliminary to the making of reconstruction plans.

The Australian Flag. The Australian flag has the Union Jack in the upper right-hand corner. The field is either red or blue. Immediately below the Union Jack is a large seven-pointed star, one point for each of the states and the seventh for the territories. In the left portion of the field are five stars representing the Southern Cross, only to be seen in the heavens after one has crossed the Equator. The flag with the red field may be flown by anyone, but that with the blue field is reserved for use by the government, its various services, and noncommercial organizations. The flag was designed by Ivor Evans, a fourteen-year-old schoolboy. In 1901 the new Commonwealth held a competition for designs in which thirty thousand suggestions from all over the world were submitted. Evans's design won first place. He submitted both red and blue versions.

The National Capital. An odd experience one can have in Australia is to open a Sydney morning paper and find an article headed, "Melbourne Is An Issue in This Election." Or one can open a Melbourne paper and read a leader declaring that Sydney has "insulted" Melbourne by roaring in that fashion. The bickering between Sydney and Melbourne has been going on since the days of the gold rushes, rising to peaks of violence at various odd times over issues great and small. A favorite Melbourne "insult" of Sydney is the allegation that it is excessively "Americanized." Sydney's reply is that Melbourne is stuffy and stodgy. (I have had to listen to both sides of the argument.) In late years any serious disagreement has seemed a thing of the past, and a good thing, for it is not only silly nonsense, but a major contribution to national disunity. The flare-up of 1940 was deplorable, but nevertheless it happened and was ten times as violent in private conversation as in the press.

One large conclusion can be drawn from the Sydney-Melbourne "war": Australia's national capital, Canberra, has not yet become either the actual center of the national administration or the symbolic center of the national spirit. This causes bad feeling against Melbourne, where many government departments are located.

A curious consequence of the Sydney-Melbourne rivalry was the provision of the Constitution that neither city should become the permanent national capital. In Chapter VII, Section 125, it is stated:

The seat of the Government of the Commonwealth shall be determined by the Parliament, and shall be within territory which shall have been granted to or acquired by the Commonwealth, and shall be vested in and belong to the Commonwealth, and shall be in the State of New South Wales, and be distant not less than one hundred miles from Sydney.

Such territory shall contain an area of not less than one hundred square miles, and such portion thereof as shall consist of Crown lands shall be granted to the Commonwealth without any payment therefor.

The Parliament shall sit at Melbourne until it meet at the seat of Government.

It was to satisfy this provision that Canberra was brought into being. But as not all the Federal departments had been transferred from Melbourne to Canberra when the Second World War broke out, many of the new administrations were established in Melbourne near the related departments. Hence . . .

Canberra is the most beautifully situated capital city I have ever seen, and if it is developed according to the elaborate plan now being followed, it will in time be one of the outstanding examples of successful city planning in the world. It is being built in a 25,000-acre natural basin formed by quite low pyramidal and table-topped hills, a few of which are high enough to be points of observation, Mount Ainslie and Black Mountain. It is from these two mountains, one version has it, that Canberra takes its name, for while the origin of the word is obscure, it is thought to mean "a woman's breasts" in an aboriginal dialect. The Australian Capital Territory, within which Canberra is located, was not formally accepted from New South Wales until 1910 and the name Canberra was not attached to the city until 1913. The Territory contains 570,000 acres, much of it quite uninhabited.

The name Canberra was given the city after at least two alternatives were rejected, Myola and Shakespeare. It is speculated that an accurate transliteration would give some such spelling as Kamberry, Caaberra, or Kamberra. In Australia today it is usually pronounced Căn'bră.

In 1911 the Australian government circulated throughout the world the conditions of a contest for a design for the new city. The competition was won by Walter Burley Griffin of Chicago, an associate of Frank Lloyd Wright. Griffin went out to Australia to supervise the execution of his plan and remained there. (He died in 1937 while working on a great library in Lucknow, India.) While it cannot be said that Griffin's course in guiding the project was uniformly smooth, the present city is beyond question his creation. The fact that the city exists only in outline today is neither attributable to Griffin nor to the dilatoriness of the Australians. Construction was naturally suspended during the First World War, the depression caused another slackening of activity, and Australia failed to grow at the pace expected by the optimistic generation that launched the project. Those who did the original planning expected that the population of the city would reach fifty thousand during the first decade of occupation, but it acutally reached only ten thousand.

The delay occasioned by the World War prevented the transfer of any governmental activities to Canberra until 1927. From 1901 to that year the actual capital of Australia was Melbourne. On May 9, 1927, the twenty-sixth anniversary of the opening of the first Federal parliament, the first session at Canberra was opened with great ceremony by the Duke of York, now King George VI. To symbolize the continuity of parliamentary tradition, the Parliament of the United Kingdom sent a replica of the speaker's chair in the House of Commons for use in the Canberra House of Representatives. In 1927 Australia was very near the height of its great postwar boom, and the Duke's progress through the country can only be described as triumphant. The whole tone of the nation—I was there at the time—was strikingly optimistic. There were undoubtedly many thousands who looked upon Canberra for the first time that May day who fully expected that in a few years the city would redeem its magnificent promise. But the very next year Australia dipped into the Great Depression.

Aside from the natural and normal decentralization of Federal functions in a huge country like Australia, it has proved difficult to bring together in Canberra all those government offices which should be there. If the Australian situation of today existed in the United States, the Treasury would be in Washington and the War Department in Philadelphia! While there is a kind of Canberra patriotism, there is also an anti-Canberra sentiment which takes the form of describing the whole project as a "white elephant." The city was attracting more and more interested tourists when the present war broke out, but Canberra cannot yet be said to have captured the popular imagination as the symbolic center of the nation.

Yet no visitor to Canberra fails to get a pleasant and enduring impression of it. Burley Griffin's plan was designed to make full use of all the natural beauty of the site and to enhance the man-made works he envisaged rising there. The city is laid out in relation to two circles, one of which is to be the center of government buildings, the other the center of commercial activities. From the circles the main avenues radiate, running into minor "circles" and other decorative diversions, something after the pattern of the city of Washington, but skillfully avoiding, to my mind, all artificial rigidity or absurd over-artfulness. The avenues and streets are named for figures in Australian history and the capitals of the states, with a sprinkling of aboriginal place names. The residential areas are scattered rather than concentrated, thus giving the city an enormous spread which is disadvantageous under present conditions. One is frequently called upon to traverse great open spaces when going from one part of the city to another. The same difficulty is apparent with the government buildings themselves. Located today in accordance with the plan—all in all a wise measure —they tend to be lost in the immensity of the spaces between them. It is a trifle odd to come upon the first wing of the National Library standing up with soldierly rigidity in the midst of a vast paddock.

But with all the obvious and pointed-to-with-scorn difficulties of present-day Canberra, it remains a singularly beautiful place. One has a sense that on some tomorrow this will be not only a superb site for a city, but actually the site of a superb city. The very magnificence of the conception should give Australians a sense that here, if anywhere on their continent, they can translate the Australian dream into enduring steel and stone upon which the ages can look down.

Part Three

AUSTRALIA IN THE WORLD

11. THE TIE TO BRITAIN

AUSTRALIA is a British dominion. This simple declaration is not a very useful definition for Americans, who usually have but the vaguest ideas about dominion status. One reads the queerest observations in the American press about the relations of the dominions and the United Kingdom. They are not made by Anglophobes only. Anglophiles go equally far astray. In their anxiety to be friendly to the United Kingdom, Anglophiles often quite unconsciously tread hard on the toes of the dominions. The basic error in American thought is to concentrate attention upon the United Kingdom and to look at the whole British political system from the center outward. This leads to exaggerating the power of the United Kingdom in relation to the dominions and minimizing the self-governing power of the dominions. A far better approach is from the dominions to the center. Americans are confirmed in their confusion when they hear Englishmen carelessly refer to the dominions as "the colonies."

The major problem of British imperial relations is to reconcile the tremendous pull of London with the necessity of granting a large measure of freedom to the more mature outlying portions of the British community—*imperium et libertas*. There are many gradations of freedom within the British system, from the dependence of the Crown colonies to the almost complete autonomy of the dominions. Because of this, outsiders all too frequently have a muddled conception of imperial relations. Most tightly tied to the United Kingdom is its colonial empire. Slightly more freedom is granted to India. The greatest measure of freedom has been taken by the dominions. Broadly speaking, the British behemoth—the huge, sprawling friend and hobgoblin of mankind, occupying 26 per cent of the world's land surface, containing 22 per cent of the world's people—looks like this:

I. The British Empire:
: The United Kingdom and its Colonial Empire.
: India.
II. The British Commonwealth of Nations:
: United Kingdom and dependencies.
: Canada.
: Australia.
: South Africa.
: New Zealand.
: Eire.

It is wise, for purposes of understanding, to separate the Empire from the Commonwealth. They are really quite different systems.

The political metaphysics of the British Commonwealth are the product of a long evolution, and the driving force behind the evolution is the increasing maturity of the overseas British nations. The leader in defining the status of the overseas communities has been Canada, the senior dominion and the one which has been consistently most mature. She has been ably seconded by South Africa. The laggard members of the British Commonwealth in this regard have been Australia and New Zealand. Eire, a late and reluctant member of the Commonwealth, by accepting the most advanced interpretations which can be placed upon Commonwealth relations, seems to say that if she cannot have absolute freedom she will get as near to it as possible. The attitude of Eire is colored by a sense of being an ancient nation which for generations was held in armed subjection. Only in South Africa is a comparable feeling found and there chiefly among the Boers. The outlook of the French Canadians is different. Their struggle is to maintain their special privileges under the Canadian Constitution and their cultural identity as a North American people. They do not ardently aspire to freedom from the British connection. In Australia the group that aspires to complete freedom is an almost invisible minority today—it was larger during the "nineties." In New Zealand such sentiment is confined to stray individuals.

The written formulation of the existing pattern of relationships is the Statute of Westminster, passed by the Imperial Parliament in London in 1931. This law grants to the several dominions the powers they require to become autonomous nations. They do not lack constitutional right to use these powers, but they cannot sustain independence in a competitive and predatory world. The one power which does not seem to be the right of any dominion is that of secession from the Commonwealth. It was specifically denied to Eire by great Britain in 1921; but that was before the passing of the Statute of Westminster. Possibly the right exists today, not explicitly in any law, but as an anterior right without which the freedom of any community is incomplete. The most aggressive members of the British Commonwealth today rest content with their indisputable right to follow policies which accord with their own ideas of their national interests, regardless of the lines followed by the other members of the Commonwealth. The determining factor in the relations of the members of the British Commonwealth is not the relations of the overseas members with one another, but the relations of the dominions with the United Kingdom. As the trade figures show, Australia is not intimately attached in the economic realm to Canada, South Africa, Eire, or even her near neighbor New Zealand. But she is attached with decided intimacy to the United Kingdom.

A Canadian official once expressed the situation to me by saying that the dominions are like the members of a large family who all write home to Mother, but rarely to one another.

The single, final, *constitutional* symbol of the association of the members of the Commonwealth is a common allegiance to the Crown. All acknowledge this. But there is no King of the British Commonwealth; there is rather a King of Canada, a King of Australia, a King of the United Kingdom, who is a single person, at the moment George VI. As King of several autonomous nations, the King may acquiesce in one line of policy in one dominion and in an absolutely contradictory line in another. This may sound like elaborate hocus-pocus; it is rather an exposition of the political metaphysics of the British Commonwealth. If it seems intolerably evasive and difficult to follow, consider the celebrated Balfour Declaration of 1926 from which all these things in some sense flow:

They are autonomous Communities within the British Empire, equal in status, in no way subordinate one to another in any aspect of their domestic or external affairs, though united by a common allegiance to the Crown, and freely associated as members of the British Commonwealth of Nations.

The powers in the hands of the British dominions were not suddenly thrust upon them in 1931, nor yet in 1926 when Lord Balfour wrote his declaration. They were acquired over long years. The Statute of Westminster simply expressed what the British community had become as a result of evolution. The evolution still goes on, and at some future date, barring cataclysm, a still more radical declaration of relationships will certainly be made.

The United Kingdom does not rule the dominions in the direct and unmistakable way that she rules the Colonial Empire, nor can she reserve from their control crucial powers as in India. She, nevertheless, has in the dominions the enormous prestige of the mother country and the single member of the association which has the tradition and machinery of an autonomous nation. She retains a *functional* superiority which by status alone she could not claim. Her functional superiority is particularly marked in the field of foreign affairs. In this field the overseas dominions are least mature.

It is precisely because the dominions have a functional inferiority in the field of foreign affairs that a great deal of argumentation has circled around this matter. Let us look into the situation. The first move of primary interest to us was made by Sir Robert Borden at the Imperial War Conference of 1917, at which he offered the famous Resolution IX. This resolution declared that in the future the dominions must be granted "an adequate voice in foreign policy and foreign relations." From Sir Robert's resolution to the present day this has been a critical problem. After 1917 the following important events have had crucial influence on the evolution of the situation:

I. The admission of the dominions to the Versailles Peace Conference, and to the League of Nations, 1919.

II. The Chanak incident of 1922, when for the first time a dominion refused to stand by the remainder of the Empire in a serious emergency. The initiative on this occasion was taken by Canada, and South Africa gave support, while Australia followed a traditional line.

III. The Treaty of Locarno, 1925, was the occasion for giving formal international recognition to the idea that the members of the Commonwealth have separate responsibility in foreign affairs. Article 9 of this treaty reads: "The present Treaty shall impose no obligation upon any of the British Dominions, or upon India, unless the Government of such Dominion, or of India, signifies its acceptance thereof.

IV. The Balfour Declaration, made at the Imperial Conference of 1926; and the Statute of Westminster, 1931.

V. The outbreak of war in 1939.

The conclusions on the matter of foreign affairs may be formulated thus: (1) a clear distinction was established between the foreign policy of the United Kingdom and that of the dominions, a distinction based upon a recognition of differing national interests; (2) the right was established for dominions to dissociate themselves in whole or in part from any policy that the United Kingdom may enunciate, or a particular overseas dominion may enunciate, in pursuit of its national interests; and (3) the right of the dominions to formulate independent foreign policies of their own—apart from that of the United Kingdom to which they generally subscribe today—has been implied, but not yet acted upon except in very minor ways.

The critical issue in foreign affairs is that of war and peace. All matters of foreign policy influence it to some extent. The crucial point about dominion-United Kingdom relations therefore became the extent of the obligation to participate in war. If the United Kingdom declared war, would the dominions automatically be at war? Most British theorists seemed to think so in the pre-war period. A minority did not and argued that it was possible for a dominion to declare its neutrality. The argument turned upon the question of the "divisibility" or "indivisibility" of the Crown. If the Crown is divisible, then of course the dominions could follow contradictory policies even with regard to war; if indivisible, then when the Crown declared war, the dominions were automatically at war. The partisans of divisibility were, naturally, the partisans of full autonomy for the dominions; while the partisans of indivisibility were the traditionalists. (The Crown and the King are not identical concepts. The King exercises the functions of the Crown.)

The outbreak of war in 1939 clarified the matter. Setting aside the extreme case of Eire, which declared its neutrality, the differing conceptions of the correct answer can best be illustrated by what happened in Canada and Australia when the Crown declared war for the United Kingdom. In Canada the theory that when the United Kingdom is at war the dominions are at war was rejected. Americans will recall that the first proclamation under the neutrality laws in which the belligerents were named, did not include Canada. When Canada finally declared war, *on her own motion,* she was promptly named a belligerent. Canada, therefore, by her action in the crisis of 1939 clearly established the constitutional point that a declaration of war by the Crown on the advice of His Majesty's Government in the United Kingdom does not automatically commit a dominion, or the dominions, to war. In Australia the Prime Minister and Cabinet, immediately on receiving the news that the United Kingdom was at war, advised the King to declare war on behalf of Australia. So promptly did Australia act that she was included in the first American neutrality proclamation. Parliament was notified of a *fait accompli,* not that it would have overruled the decision had the matter come to a vote. (Only a few Australians criticized the procedure.) This is acting in harmony with the theory that when the King is at war, Australia is at war. But the important point is that both dominions accepted the policy of the United Kingdom government. How was this acceptance accomplished?

In an effort to preserve unity on the major points of foreign policy, an elaborate system of consultation and co-operation among the dominions of the Commonwealth has been built up over the years. Formal reviews given at the Imperial Conferences since 1911 are constantly supplemented by telephone, cable, mail, and personal contacts by liaison officers in London. For facilitating this distribution of information there are, the Dominions Information Department in the Foreign Office and the Foreign Affairs Department in the Dominions Office. The latter prepares the outgoing dispatches to the dominions.

This cumbersome system has been severely criticized in the dominions. It functions badly at moments of crisis, and there is a widespread feeling among the people at such times that they are more apt than not to be confronted with a *fait accompli* rather than an opportunity to debate the question at issue. This feeling is also often expressed in the parliaments of the dominions, and leads to the allegation that the decisions vital to the dominions—made in times of crisis—are taken by men far removed from the people of a dominion. Their grievance is against the Foreign Office of the United Kingdom government, and also the government of the dominion in question. Parliament and the people feel quite outside the sacred circle. It is for this reason that during a major war the Prime Ministers of the dominions often spend considerable time in London. They are trying to get closer to the inner circle in which vital decisions are made. There has also been a demand for some Imperial council or committee, on which the dominions are directly represented, to take over the direction of the war.

But thus far in British history the continued supremacy of the United Kingdom has been so decided that, while there are ominous creaks and groans at various times, a major crisis still brings most of the dominions to the side of the United Kingdom. Conspicuous among the dominions which wholeheartedly place themselves there is Australia.

12. THE FIRST WORLD WAR

WHEN the First World War broke out in 1914 the Australians lacked a formal "foreign policy." It was a matter they did not decide for themselves but left very willingly to the care of the United Kingdom government. The policies which they had evolved which had international implications were either logical outgrowths of purely domestic issues or of their geographical position in the Pacific. Yet when the testing time came it was made clear, especially at the Versailles Peace Conference, that these policies were clearly enough *foreign policies* (or collectively, a foreign policy) and that some of them were expressed in a fashion that required vigorous defense against unsympathetic or hostile critics.

Arching over all the other policies was the identification of Australia's interests with Britain's. This was, and still remains, the foundation of Australia's international outlook. While she might have a keener interest in some phases of British policy than in others, it was not felt that Australia should entertain policies of her own that ran counter to British Imperial interests; and by the same token, it was expected that Britain would not, in pursuit of Imperial interests, support policies which ran counter to Australia's conception of her needs. On occasion it might be necessary to prod the United Kingdom into taking action favorable to Australia, but the fact that prodding was necessary was not interpreted as anything more reprehensible than bureaucratic blindness due to the remoteness of London from the South Pacific. And certainly no responsible Australian leader would have deliberately advocated a policy so peculiar to Australia that it could not be harmonized with the larger Imperial outlook. Even if this might appear to be the case when viewed from London, the Australians were always prepared to demonstrate that what strengthened Australia also strengthened the Empire.

From very early in their history the Australians have taken an interest in the islands near their continent. The "island policy" has always been based on the idea that Australian security is menaced if any of the islands are allowed to fall into the hands of powers actually or potentially hostile to the British Empire in general and Australia in particular. The islands to the east, northeast, north, and northwest of Australia have for many years been thought of as a natural protective bastion and as natural bases for attack upon Australia should the wrong nations be in possession of them.

The commission of Captain Arthur Phillip, the founding governor, gave him authority over "the islands adjacent to the eastern coast of New Holland." At times this phrase was loosely interpreted, and the British authorities asserted the right to interfere in islands as far away as Tahiti. But for many decades after the British were established in Australia, the question of who was in possession of the South Pacific islands was not a very pressing one. Indeed, if the matter had been left to the Imperial authorities, not only the minor islands but also many of the major ones would have slipped from the British grasp. It was the Australians and, later on, the New Zealanders, who kept the islands within the British system. (New Zealand formally passed under British control in 1840, after having been in the nominal charge of the governors of New South Wales for many years. Permanent settlement began in the same year.) Often talking and acting in a fashion contrary to the wishes and opinions of the London authorities, the colonists insisted that the British flag must fly over the entire South Pacific. In his *Democracy in New Zealand* (1904), Andre Siegfried wrote, "According as the policy of colonial expansion developed among the Powers, they realized, as a sure instinct had from the first warned them, that it was necessary for them to remain, as far as possible, alone and without troublesome neighbours in the South Pacific. In this way the programme 'Australasia for the Australasians' developed into 'Oceania for the Anglo-Saxons.' "

In succession the Australians (and New Zealanders) opposed the incursions of France and Germany. The Australians succeeded in forcing radical changes of policy in islands that France did succeed in taking over. It was long continued Australian pressure through London that in 1898 persuaded the French to cease using New

Caledonia (a possession from 1853) as a penal colony. While most of the islands came under the Crown as a result of discovery, many to which Britain had some claim might well have passed to other nations. Important possessions which the Australians played a part in securing include Fiji (1875) and an important portion of the great island of New Guinea (1884). It was Australian pressure, also, which resulted in a joint French-British administration in the New Hebrides from 1887. The New Guinea possession passed in 1906 from the United Kingdom government, which after 1888 had administered it as a Crown colony, to the young Australian Commonwealth. This was the first Australian colony.

As the nineteenth century approached its end, the islands of interest to the Australians were in the hands of the British, which was entirely satisfactory; the French, of whom they had lost suspicion; the Dutch, of whom they had never had much suspicion; the Portuguese (in Timor), allies of the United Kingdom; the Germans; and the Americans. The Germans were established in New Guinea and associated islands east and north right up to the Philippines from 1884 and 1898, and in Samoa from 1899. The Americans came into possession of a few islands of the Samoan group in 1899 and held the excellent harbor at Pago Pago.

Although the White Australia policy developed after the islands policy had become a part of the Australian tradition, it hardly holds second place. It rather has a central position in the Australian outlook. Its genesis has been stated—it came into existence as a result of conflict between white and Chinese miners on the gold fields. After experimenting with exclusion laws, several of which were frowned on by the Imperial authorities, the Australian colonies succeeded, in 1888, in establishing their right to bar orientals from their territory. By degrees the principle was extended to exclude the brown islanders and any black people who might attempt to settle in the Commonwealth. The question of black people has always been more or less academic, but as the Queensland tropics had been originally developed with island (or Kanaka) labor on great sugar plantations, the brown people caused, in their day, very heated discussion. When the Commonwealth was established the authorities set about repatriating the Kanakas in Queensland, and all but a tiny remnant had left by

1907. Australia had firmly established her position as a Pacific country reserved for settlement by white people only. Under the immigration law the exclusionist policy is sustained by the subterfuge of a language test for intending immigrants. In recent years attempts have been made to use it to exclude persons considered undesirable because of politics or morals as well as pigmentation.

Finally, there was trade policy. From the beginning Australian trade has been chiefly with the United Kingdom. For various reasons, trade with the East did not become particularly important before 1914, though the necessary shipping connections had long existed. In the five-year period between 1909 and 1913 only 4 per cent of Australia's imports came from the East and but 5 per cent of her exports went there. At that time the United Kingdom was supplying 60 per cent of the imports and taking 45 per cent of the exports. The Australian interest, therefore, was the keeping of trade routes to England free from foreign interference.

Aside from some uneasiness occasioned by Japan's military success against China in 1894, the Asiatic menace to Australia was hardly a pressing reality by 1914, though it was even then talked about in the newspapers and magazines. Japan was the only oriental nation which could menace Australia militarily. (It is odd but true that while Australia is a young nation Japan as a country of world political significance is even younger.) The Australians looked upon the Anglo-Japanese Alliance of 1902 as a kind of guarantee of immunity from any possible pressure by Japan. The primary object of such pressure, it was thought, would be the forcing of a relaxation of the White Australia policy, against which Japan had already begun to grumble. Though the ambiguities in the alliances of 1905 and 1911 aroused some suspicion that Australian interests had been subordinated to Imperial interests, especially those on the continent of Asia, and some fear that if war broke out Australia might be attacked by the opponent of the Anglo-Japanese combination, such suspicions were temporarily dissolved when Japan joined the Allies in 1914.

At the outbreak of the First World War Australia's international situation was about as follows: while policies had been developed which had international implications, it was not considered that Australia had a foreign policy peculiarly her own; it was rather considered that the Australian policies were in harmony with the larger Imperial interest and as such, their support was part of the general Imperial task, not a unique and separate duty of Australia.

Although the Commonwealth was geographically a Pacific country, few Australians argued that it had national interests apart from the United Kingdom for that reason. Indeed the story of Australian development had underscored again and again that Australia was far more firmly integrated with the United Kingdom than with her Pacific neighbors. She had, as a matter of fact, sought to preserve her separateness from the Pacific context and had deliberately cultivated her integration into the European-Atlantic world. Whether one considered the national origin of her people or the nature of her cultural and political heritage or the direction of her trade or the character of her financial ties, that point was strongly supported. It was the crucial factor in determining Australia's reaction to the war.

There remains the question of what contribution Australia had made up to 1914 to the defense of the Empire and herself. Most of her development had taken place in the era of Pax Britannica under the protecting shadow of British sea power. She had every reason to suppose that she would be protected by British men-of-war if ever worst came to worst. Yet it would have been reprehensible had she simply handed over the defense problem to the United Kingdom. She had, as a developing nation, to make some contribution to her own defense.

From 1788 to 1870, when the last redcoats departed for England, Australia was garrisoned by British troops, and such ships-of-war as were in her ports were vessels of the United Kingdom. Between 1870 and the establishment of the Commonwealth the defense of the continent was, aside from the general protection of British power, based upon a militia system, each colony maintaining its own forces. Not until the Boer War in 1899 was there any cooperation between the various forces. But in 1889 a British military man, commissioned to examine the Australian defenses, had pointed out the need for a continental defense policy. This idea played an important role in the campaign for federation. Under the constitution of the Commonwealth the Federal authorities are charged with, "The naval and military defence of the Commonwealth and of the several states" and are given power to take control of the state railways for defense purposes.

But it takes more than constitutional provisions to defend a country. The Australian defense system remained in a very backward condition until about 1907 when William Morris Hughes and other nationalistic Labour party leaders, in association with various liberals and conservatives both in and out of politics, began to make real progress in their campaign for a system of compulsory, unpaid, peace-time, military training. The Defence Act of 1909 made provision for the establishment of this system, and Australia was the first English-speaking country to adopt it. The impelling factor was the rising tension between England and Germany. The bill was introduced by a Liberal party government, but it was felt by the advocates of the compulsory training system that it did not go far enough. Lord Kitchener was therefore called in to make a report on defense needs, and in 1910 a Labour government gave effect to his recommendations. Under the amendments then made to the Defence Act, all "male inhabitants of Australia (excepting those who are exempted by this Act), who have resided therein for six months and are British subjects, shall be liable to be trained as prescribed. . . ." The act provided that males from twelve to twenty-six years were liable for training and that they should progress from the Junior Cadets to membership in the Citizen Forces. Under later amendments it was provided that each year the boys and men should train from ninety hours for Junior Cadets to sixteen days for the Citizen Forces. In addition there was a small regular army, and from 1903 all male inhabitants of Australia aged eighteen to sixty were liable for service with the home defense forces *in time of war.* In 1911 a school for training army officers, modeled on America's West Point, was opened at Duntroon in what was to become the city of Canberra. Thus, while Australia was maintaining but a small regular army in 1914, she was a bit ahead of most countries of the English-speaking world in the training of her male civilians for war service.

The naval defenses of Australia went through a somewhat similar evolution. From 1887 to 1909 British naval vessels stationed in Australian waters were partially subsidized by the Australian authorities. In 1909, largely as a phase of the Anglo-German naval rivalry, British naval defenses in the Pacific were re-planned; and, after some conflict over policy, Australia began to assemble a navy of her own, which would, however, be automatically incorporated into the Royal Navy on the outbreak of war. The Fisher Labour government had taken the initiative in 1908 and ordered the first vessels. In 1914, therefore, Australian naval units were available for immediate service in the South Pacific and Indian Oceans, and they played a gallant role in eliminating the German Pacific Squadron. They included one battle cruiser, two light cruisers, two destroyers, and two submarines.

In the fiscal year 1913-14, Australia, with a population of 4,972,000 was spending £4,752,000 on defense.

A Liberal party government led by Sir Joseph Cook was in power when the United Kingdom government declared war in 1914 and automatically committed Australia to belligerency. The Australians, according to an official historian, almost unanimously supported the war. The leader of the Labour party, Andrew Fisher, declared that Australia would defend the Empire "to our last man and our last shilling." (This became one of the most famous of political phrases. On the outbreak of the Second World War, Prime Minister Menzies repeated it several times in defining Australia's attitude.) There was, therefore, no criticism of the Cook government for immediately offering to the United Kingdom to "despatch an expeditionary force of twenty thousand men of any suggested composition to any destination desired by the home government. Force to be at complete disposal of home government. Cost of despatch and maintenance will be borne by this government."

From this small beginning came the great Australian expeditionary force, which under the name of the "Anzacs" made Australia world-famous. (The word "Anzac" refers to the Australian and New Zealand Army Corps, and it is therefore incorrect in the technical sense to apply it to Australian troops alone, whether in the last or the present war, but the loose usage has become widely accepted, even in the two dominions. The correct name for the Australian expeditionary force in the First World War and this one is the Australian Imperial Force, the A.I.F.) Before the war was over Australia had raised 416,000 troops and dispatched 330,000 overseas. Total casualties were 226,073, and killed, dead, and missing totaled 59,258. The percentage of casualties to numbers engaged was 68.5 per cent, the highest experienced by British forces. Almost two-fifths of the Australian males between eighteen and forty-four enlisted. Approximately 80 per cent of these came from that portion of the population which normally supported the Labour party and from which the unions recruited most of their members. All were volunteers. These points are very important in the light of events on the home front during the war.

Australian troops served in Egypt, at Gallipoli, in Palestine and Mesopotamia, in France, at Archangel in northern Russia, in the Caucasus, and in New Guinea. They took an especially conspicuous and gallant part in the ill-fated expedition against the Dardanelles in 1915, where they were pitted against the Turks. (One of the Turkish leaders was Kemal Ataturk, the maker of modern Turkey.) Gallipoli is a word that summons up poignant memories for Australians. From April to December 1915, they and their fellows battled manfully to wrest the control of the straits from the enemy, only to be forced to withdraw with the objective unreached. But, though defeated, the Australians established themselves in the world's imagination as the most daring fighters of modern times. They neither gained nor coveted particular honors as a "fighting machine." Their quality was rather revealed as the exceptional initiative of the individuals composing the army.

Not until the spring of 1916 did Australian troops appear in France. Beginning in July of that year, they were heavily engaged in battle, first blood being drawn in the Battle of the Somme. In 1917 they participated in the successive British assaults on the Hindenburg Line, and in 1918 they played a strategic role in resisting the powerful German spring offensive, as well as in the final breaking up of the Hindenburg line in the autumn. While the majority of the Australian troops then in active service were in France by the end of 1917 (110,000 in France, 17,000 in the Near East), the campaigns in Palestine, especially those in which light horse troops were engaged, were of great importance to the British cause. The Australians took part in the campaigns for Gaza, Beersheba, and Damascus. All in all, the Australian troops won the right to claim battle honors for such various engagements as those at Kabakaul in New Guinea, Lone Pine, Hill 60, and others at Gallipoli, Fromelles, Messines, Passchendaele, Villers-Bretonneux and Mont St. Quentin in France, and Beersheba, Gaza, Jerusalem, and Damascus in Palestine. Among their most famous leaders were Lord Birdwood of Anzac, Sir John Monash, and Sir Henry Chauvel.

On the home front the Cook Liberal government was ousted from office in September 1914 by the Labour party under the leadership of Andrew Fisher, who became Prime Minister. A year later Fisher resigned to accept the post of High Commissioner in London and was succeeded by William Morris Hughes, thus bringing to the prime-ministership the most remarkable political figure in Australian history, and one about which all Australians hold passionate opinions, pro and con, to the present day. Mr. Hughes was born in Wales in 1864, arrived in Australia in 1884, and after working at such various jobs as drover, boundary rider, seaman, cook, fencer on a sheep station, actor, locksmith, umbrella mender, journalist, and bookseller, he became a union leader. He organized the hotel, club, and restaurant workers in Sydney and served as secretary for the waterside workers' union. In 1894 he entered state politics in New South Wales and in 1901 transferred to the Federal House of Representatives, in both instances being a Labour member. He served as Prime Minister of the Commonwealth from 1915 to 1923, twice winning general elections after rising to the post on Fisher's resignation. Today he is still a member of the House, the only man who has held a seat continuously since Federation. For political longevity and agility, Mr. Hughes has no equal in Australian history. What inspires controversy is the nature of his record, not the length of it.

While this remarkable man rose to power through the labor organizations he crossed to the opposition side at a critical time in Australian history. Temperamentally and intellectually akin to that other famous Welshman, David Lloyd George, in many respects, and to Georges Clemenceau in his passionate and harsh nationalism, Hughes became in war time less and less the reformist labor political leader and more and more the inflamed "Imperial-ist-nationalist." The nationalist element in his make-up was always important, as can be seen in his classic pamphlet *The Case for Labor* (1910), but in war time it completely overwhelmed all else in him. This man who became Prime Minister only because of the free vote of his colleagues in the Labour party caucus which raised him to party leadership, was prepared within a year to split the Labour party from top to bottom, drive it from office, and go on to form an alliance with his erstwhile opponents and end his days as a perennial member of conservative cabinets.

Even before Hughes was elected to leadership of the party there was distrust of him, particularly among the unionists. He did noth-ing from that moment to conciliate his opponents. In the latter part of 1916 he posed an issue which he well knew would arouse bitter feeling—conscription for overseas service. Compulsory mili-tary training and compulsory service within Australia had both been opposed, but the feeling aroused was as nothing to what con-scription for overseas service was to stir up. When, therefore, Hughes proposed to put this issue to a vote, Australia was im-mediately launched upon the open seas of bitter controversy, en-venomed by every consideration which can separate men living in a modern community one from the other—class, political, religious —in the midst of the war. It was a free-for-all in which no quarter was given by either side. Instead of attempting to insure that a rational judgment would be made, Mr. Hughes further inflamed public opinion by exercising his exceptional talent for invective on all those who dared oppose the measure on which he had set his heart. Even the official historian of the home front is moved to declare, "He was indiscriminate. His attitude was that all his opponents were tarred with the same brush. . . . Mr. Hughes sometimes seemed to confuse the Imperial cause with his own, as though in breathing forth fire against his own enemies he was assisting in the defeat of the enemies of the Allied Powers." But in spite of Mr. Hughes' best efforts, his proposal was defeated. The people declared that they did not want men conscripted for over-seas service.

The conscription issue brought to a head the conflicts within the labor movement. Even before the referendum was taken, F. G.

Tudor, a member of the Hughes Cabinet, resigned his office. Finally, out of a cabinet of ten, six resigned, leaving Mr. Hughes and three others in nominal possession of the government. Hughes and all Labour party members who had supported conscription, including members of the state parties, were expelled from the party. The mass expulsion eliminated some of the oldest and most distinguished members, including founding members, among them W. A. Holman, at that time Premier of New South Wales. All told, thirteen Federal Labour members of the House followed Hughes out of the party. They formed what they called the National Labour party (a revealing name) and carried on with the support of the Liberals. In January 1917 this party was dissolved and replaced by the Nationalist party, formed of the expelled Labour party people and the Liberals, at the instance of a group of Victorian political leaders. (The Nationalist party lasted until 1932, when it was succeeded by the United Australia party.) When a cabinet was formed the following month with Mr. Hughes as Prime Minister, the ex-Labour group found itself in a minority. Of the ideas around which this party rallied, several were to influence strongly Hughes' course at the Paris Peace Conference—control of the Southern Pacific and White Australia. Nowhere in the program was there any specific commitment to Labour's reformist ideas. In a way, this is also the moment when that shift of emphasis from betterment of conditions to the use of the state power to encourage private enterprise took place. When ratified by the people, it put the Labour party at a disadvantage for many long years.

After its purge, the Labour party elected Mr. Tudor to leadership, a post he held until 1922. In the general election of May, 1917, it suffered defeat at the hands of the Nationalists. The result is usually interpreted as a rebuke for Labour and as proving the oft-quoted allegation (first used as an election slogan on Nationalist posters) that in expelling Hughes and his fellows, the Labour party had "blown out its brains." If Labour blew out its brains, they were quickly picked up by the opposition which, having no man comparable in capacity to Hughes promptly elevated him to leadership. Just as promptly the opposition found it had no particular use for many of the other representatives of Labour's brains, for six of the Labour men who had portfolios in Hughes' short-lived National Labour party cabinet, failed to win places in the first Nationalist cabinet. What Labour apparently lost in the 1917 election was the "floating vote" which, under war-time conditions, was naturally more nationalist than Labour. Labour's actual loss over 1914, when it took office, was one hundred thousand votes. Because of a shift in public attitudes, it was a long time in recovering the suffrage of the floating voters.

That Mr. Hughes did not completely command the voters even after his extraordinary triumph was shown by the fact that when in December, 1917, he held a second referendum on the conscription issue, the pro-conscription forces were even more decisively defeated than fourteen months earlier. Obviously many who voted for him in the general election had assumed that he had accepted the verdict of the 1916 referendum. In 1920, when Mr. Hughes again went to the country as Prime Minister, he had behind him the prestige of having won the war and also great victories at the Paris Peace Conference. He was therefore victorious. But in 1923 he was displaced as leader of the conservative forces by Stanley Melbourne Bruce.

William Morris Hughes at the Peace Conference, says Professor Paul Birdsall, the American historian, writing in 1941, ". . . was the living embodiment of everything that was anti-Wilsonian; he gloried in savage attacks on the President's plans for a new world order; he was as hard-boiled a nationalist as any at the Paris Peace Conference." This is intended to be a harsh and scornful judgment, as the context unmistakably shows. But the Australians take a very different view of the matter. Even Mr. Hughes' opponents, who are ready enough to attack him on almost all other scores and who accept Brian Fitzpatrick's observation that he "may one day be classed as amongst the most fateful figures in Australian political life," are prepared to defend his record at Paris. Dr. H. V. Evatt, who has in his writings indicted Hughes again and again for his domestic sins, is yet prepared to say, "Whatever criticisms history will pass on Mr. Hughes as war-time Prime Minister . . . it should never fail to recognize the work he did for Australia at Versailles." Another Australian might have avoided Hughes' personal faults of manner and manners, especially in dealing with Woodrow Wilson, but he would nevertheless have striven for the same things that Hughes fought for and, in large measure, won.

The Australian nationalism that Hughes expressed at Paris was particularistic and aggressive in relation to the non-British world, but it was not a nationalism which led its proponents to seek to escape from the British Imperial political system. Mr. Hughes and the Australian people generally were not nationalists of what they call the "cut the painter" school. Indeed they were not, in the postwar period, particularly anxious to follow up the recognition of their claim to representation at the Paris Peace Conference with further advances toward autonomy. Australia accepted separate membership in the League of Nations, which Mr. Hughes disesteemed; but she took little or no part in forwarding the other developments toward a new definition of dominion status. She has never formally adopted the Statute of Westminster. Said Hughes in 1929, "Against this folly I have always set my face. . . . I have always held that we can maintain the unity of the Empire only if we exercise the rights we all possess with the utmost discretion and watch that our acts do not deleteriously affect the Empire or any part of it." At Versailles, therefore, Mr. Hughes conceived of himself as advancing Australia's national interests *and also* the interests of the Empire. His most vigorous work was done in an effort to insure that Australia would control the former German islands near the Australian continent, and be allowed to continue the White Australia policy without let or hindrance by any outside power whatever.

Mr. Hughes' bitter feeling against the Wilson peace program began, according to Sir Ernest Scott, with his reaction to the Fourteen Points. Hughes was particularly offended by the points on reparations and annexations, for he felt that they represented the thinking of "a leader whose people had not borne the main suffering of the war and that they were grossly unfair to those who had. . . ." When the time came he reproached the Americans in exactly these terms, the first important political leader to do so. He eventually played a part in blowing up reparations to the fantastic size which drove John Maynard Keynes to write his brilliant *Economic Consequences of the Peace*. What is really important is that we have here the genesis of the Hughes-Wilson quarrel over the disposition of the German Pacific islands.

Early in the war Australian troops took over the German portion of New Guinea and the associated islands south of the equator, including the small but valuable island of Nauru. (New Zealand at about the same time took over German Samoa.) It was also understood that Australian forces should go on and occupy the German islands north of the equator as well. But on November 24, 1914, the London authorities instructed the Australians not to proceed with this task. Instead it was undertaken by Japan. As early as February, 1915, the United Kingdom government consulted the Australian authorities as to their attitude should Japan retain these islands at the close of the war. Prime Minister Andrew Fisher apparently gave the answer that Australia would not object. On February 1, 1917, when Japan was pressing the United Kingdom government for a formal declaration on the subject, Australia was again consulted, and Prime Minister Hughes assured the home government that Australia would not object if Japan were given only islands *north* of the line. On the 17th Japan was told, "on the occasion of the Peace Conference [His Majesty's government] will support Japan's claim in regard to the disposal of Germany's rights . . . in the islands north of the equator; it being understood that in the eventual peace settlement the Japanese government will treat Great Britain's claims to the German islands south of the equator in the same spirit."

Apparently the motivation behind Hughes' assent to this arrangement was a decision to demand that Australia be allowed to *annex* the German territories south of the line and in her vicinity on the ground that they were required to assure Australia's security. At the Paris Peace Conference, Hughes put forward this claim at the earliest possible moment and precipitated the first great crisis of the conference, for he ran head-on into Wilson's desire that territories of this character be dealt with under the mandate principle. Hughes, however, had the support of Prime Minister Massey of New Zealand, who wanted German Samoa, and also Prime Minister Smuts of South Africa, who, though he supported the mandate idea, hoped to be allowed to annex former German possessions contiguous to the South African Union. Since the prime ministers based their claims on the argument of *security,* they were also supported by Canada, which had no territorial claims of her own. After a long and unseemly wrangle, Mr. Hughes was defeated as far as annexation went. But only after a new type of mandate had been invented, called "C-class." When he was assured that it was, in Australian terms, "the equivalent of a 999 years' lease as compared with freehold" he accepted it, though grudgingly.

The basic ideas incorporated in the definition of a C-class mandate were first phrased by John G. Latham, a member of the Australian delegation to the conference. (He is now Sir John Latham, Australian Minister to Japan.) The essential idea was that holders of C-class mandates could make the territories integral parts of the home country in an administrative sense. It was thus made possible for Australia to substitute the closed for the open door with regard to trade and immigration in her mandate. But as Australia won the closed door in her islands, the same right could not be denied the Japanese in theirs. The consequences have been fateful.

One island which was coveted by Australia was distinguished from the others and dealt with as a separate problem. This was Nauru. Its disposition became an issue between Australia, New Zealand, and the United Kingdom and, says Sir Ernest Scott, "evoked much strong feeling" which "nearly developed into a quarrel." The immediate cause was that Nauru is the most important source of phosphate rock in the South Pacific, and phosphate rock is the basis of the principal fertilizer used in the agriculture of the South Pacific dominions. Naturally Australia aspired to control Nauru, for that would insure not only adequate supplies of rock but also the profits of exploitation. New Zealand, however, was equally dependent upon Nauru for phosphate and strongly resented the idea of an Australian monopoly. And the United Kingdom entered the picture because, while the island had been held by Germany before the war, the company which was engaged in exploiting the phosphate was British. In the end the League assigned a C-class mandate for Nauru to "His Britannic Majesty" and the three countries compromised their differences by forming a joint government corporation which bought out the private company and assumed the task of exploitation. The proportionate interests were United Kingdom 42 per cent, Australia 42 per cent,

and New Zealand 16 per cent. Nauru was the most valuable former German possession that passed into British hands in this
general region.

If Mr. Hughes found himself in accord with the Japanese on the
question of the islands, he fought them hard on another. The
Japanese sought to have incorporated into the Covenant of the
League a declaration to the effect that the members would accord
"to all alien nationals equal and just treatment in every respect,
making no distinction either in law or in fact on account of their
race or nationality." They played many variations on this idea in
the course of their campaign for its adoption. The most open and
outspoken opponent of their aspiration was William Morris
Hughes, who saw in it a direct challenge to the White Australia
policy. Woodrow Wilson tried to compromise the issue by assuming that the declaration would merely be a pious declaration of
faith and not necessarily a principle on which the Japanese would
act. He apparently believed that the vexing question of Japanese
immigration could best be dealt with by "gentlemen's agreements."
But Hughes would have none of *American* hocus-pocus. Yet he
did not want to bear the burden of being the only opponent of the
idea. He therefore tried to force Wilson's hand by arousing against
him the well-known sentiments of the Pacific Coast Americans.
Says the Australian official historian: "Mr. Hughes . . . had been
privately endeavouring to force Wilson's hand by appealing to the
representatives of the American press—particularly those from the
Western States. . . ." In the end the provision was carried by a
two to one vote, but Wilson ruled that it had been lost because it
was not unanimously approved and nothing not unanimously accepted could be incorporated into the Covenant. This decision,
Hughes wrote later, "amazed and angered the Committee," and
instead of rejoicing in his unexpected victory he, to this day, con-
siders the episode a prime example of Wilson's deviousness and
duplicity!

Mr. Hughes was victorious in two of his great campaigns at the
Paris Peace Conference, and this accounts for the Australian approval of his conduct there. But he nevertheless returned to Australia in a somewhat disconsolate mood, for, to his mind, the peace
was not sufficiently punitive. Above all, he felt he had been de-

feated on reparations. He had hoped to get full compensation from Germany for Australian expenditures in the war. Sir Ernest Scott says that Mr. Hughes' most extreme statement of Australia's case was the observation that "every Australian who had placed a mortgage on his house to buy a war bond was as definitely entitled to reparation as was every Frenchman whose house had been burned by the Germans." Speaking before the House of Representatives on his return from Paris, Mr. Hughes said: "Our claim was for £464,000,000. This is made up of £364,000,000 actual war expenditure, and £100,000,000 being the capitalized value of pensions, repatriation, and loss to civilians and civilian property, and so on, incidental to the war. At one stroke £364,000,000 of that amount was struck out. . . . The position of Australia, then, is that our claim is cut down from £464,000,000 to £100,000,000 or thereabouts. . . . Probably—or possibly—we may receive between now and the end of April, 1921, anything from £5,000,000 to £8,000,-000. I say may. How much we shall get afterwards, I do not know." Actually up to the suspension of the Young Plan in 1932, Australia got £5,571,720. Since the same year principal and interest payments on a war debt of about £80,000,000 owed the United Kingdom have been suspended. The Commonwealth government entered the war with an infinitesimal public debt—up to that time the states had incurred most of the Australian public debt—and came out of it with the gigantic total of £381,300,000 (1920). These were the dregs of glory.

13. THE SECOND WORLD WAR

THE verbal expression of the Australian outlook on world affairs changed remarkably little between wars. The emphasis on the tie to Britain is still of central importance. It is therefore also still emphasized that Australia is an integral participant in the Imperial defense scheme, contributing heavily to it, fundamentally dependent on it. And it is still emphasized that Australia is more firmly integrated into the European-Atlantic world than with her Pacific neighbors.

But times have changed during the last quarter-century, and Australia has changed with them. In 1913 no one raised the point that the United Kingdom would only a little longer be the certain outlet for increases in Australian primary production. By 1938 only a few hardy traditionalists disputed it. In 1913 few thought that manufacturing was the real basis of Australia's future development. By 1938 that view was generally accepted. In 1913 no one would have forecast that borrowings on the internal money market would shortly be more important than loans secured overseas. By 1941 this was a commonplace. In 1913 no one would have said that primary responsibility for Australian defense must rest with the Commonwealth, Imperial aid being supplementary. The reverse was thought to be the case. By 1938 the point was beginning to be appreciated; and in 1940 the Prime Minister stated that the defense of Australia by Australians is a "first" duty, implying that it takes at least equal rank with Imperial collaboration. In 1913 few would have said that the destiny of Australia may be decided by what happens in the Pacific. In 1941 the point is being underscored every day.

Yet it still remains true that Australia is tightly tied to Britain, in trade, finance, culture, and politics. It is still true that however strong Australian defenses have become, she cannot hope to fend off her enemies standing alone. She must have Imperial aid, or a helping hand from some friendly foreign power. It still is true that, in spite of her geographical position in the South Pacific, what happens to the United Kingdom in Europe is of crucial importance to her. What happens in Europe will probably determine what happens in the Pacific.

Thus, while Australia's position appears to be the same in this war as in the earlier one, the more one penetrates below the surface, the more one appreciates that it is different. It is the differences which are of basic importance to any understanding of Australia's situation today.

Two factors in the change stand out with especial vividness. The first is the rapid growth of Australian industry—and hence of her defensive power. This alone has transformed her international political position. The second is the changed Australian outlook on Australia's position as a nation in the Pacific Basin.

Australian manufacturing at the outbreak of the First World War was in a low state of development. The most important industries were wool spinning and weaving, clothing, food and drink preparation, and printing. The government owned an explosives factory at Maribyrnong, a factory for making harness and other leather equipment at Clifton Hill, and a clothing factory at Melbourne in Victoria, as well as a small arms factory at Lithgow in New South Wales. Otherwise it had to rely upon private industry. It is not surprising, therefore, that Australia got but a little distance beyond providing its troops with uniforms, hats, shoes, small arms, rifles, and the ammunition for the latter two. The problem of equipping the Australians for front-line combat fell chiefly on the United Kingdom. Even the problem of civilian supplies became very difficult, so extensive was the dependence upon imports. The most common household articles became scarce, and prices rose to high levels. Although heroic efforts were made to increase and diversify war and civilian production, both problems were far from solution when peace returned. Lacking equipment for them at home, Australia sent six thousand skilled workers to English factories. The new plants which were brought into production during the war were either devoted to consumer goods or to the manufacture of supplies for the primary industries. The great industrial event of the time was the coming into production of the steel works at Newcastle in 1915, without which conditions would have been infinitely worse than they were.

When the present war broke out the situation was completely different. Between wars there had been a steady expansion of industrial plants and periodical upswings of a striking character, as after 1932 during the Great Depression and in the year or two before 1939. The steel works at Newcastle became the largest in the British Empire and able to produce the widest variety of steels of any plant as well. A second steel plant at Port Kembla had also been built. Today these plants provide the foundation of Australia's industrial war effort. Spreading out from them is a complicated set-up of steel processing and utilizing industries. As the capacity of private industry to sustain modern war production increased, so also did the government expand its plants. In July, 1928, it put itself in a position to produce, in addition to First World War supplies, big gun fuses, detonators, cartridge cases, and aircraft bombs. At an ordnance factory established four years earlier it could produce guns, shells, gun carriages, and military vehicles. In 1939, therefore, the problem was a matter of changing over from peace-time to war-time production of an industrial economy which had made considerable strides toward maturity.

The basic difficulties were two—the problem of machine tools, and the problem of finding metal and other supplies still imported from overseas. The first was in a measure eased by successfully improvising a machine-tool industry from very small beginnings, and the second is being progressively eased by bringing local resources into production as rapidly as the difficult circumstances allow. Australia has not broken either bottle-neck, nor is she likely to do so during the course of the war, but she has gone a tremendous distance toward solving her problems as a mere enumeration of the war supplies in quantity production will illustrate.

small arms ammunition	military clothing
shells up to 12 in.	boots
antiaircraft shells	steel hats

air bombs
mines
torpedoes

small arms
bren guns
antitank guns
antiaircraft guns
Vickers guns
field guns
trench mortars
naval ordnance
mine-throwers

leather equipment

bren gun-carriers
army vehicles
trucks

radio equipment
radio locators

paravanes and antimine devices

trainer planes (Tiger Moths)
advanced trainers

bombers (all-Australian Wacketts; and Bristol Beaufort torpedo
bombers, redesigned to take American engines.)

freighters (9,000 tons each; 60 planned)
naval patrol boats (800 tons each; 50 planned)
destroyers (Tribal class)

In mid-1941 plans are well advanced for the production of medium
tanks, steel armor plate, and optical glass, the latter with the aid
of German and Czech refugees. A remoter possibility is fighter
planes. An index to the situation is the fact that an Australian-
equipped mechanized division is planned.

Much of this production is achieved by utilizing *small as well as
large* engineering plants, including railway workshops, for the production of component parts, and then assembling them at central
points. In the production of the antitank gun, for example, fifty
engineering shops in four states make contributions of one kind or
another. But existing plants could not cope with needs. The government on its own account has built three new explosives factories, a new small arms factory, and a new cartridge case factory.
Private industry has also expanded plants, frequently along lines
envisaged in peace time, thus bringing forward plans to completion
from three to five years in advance of the prewar schedule. Since

capital issues are controlled by the government, funds which might otherwise be diverted into consumer-goods industries are available for war industries. All told, 170,000 hands were employed directly in war production in 1941.

Australian manpower, foodstuffs, and raw materials are available in greater quantities than during the First World War. There may be no skilled workers for transference to England, and the army may contain fewer men of high technical skill, for they are retained in industry, but there are plenty of soldiers available. Australia has 1,200,000 men of military age—19 to 40. As in the last war, recruiting for overseas service is entirely voluntary, and any hint that conscription may be advocated brings an immediate negative response from the trade unions. In a very accurate sense, the present Australian army is a more useful army to the United Kingdom (and Australia herself) than the first A.I.F., because it is Australian equipped in considerable measure. Although peace-time compulsory training was suspended by a Labour government in 1929 as an economy measure and not resumed up to the outbreak of war even by succeeding conservative governments, Australia's defenses were progressively strengthened beginning in 1934. From 1937, as the Far Eastern situation deteriorated, defense activity was stepped up to a remarkably high level for peace time, though the expenditures now seem very small when compared to war-time requirements. In 1938 the voluntary militia totaled 70,000 men. After the outbreak of war a home defense army on a compulsory basis was formed, the aim being a force of a quarter-million. By mid-1941 Australia had over half a million men under arms at home, in Egypt and North Africa (protecting the Suez Canal), Syria, England, and Malaya. Voluntary enlistment for overseas service had been maintained at a high level.

The Australian navy is also on a level superior to that of the First World War. At the outbreak of hostilities it included three cruisers, two sloops, a destroyer flotilla, and auxiliary patrol boats. Since the outbreak of war, personnel has been increased about two and a half times. Australian-built ships are constantly increasing its strength. In addition to contributing to Empire defense (as in the Mediterranean) Australia has 11,300 miles of coast line to patrol. A huge graving dock is being built at Sydney, which will be capable of taking battleships for repair.

Military aviation in Australia dates back to before the First World War. An Australian, Lawrence Hargrave (1850-1915), is recognized as being among the world's pioneers of aerodynamics. During the 1914 war Australian pilots and ground crews served on all fronts, using British-built equipment. In civil aviation after the war Australians made a notable record, their heroes of the air including Sir Charles Kingsford-Smith, the leader of the first flight from the United States to Australia across the Pacific in June 1928. (Two of his companions were Americans.) As Australia is peculiarly adapted to flying and the vast distances encourage it as a means of fast communication, commercial aviation was rapidly developed between wars. Much pioneering in freight carrying by air was done by Australians in the mandate of New Guinea as a phase of the development of the gold fields of the interior. In the present war, therefore, it is only to be expected that there would be a rapid development of the air arm. Both on its own initiative and in collaboration with other British countries under the Empire training scheme, Australia has carried out a program of expansion only limited by the availability of planes. In the 1937 general election the Labour party tried to establish the point that the basis of the defense of Australia must be air defense. Although at that time the claim was disputed in the interest of partisan politics, after the outbreak of war the emphasis placed upon aviation justified Labour's position. At the present time there are 32 air schools. The air arm has had 160,000 volunteers from whom to select its personnel. It has already sent aviators to every fighting front and to Malaya, as well as increasing the home defense forces, including a coastal and island patrol which uses Catalina Flying Boats, imported from the United States via a Pacific "ferry service" employing Australian fliers. This service has emphasized to the Australians the defensive importance of the air base at Canton Island, developed by the United States.

When war broke out Robert Gordon Menzies was Prime Minister of Australia. Mr. Menzies had long been recognized as a man of exceptional ability, though few people had ever regarded him as a popular political leader. He had succeeded to the prime-minister-ship in April, 1939, after the death of Joseph A. Lyons, but because of the exigencies of politics, his coming to office as leader of the United Australia party had broken up the alliance between the U.A.P. and the Country party. Standing alone, the U.A.P. was a minority group in the House, commanding but twenty-seven votes. As time passed this was recognized by the conservatives to be a dangerous situation, especially since Labour's political power appeared to be waxing, and so, after a change of leadership in the Country party, the coalition was resumed, giving the government forty-one votes in the House. (The event which precipitated this was the winning by Labour of the seat in the House vacated by Richard G. Casey on his appointment as Minister to the United States.) Labor was divided into two groups, the Federal Labour party with twenty-seven votes, and a splinter labor party based on New South Wales, with five votes. There was one independent. Both labor groups supported the Government on all *major* issues of war policy.

In the months before the general election of September 1940 the Menzies government was subjected to severe criticism for poor administration, especially by the press of Sydney. The election was not fought over participation in the war, but rather over the administration of the war effort. Both sides appealed for a clear-cut decision, but the result was a stalemate. The government parties were able, after supplying a speaker, to command thirty-seven votes in the House, while the Labour parties (shortly to be united by the readmission of the splinter group to the Federal party) commanded thirty-six. There was still one independent, but his power had been enormously increased. He showed an inclination toward Labour. This situation naturally made for uncertainty as to the future of the Menzies government and for a dangerous instability in the politics of the Commonwealth. The situation was not improved when Labour swept the polls in a state election in New South Wales. Only a Prime Minister able to command loyalty beyond the limits of the government parties could hope successfully to govern, in spite of Labour's avowed intention to support the government on all important aspects of war policy. The Labour party leader, John Curtin, was a benign man with no liking for trouble for trouble's sake.

There was little in Mr. Menzies' record to lead anyone to conclude that he could achieve the miraculous kind of leadership required. He was the reverse of popular with labor, and he inspired little enthusiasm among the masses of the people. Nevertheless he continued to be Prime Minister until the end of August, 1941. This was a triumph of sheer brain and will power, an exceptionally interesting demonstration of what a man can do when great events summon him to high effort. Finally confronted with clear evidence that he could no longer successfully rule, Mr. Menzies resigned. In the final phase he was attacked by members of his own party as well as by Labour. The immediate issue which caused his downfall was his desire to make a second war-time trip to London to represent Australia in the councils of the Empire. Labor argued, however, that if the Pacific situation was as desperate as represented, the Prime Minister should stay in Australia. But since all hands agreed that a representative of Australia with greater powers than the High Commissioner should be in London, a minister plenipotentiary could be sent as liaison officer between the cabinets. Mr. Menzies could take that office if he so chose. He did not choose to do so. He remained in the Cabinet as Minister for Defence Co-ordination.

Menzies was succeeded by Arthur William Fadden, leader of the Country party, but selected for the prime-ministership by the votes of the combined government parties. Mr. Fadden, a mere neophyte in Federal politics as compared with Mr. Menzies, held the office of Treasurer in the Menzies Cabinet and acted as Prime Minister during Mr. Menzies' absence in London and Washington in early 1941. A member of the House since 1936, he only rose to full ministerial rank in 1940, on the basis of his election to the leadership of the Country party, a post which, he told me, he accepted with great reluctance to settle an unbreakable tie between two senior members of the party! During Mr. Menzies' absence he proved himself able to command co-operation from Labour more readily than his chief. He is a man of more genial personality, has more of the "common touch," and he has fewer private commitments. But, like his predecessor, he also held office only so long

as his government raised no major issue which would provoke
dissident members of the government parties to cross the floor and
vote with Labour. Such an issue arose during the consideration of
the budget in early October.

Mr. Fadden chose to make a Labour amendment to the budget
an issue of confidence. Two "independents" (one of whom had
assumed that status on Menzies' resignation) "crossed the floor"
and voted with Labour, tipping the precarious balance against the
government. The Fadden government fell after a life of thirty-
seven days, and was succeeded by Labour. John Curtin became
Prime Minister. The Labour party caucus elected a "ministerial
team" and the actual assignments of portfolios was announced on
October 6th. But Labour won office, and can hold it, only by vir-
tue of the votes of "independents" known not to accept all of
Labour's policies. The Labour tactic would therefore appear to be
to administer the war effort in the very best fashion possible. The
Labour Cabinet includes men of great ability. If it demonstrates
that it can efficiently run the nation, then it can "go to the country" with confidence if an election is precipitated. Labour entered
office on a rising tide of pro-Labour sentiment. The task before
it was to keep it running until an election could take place and
give Labour *power*—a majority in the House—as well as office.
Labour returned to office after nine years and nine months in the
opposition.

The rush of events, climaxing with the outbreak of war in December, has been met by Labour with a skill and decisiveness
which have given it a more secure hold on office than the situation
in the House would argue. It is not now likely that an election
will be held before the life of the present parliament automatically
expires in late 1943. If Labour should win this election—as now
seems highly likely—John Curtin will continue as Prime Minister.
Should the conservatives win a clear victory Mr. Fadden will have
a strong claim to the prime-ministership. That is indicated by his
election as leader of the opposition forces to Labour in the House.
(After Mr. Fadden's fall Mr. Menzies lost the leadership of the
U.A.P. to William Morris Hughes, this appearing to eliminate
him as a serious competitor for the prime-ministership.)

In an effort to achieve a measure of stability in the conduct of the war effort, the National War Council, on which all parties in the House are represented, has been established. It was first suggested in a resolution passed at the Federal Labour Conference in June, 1940. But it was only accepted by the Menzies government after the election of September, 1940, when it was no longer possible to hope that Labour would accept a counterproposition of five or six portfolios in an all-party war cabinet. Although an intensive newspaper and political campaign designed to force Labour's hand was conducted, it adamantly refused to abandon its position. The Federal Labour Conference had declared, "That the Labour party should maintain its integral identity in the people's interest." This was in harmony with Labour's long-standing attitude toward coalition governments, not a purely political dodge to embarrass the Menzies government. The War Council was finally set up in late October, 1940.

It discusses all important questions of war policy and votes on them, thus achieving a large measure of national unity in this vital field. But it accepts no executive responsibility. That continues to devolve upon the government. The sharp criticism of the course of events in Greece and Crete, in which Australian soldiers took such a conspicuous part, was in large measure voiced by Labour members of the War Council. These men, and of course the other members of the party, did not consider that their participation in the council in any measure limited their right to criticize the government in the House. The difficulty over Greece and Crete did not arise from any feeling that Australian soldiers should not have been sent there, but rather over two points—first, the War Council was not consulted before the troops were dispatched, the Cabinet taking full responsibility; and second, that the troops had been sent to do a difficult job with inadequate equipment and no proper support in the air. The first was looked upon as derogatory to the council's dignity, the second as a reckless misuse of Australia's manpower. Within the council Labour naturally attempted to mold war policy along its own lines; and it also continued this campaign in the House. Moreover Labour did not remit its efforts to get its program on non-war domestic matters adopted. It continued to exert all pressure to that end. A notable success was the launching of a scheme of family endowment in 1941.

Since Australia had been, long before war broke out, notable for the elaboration of governmental and private controls over economic activities, it was in war time not entirely a question of improvising controls. It was rather a matter of adapting the peace-time controls to war purposes and adding those which the war system required. Australia has developed a system of governmental controls far more elaborate than anything likely to be adopted in the United States, even should this country enter the war. The government, among other things, controls food and commodity prices and rents and also influences wages through the arbitration courts. Through heavy taxation it controls purchasing power. It directs the investment of capital, determines the rate of interest, governs imports and exports, and has absolute power over foreign exchange, watching dollar exchange with especial care. It directs the farmers as to what to grow and what not to grow and how much; it buys up produce and takes a hand in its storage if shipping is not available; it determines which peace-time industries shall continue operations and which shall close down or change over to war production. It directs labor into the channels where it will be most useful. In fact, it is stated that the Australian economy is far more elaborately governed by the political authorities than that of the United Kingdom. The influence of this development from prewar beginnings, themselves remarkable, cannot fail to have a profound effect on postwar policy. Labour will probably extend and elaborate the controls and may give them a more decidedly "socialist" slant. Certainly Labour will tackle the matter of excess profits more forthrightly than its predecessors.

The Australian trade unions are pro-war. That statement requires little qualification beyond a recognition of the fact that the left-wingers have swung to and fro as the policy of the Soviet Union has shifted—or been shifted. The unions have nevertheless consistently aimed at preserving their hard-won privileges. They have permitted relaxation of their rules and job practices only in return for specific assurances that the change is purely temporary. Strikes are not prohibited. The unions provide the major part of the support given the Australian Council for Civil Liberties. Those leaders who have always held to the socialist objective still do so. They argue, in the current situation, that the war effort cannot be finally successful nor the war won, short of the adoption of the socialist system of production. (Even members of the Labour party recently raised the cry that the BHP should be nationalized.)

The outlook of the unions on the war is well presented in a resolution of the Australian Council of Trade Unions, passed by a vote of 128 to 71, on June 5, 1941. The vote should prevent anyone from overlooking the point that some unions are cautious in their outlook on the war question because they are radical and others more co-operative because they are conservative. All unions will feel a little better about the war since it is being fought by a Labour government.

We record our uncompromising determination to continue the struggle against the aggressor Powers who are endeavouring to destroy personal liberty, industrial and political freedom, the right of collective bargaining, and associationship, and therefore pledge the trade union movement to work for a swift and complete victory for the cause of Democracy against aggression and oppression.

We affirm that in order to prevent the possibility of individual profiteering by the war there should be brought about the immediate nationalization of the arms industries and the utilization of the national credit.

We demand a substantial immediate improvement in the standard of life and freedom of speech and assembly.

We express our deepest sympathy to the relatives and friends of members of Australia's oversea forces who have given their lives or suffered from wounds or illness whilst fighting to preserve Democracy, and we express our highest appreciation of the bravery of Australia's volunteer forces in oversea conflicts.

We express horror and condemnation of the barbaric and ruthless method by which the forces of Nazism and Fascism are endeavouring to gain world control and domination.

Between wars Australia became more and more concerned with the course of events in the Pacific Basin. The tide of Australian opinion ran, in these years, now in the direction of friendship for Japan—the focus of all thinking about the Pacific—now in the direction of hostility. The long-term expectations of Australia with regard to the Pacific therefore differed from time to time.

Today her situation can be summarized thus: what Japan can do to realize her aims in eastern Asia and the South Pacific depends in large measure upon the course of events in Europe. If the United Kingdom should be fatally weakened, or defeated, then Japan would probably use force to realize her ultimate aims. That would immediately jeopardize Australia's position as an independent nation, even if Japan should come temporarily to rest in the Netherlands East Indies. Australia's stake in the *status quo* in the region centering upon Singapore is, therefore, very great indeed. In seeking to support her position as a nation located on the fringe of the geographical area Japan seeks to dominate, Australia is therefore actively collaborating with the United Kingdom, not only in the British Isles, the Near East, and North Africa, but also at Singapore and in Malaya. Australian flyers have been at Singapore since early in the war. Australian troops began to arrive there in numbers, fully equipped, beginning on February 19, 1941. As a phase of its defense in the north, Australia has extensively developed Darwin in Northern Territory as a naval and air base.

Australians in general have never been really reconciled to having the common frontier with Japan which the disposition of the formerly German islands in the Pacific brought into being, in spite of the fact that the frontier is removed from their continent by the great island of New Guinea and a stretch of ocean. There has been constant conflict between Australian and Japanese pearl-shell gatherers operating in the richest field in the world off the northern and northwestern coasts of Australia. The Australian fleets operating from Broome, Darwin, and Thursday Island have endured devastating competition from the Japanese fleet operating from Palau in the mandated islands. No satisfactory arrangements to govern the industry were ever concluded. It was well on its way to chaos through overproduction when war broke out. (Incidentally, New York is the world's greatest marketing center for this shell.)

But Australian suspicions of the Japanese especially increased as air transport developed and intensified in proportion as Japan took an anti-British position in world politics. Perhaps the majority of Australian publicists are convinced that the Japanese have fortified strategic points in their islands, especially Jaluit in the Marshall's and Truk in the Carolines. They describe the islands as a dagger pointed at Australia. They view them as affording a protected highway, only broken at Guam, leading from Japan to Australia along a line over two thousand miles east of Singapore.

After openly disagreeing with Japan over the so-called "racial equality" issue at the Paris Peace Conference, Australian opinion swung around to a more favorable view of Japan in 1921. In that year the question of renewing or abandoning the Anglo-Japanese Alliance came up for debate at the Imperial Conference. Mr. Hughes, still spokesman for Australia, advocated renewal, one of his most important arguments being that however reluctant he was to offend the Americans, who objected to the alliance, the fact remained that the United States was an unreliable quantity in international affairs. (Mr. Hughes' views of the United States, not too favorable in any respect, are fully set out in *The Splendid Adventure* (1929).) For that reason if Britain wanted a friend in the Pacific, Japan was the friend sought. She had observed her bond in the World War and undoubtedly would do so in the future. Mr. Hughes was especially critical of the Canadians for speaking, as he put it, with the voice of the unreliable Americans in Empire councils. But he lost. Before the Imperial Conference was finished with this business, he was in a minority of one. The alliance was not renewed. Instead the Pacific problem was dealt with at the American-instigated Washington Conference.

The Australians were not enthusiastic about the Washington treaties, least of all the conservative Australians for whom Mr. Hughes spoke. Labour took a rather more favorable view, since it deprecated entanglements with the Japanese. In the conservative Australian view, what they got for the certainties of the Anglo-Japanese Alliance was the so-called Four Power Treaty which guaranteed the *status quo* with regard to the "insular possessions and insular dominions" of the contracting powers; and the article in the Naval Treaty which provided for a standstill agreement with regard to fortifications and naval bases in the territories and possessions of the parties, homelands excluded. But the Australians felt that the terms of these treaties were nebulous, and they deplored the lack of sanctions or, in plain words, the lack of provision for the use of force to maintain rights. (In October, 1940, when I had a long chat with Mr. Hughes in Canberra, he was still of the opinion that the Anglo-Japanese Alliance should have been renewed, thus, in his opinion, blocking the development of anti-British policy in Japan.)

After the Washington Conference, Australia's Pacific relations were chiefly thought of in terms of trade until just the other day. Between wars, Australia's trade relations with the East increased in volume, especially her trade with Japan, the Netherlands East Indies, and Malaya. The trade with Japan quite overshadowed the rest. Especially active interest in Eastern trade was taken in the years 1931-1935, during which three important government missions investigated prospects in the East. One was headed by Sir John Latham, now Australian minister at Tokyo. Trade commissioners were appointed to China, Japan, and Netherlands East Indies. But the course of trade was not smooth, for in 1936 came the trade war with Japan. With all the chances and changes, however, as of 1937-1938 Australia was drawing 14 per cent of her imports from the East and sending 8 per cent of her exports there. (It should be noted that the quantum of Australian trade increased between wars.) Her trade with the Pacific Basin countries also increased.

By 1937 the Australians were again concerned by the trend of political events in East Asia. They had greeted Japanese activities in Manchuria with mixed feelings, one very powerful paper arguing that it would be all to the benefit of Australia should Japan exhaust her energies there. But the attack on China was viewed in a quite different light, although the Australians in general were slow to recognize that British and Australian interests were jeopardized by Japan's course. The gist of Australian public policy during the three difficult years after 1937 was to temporize with Japan in the hope of deflecting Japanese anger from Australia. The fact that Australia has always wanted friendship with Japan introduced a note of ambiguity into policy when Japan's own actions made friendship with her increasingly difficult. Perhaps the best indication of the nature of the Australian reaction to Japan's policy in its early stages was the proposal, made by Prime Minister Joseph Lyons at the Imperial Conference of 1937, for a "regional understanding and a pact of non-aggression by the countries of the Pacific conceived in the spirit and principles of the League of Nations." This proposal was made abortive by the outbreak of war in China, but the sentiments expressed continued to influence public opinion in Australia for many months thereafter.

When Robert Gordon Menzies became Prime Minister, he made a clear declaration of Australia's outlook on the Pacific. In his first policy speech in April, 1939, he included two paragraphs which may turn out to be one of the most important declarations on foreign policy ever made by an Australian leader. He ratified the ideas long expressed by the Australian intelligentsia but hitherto not publicly recognized by the political authorities. Mr. Menzies said:

In the Pacific we have primary responsibilities and primary risks. Close as our consultation with Great Britain is, and must be, in relation to European affairs, it is still true to say that we must, to a large extent, be guided by her knowledge and affected by her decisions. The problems of the Pacific are different. What Great Britain calls the Far East is to us the near north. Little given as I am to encouraging the exaggerated ideas of Dominion independence and separatism which exist in some minds, I have become convinced that in the Pacific Australia must regard herself as a principal providing herself with her own information and maintaining her own diplomatic contacts with foreign powers. I do not mean by this that we are to act in the Pacific as if we were a completely separate power; we must, of course, act as an integral part of the British Empire. We must have full consultation and co-operation with Great Britain, South Africa, New Zealand, and Canada. But all these consultations must be on the basis that the primary risk in the Pacific is borne by New Zealand and ourselves. With this in mind I look forward to the day when we will have a concert of Pacific powers, pacific in both senses of the word. This means increased diplomatic contact between ourselves and the United States, China, and Japan, to say nothing of the Netherlands East Indies and the other countries which fringe the Pacific.

It is true that we are not a numerous people, but we have vigor, intelligence and resource, and I see no reason why we should not play not only an adult, but an effective part in the affairs of the Pacific.

It was on this basis that the Menzies government appointed ministers to the United States, Japan, and China in 1940 and 1941.

But the Australian influence on British policy was, well into 1940, definitely on the side of temporizing with Japan. The fear was that if war broke out between Britain and Japan the burden of the fighting would fall on Australia and she could not long sustain the weight. An influential section of the public supported this view, even alleging a fear of actual invasion of the Australian continent by Japan. (Though this idea has long been discounted by military experts, it is still alive in Australia. In May, 1941, Sir Robert Brooke-Popham made this statement:

"Even supposing the enemy passed by Malaya to attack eastern Australia, the invasion of Australia is hardly a practicable proposition. Such a force would meet opposition over thousands of miles of sea-lanes. When it reached its destination, owing to the huge force of transports it would require, it would be vulnerable. Its attempts at landing would be strongly resisted. A very large naval force would be needed to protect transports and supply craft for a landing force big enough to get a footing. These supporting naval forces could themselves require fuel tankers—a vicious circle of requirements."

But this implies outside aid for Australia in such a contingency. If Australia stood alone, she might succumb. Is Australia ever likely to stand absolutely alone?) It was hoped that if Japan were handled with gloves she would become friendly. A friendly Japan is what all Australians want.

This outlook led Australia to support the closing of the Burma Road on July 17, 1940. The Minister for External Affairs publicly stated that Australia had played a decisive role in the making of that move. But as the gesture did not change Japan's attitude, there was practically no Australian opposition to reopening the road on October 18, 1940. Yet as late as March, 1941, Mr. Menzies, speaking in London, hinted at further temporizing. This expression of opinion immediately provoked hostile criticism in political circles inside and outside the government and in the newspapers in Australia. By that time almost all Australians were whole-heartedly against further temporizing, for it plainly did no good. Moreover, the Australians were then taking a more hopeful view of American policy than had hitherto been the case. The turning point had come (as it came in America to an almost equal extent) when Japan rejoined the Axis in September, 1940. When, in late April, 1941, Mr. Tatsuo Kawai, the Japanese Minister to Australia, publicly advocated friendship with Japan, he was met with the following public statement by the Minister of External Affairs. It epitomizes the Australian position today.

The paramount concern of Australia is that we are now engaged heart and soul in a war on the side of Britain against Germany and Italy, with whom Japan has allied herself. It must be obvious that our relations with Japan cannot disregard this important fact. While Australia has her own specific interests in the Pacific region, let me say quite plainly that for all Australians the overriding fact now is that they are grimly at war, and that no considerations whatever would lead them to act in any way other than as a partner of the British Commonwealth.

A focal point of Australian-Japanese tension is the island of New Guinea. Late in February, 1941, Yosuke Matsuoka, then Japanese Foreign Minister, made some ambiguous remarks about Oceania, and special mention of New Guinea. That great island, second largest in the world, only exceeded in area by Greenland, is one of the great unknowns in the economy of the South Pacific. The Japanese allege that they can do far more with it than has thus far been accomplished. It is but a hop-skip-and-jump from the southernmost islands of their mandate.

Today two nations control New Guinea, the Dutch and the Australians. The Australian portion, the eastern, is divided administratively into the colony of Papua (capital, Port Moresby) and the Mandate of New Guinea (capital, Lae). The Dutch portion has its capital at Manokwari and consists of 153,000 square miles.

New Guinea has proved something of an enigma to the powers controlling it. It is extraordinarily mountainous and hence almost all development has been along the seacoasts. That is why it is possible for the Archbold expedition of 1938, an American undertaking, to discover a hitherto unknown valley with a native population of sixty thousand. The coming of the airplane has facilitated both exploration and development, but land transport still remains a basic necessity both difficult and extremely expensive to provide.

Australian Papua has a white population of 964 males and 524 females. The most recent figures available show that only 57,636 acres are under cultivation, of which over forty-five thousand acres are in coconuts (mostly for copra) and eleven thousand in rubber. Other agricultural products grown are sisal hemp, kapok, and coffee. While many minerals have been found—copper, tin, iron, coal, manganese, platinum, and so on—only gold has been produced in recent years. It is just possible that the war has revived copper mining. Exports reach a total value just short of two million dollars a year. The condition of the native population is considered good. The administration receives a subsidy from the Commonwealth equal to 25 per cent of its total revenue. A defense force (strength not revealed) is stationed at Port Moresby, complementing the one at Darwin on the mainland.

The position of the Mandated Territory is rather different. The white population totals about forty-five hundred. There are seventeen hundred Chinese, a heritage from German days. The plantations embrace 260,000 acres under cultivation, almost half being in coconuts, and most of which are located on outlying islands of New Ireland and New Britain.

Only one-third of the total area under cultivation is on the mainland of New Guinea. In addition to copra and other coconut products, the principal exports are cocoa, coffee, peanuts, and rubber, marine shells, trepang, and tortoise shell, all in small quantities. By value these exports fall just short of three million dollars a year. Oil is being sought in both the Mandated Territory and Papua by Australian, British, and American interests, but no commercially significant results have as yet been reported. It is gold that makes the Territory prosperous today.

Gold was first discovered in payable quantity apparently in the early nineteen-twenties. The man responsible for it rejoiced in the name of Shark-eye Park. He was an Australian prospector of the type known as a "battler." He kept his secret for a number of years, but the field was slowly "smelled" by other prospectors. The rush did not come until 1926. Park's vision never went beyond winning alluvial gold. The larger developments are attributed to Cecil John Levien, an impecunious Australian Jewish farmer and civil servant who early foresaw that big money would be made by dredging. New Guinea gold comes chiefly from the Morobe District in the southeastern portion of the mainland. The port of the fields is Salamauna, on Huon Gulf. Air transport is based on Lae (from which Amelia Earhart took off and disappeared in 1937). The principal town on the fields is Wau, thirty-three air miles from Lae. Because of engineering difficulties there is no road from the coast to Wau.

Gold accounts for the fact that the Territory is self-supporting even though its services are more elaborate than those of Papua. It also accounts for the fact that the labor problem is acute, for recruiting has reached a level which endangers the stability of native life.

No part of New Guinea has been fully exploited to date except, perhaps, the Morobe gold field. Agriculture, presumably the basic economic activity in the tropics, has hardly begun to develop. Preliminary to any large-scale development the problems of land transport and labor supply must be solved. Then the matter of capital will arise. But the fundamental issue really is: shall New Guinea development be "forced" or shall it be allowed to follow a pattern determined by the state of the world markets for the products it is capable of producing? Whatever the answer, Australia will hang on to its part of New Guinea for defense reasons, regardless of other considerations. (There are, of course, no defense works in the Mandate, but it is well equipped with airfields for use from the base at Port Moresby in Papua.)

The position of Nauru is different again. This small but incredibly rich island is being fully exploited, chiefly for the benefit of the agricultural industries of Australia and New Zealand. (It was for this reason that a German raider shelled the island in late December, 1940, hoping to destroy the mechanical equipment.) But Japan also needs phosphate rock for its agriculture. Today it has direct access to a small supply on the island called Angaur in the Carolines. This source has only one-twentieth of the reserves of Nauru and supplies but one-fifth of Japan's consumption.

In addition to making provision for her own defense and contributing to the defense of the British Isles, the Near East, and Malaya, Australia is a member of the Eastern Group Supply Council, which began operations in March, 1941, with headquarters at Delhi, India.

The members of the British Eastern Group are Australia, New Zealand, South Africa, India, Burma, Malaya, Hong Kong, Palestine, the seven crown colonies in East Africa, and the United Kingdom. The council consists of two parts—the Central Provision Office staffed by military men, which allocates arms and munitions in the British Eastern triangle formed by the countries just named, and the Supply Council. The latter organization handles problems of production, the utilization of existing factories and the location of new ones, the buying and accumulation of stocks of materials, the problems of shipping and transport generally within the triangle, and the distribution of foodstuffs. The objectives are to assure a flow of raw materials like wool, lead, zinc, meat, dairy produce, chrome, asbestos, jute, cotton, hides, timber, rubber, tin, and manganese to the United Kingdom; to make the Eastern Group countries self-sufficient in essential war materials and equipment; to send supplies of these to active theaters of war outside the triangle when possible; and to deal with civilian needs within the triangle in such a fashion as to reduce the number of "long hauls" which put a strain on British shipping. The Eastern Group countries are, of course, rich in raw materials. But because this is a war of the factories, Australia has a preponderating influence in the council *because she has factories* in addition to essential raw materials. Australia today is an arsenal of strategic importance to British survival east of Suez.

She has a decisive role to play in any clash in southeast Asia or the Netherlands East Indies. As she has progressively stiffened her attitude toward Japan since the latter months of 1940, her resolution to play such a part cannot be questioned. Looking north to Netherlands East Indies, Singapore, and Malaya, Australia finds the key to her defense against assault from that direction. The general nature of the situation has been succinctly outlined by Sir Robert Brooke-Popham, pre-war British Commander-in-Chief in the Far East. On May 1, 1941, he said of Burma, Thailand, the Netherlands Indies, and Australia, "You cannot separate any of these territories. If anything happens to any of them, it will affect the rest. If one is attacked, the others must come in. Malaya, Sumatra, the smaller Indies islands, Borneo, and Australia must be considered strategically as one unit."

Singapore is the key to this area. The Australians took a keen interest in Singapore from the moment construction began, feeling that their safety depended upon its strength as a base for a powerful British Eastern fleet. Their own navy was, in considerable measure, planned as a unit which could co-operate with the British Singapore fleet in case of hostilities in the Pacific. But whatever the conception of Singapore, and it has varied in recent years and months—whether thought of as a fleet base, an air base, or as a powerful fortress—Australia has not failed to regard the holding of it as of primary importance to her security. The sending of airmen and soldiers there is as inevitable a move as any Australia has made in the present war.

Although it has also long been recognized in Australia that it is of the utmost importance to Australian security that the Netherlands East Indies remain in the hands of a friendly power (a thesis which is an integral part of the Australian "island policy"), little had been done to carry relations beyond trade until after the present war broke out. Indeed, most of the important non-commercial developments have occurred since the fall of France in the summer of 1940 and hence are more or less shrouded in secrecy. Australia gets many indispensable commodities from the Indies. Practically all of her supply of high octane gasoline comes from there and a considerable proportion of her rubber and quinine, and some tin. The Indies also supply most of Australia's tea, a liberal quantity of which is essential to civilian morale. Although it is a two-day run by air from Sydney to Batavia, Darwin is within three and a half hours flying time from the nearest point in the Indies.

Collaboration for defense between the Indies and Australia can be discussed in terms of geography, complementary economies, and actual military, air, and naval equipment.

In geographical terms, it is important that air communications between Darwin and Singapore are along what is roughly a line running northwest across the Indies. It would be menaced should a hostile power find a foothold there. The fact that the Dutch have, for their own defensive purposes, built numerous emergency airfields along this line, is very important to Australian and British planes flying the route, and the use of them will materially assist in keeping it open. Then again, the Dutch authorities have been building a defensive chain of fortresses from west to east along the equator, linking up the basic Indies defenses in Java with far-away Dutch Guinea. This fortified line is a contribution to the defense of Australia on the north.

Complementing these developments are the commercial air routes in this part of the world. Air communications between Australia and the United Kingdom have always followed a line north from Darwin to Singapore. Just before the war the Dutch services operating from Batavia obtained the right to enter Australia at Darwin, thus linking up Batavia and Sydney. As a phase of their activity, the Japanese have long had air services running from Tokyo into their mandated islands. In March, 1940, they reached the Pelew Islands, about one thousand miles from the Australian Mandate of New Guinea and within five hundred miles of the Netherlands Indies. A further and very embarrassing extension was surveyed early in 1941, a run west from the Pelews to Dilli, the capital of Portuguese Timor.* This proposed service, which cuts across Indies-Australia routes, was countered by a Dutch supported Portuguese line from Dilli to Koepang where it connected with the Batavia-Sydney service, and by an Australian line from Darwin to Dilli. (The Portuguese colony of Timor is in a low state of development. Its chief export is coffee. The Portuguese population of the capital, Dilli, is one hundred.) Furthermore, the Dutch proceeded to inaugurate another service which cut across the proposed Japanese line of flight at right angles. This starts at Batavia, runs through the Spice Islands to the east, and has its terminus at Lake Wissel in Dutch New Guinea. (Lake Wissel was only discovered in 1937!) A link with the Australian services in Papua and the Mandated Territory is very easy to ar-

* A Portuguese-Japanese agreement for this line was signed at Lisbon, October 13, 1941. Australian and Dutch forces occupied Dilli on December 17, 1941.

range. Thus it is safe to say that the air tie-ups between Australia and the Netherlands Indies are remarkably complete, and if they are not all of a military character today, they clearly outline the possibilities of co-operation in air defense.

That the Australian and Netherlands Indies economies are complementary hardly needs much elaboration. The bulk of Australian production is of a temperate climate character; all of the Indies production is of a tropical character. Since the Australians have not gone far in developing production in their own tropics, save in the case of sugar, Indies products are in demand. As suppliers, the Australians are in an especially good position to send temperate climate foodstuffs. Equally important is Australia's potential capacity as a supplier of manufactures, especially steel for use in the Indies munitions works, shipyards, and naval repair shops. Australia has already exported trainer planes for the growing Indies air force, and may be in a position to release bombers in the future. In any case, it is a source of airplane parts. But as long as communications with the United States are open, Australia's significance as a source of manufactured war supplies is lessened. At the moment, she is sending very little in the way of munitions, though in an emergency she might become a major source of supply.

When it comes to the actual state of the defenses, the facts are difficult to state exactly, owing to unrevealed changes in the relative positions. It seems fairly certain, however, that both the Indies navy and air force are larger and more powerful than the Australian. The navy is almost certainly stronger in all types of craft. It includes, for instance, a considerable number of submarines, of which Australian statements on naval strength make no mention. On the other hand, the Australian air force may have equaled or surpassed the Dutch force since the early part of 1941 when Dutch superiority was conceded. The Dutch army is small. The Australian forces are larger. Both Labour and conservative political leaders in Australia have made it clear that there would be no objection to sending Australian soldiers into the Indies in an emergency. Finally, the Indies has a far larger merchant marine than Australia, a fact which might be of decisive importance to the co-operation of the two governments in case of actual warfare.

While it is known that the Dutch, British, and Australian authorities have several times considered the strategic problems of the region, and undoubtedly have worked out policies of collaboration in the light of many possible contingencies, few enlightening public statements have been made. However, in March, 1941, Sir Robert Brooke-Popham stated categorically that a complete understanding had been reached between Australia, New Zealand, Netherlands East Indies, and Malaya with regard to defense. In April, 1941, talks of the same general character took place at Manila between the Americans and the British, after Sir Robert had consulted with the Australians at Canberra. The Dutch, however, did not directly participate in these talks, although Foreign Minister Van Kleffens, then en route from London to Batavia, interviewed the American authorities the following day. After surveying the situation in the Indies, Van Kleffens and his associates flew to Australia for talks with the Cabinet. These took place in May, 1941. Presumably the whole question of Australian-Indies co-operation was surveyed, but no formal statement was made. In newspaper interviews and radio talks, however, Van Kleffens made it very clear what was in his mind. Speaking over the government radio from Sydney on May 14th he declared:

Australia and the East Indies must help one another to the best of their ability. You have given us your support in the Indies, and I am glad to have this opportunity of thanking you for it. We need your munitions and your weapons, and we are ready to continue buying them in great quantities. It is good that as old friends and especially as allies we should know one another. It makes us all feel that we are not alone in a threatened world. I can assure you that the Dutch will fight to the last limit of their strength.

Two weeks later he stated to newspaper interviewers:

For the Dutch, the Netherlands Indies form part of a long line of islands extending from India and Singapore to Australia and New Zealand . . . an attack on any part of the line would be considered an attack on the whole. I cannot speak for Australia and New Zealand; but I can say that our co-operation in all matters of common interest is most cordial.

The pivot on which Australian co-operation with the lands to the north really turns is the tropical town of Darwin, for many years mistakenly named on maps as an important British base in this region. Until the other day it was merely a dismal little town which served as the capital of Northern Territory. In 1938 it had a population of around sixteen hundred. At that time there were only 5,625 persons of European blood living in the 523,620 square miles of the Territory.

Darwin, named for Charles, the Father of Evolution, was planned in 1869 as the first station in Australia on the telegraph line which was to connect Australia with Europe via Java, Singapore, and Madras. From Darwin the line went overland to Adelaide in South Australia. It was completed in 1872. But Darwin didn't boom. As the inimitable Frank Clune, the "dinkum Aussie" reporter, puts it, Darwin's "potentialities have been boosted, explored, and deplored by graziers, gold-diggers, acre-grabbers, buffalo-hunters, crocodile-catchers, political pop-eyes and hooey-hawkers of every variety, spilling a plentitude of propaganda. 'Go north, young man, go north!' was the usual advice—but most of them came south after one look at the torrid Territory." In 1911 the Commonwealth took over the Territory, together with the accumulated debts, and has administered it ever since with no economic success. Darwin is a "government town," living off subsidies of one kind or another.

Always an appalling place, largely because of the amazing contrasts of the "wet" and "dry" seasons, Darwin has never, until recent years, even justified the cost of putting it on a decent footing. What gave it a lift just before the outbreak of the present war was the fact that it was the first Australian point reached by planes coming down from Singapore, and the last point in Australia on the outward voyage. The town also became the northern focal point of continental air lines from the Eastern cities, from Perth in the west, and from Adelaide in the south. But these developments failed to bring Darwin to a very high level. The town's chief fame was as the most unimpressive gateway that any proud country has ever tolerated. Even in 1938 the principal hotel was a strong competitor for the honor of being the world's worst.

In the last three years Darwin has been transformed. Beginning in 1939, infantrymen have been stationed there (housed in an abandoned meat works, monument to the optimism about the Territory's pastoral prospects entertained a quarter-century ago.) Since the outbreak of war, artillerymen, engineers, and airmen have been added. In April, 1941, the garrison was strengthened by a movement of troops from the southeast described as the greatest ever made within Australia. Whereas formerly the civil airport alone provided landing facilities, today there is a new and ultra-modern military aerodrome. The civil port has been provided with direction-finding equipment and night lighting. From the military field, American-built bombers carry out patrol work along the northern Australian coast from Cape York, Queensland, on the east, to the little town of Wyndham, Western Australia, on the west, or from the Pacific to the Indian Ocean. The infantrymen are charged with protecting the town against surprise attack from the rear, a maneuver made possible by the fact that the coast for long distances in either direction from Darwin is uninhabited. The artillerymen have charge of protecting harbor installations. Equipment includes bren gun carriers, anti-aircraft guns, searchlight stations of two hundred and ten million candle power, and radio listening equipment for detecting planes.

The port is the Australian corner of the British naval triangle formed by Hong Kong, Singapore, and Darwin, as well as an air center for the same area. To make it really useful, the Commonwealth has had, as a war-time measure, to replace the single, fantastic old wharf which previously served the town with a new and modern one and to build as well a modern wharf exclusively for naval vessels. Storage tanks for fuel oil have also been installed. Today Darwin is a defensive point of importance.

Even the town itself is being improved. The problem of a water-supply which will function in the "dry" as well as in the "wet" season has been faced and solved. A new, lavish modern hotel has been built. But because the civilian population alone has risen to five thousand there is a housing shortage of monumental proportions. Nevertheless, according to the Australian newspapers, the place has not changed socially. It remains irredeemably raffish, dedicated to the proposition that a man is to be measured by the beer he can drink. In 1940 about one-quarter of the population received medical treatment for tropical ailments, including ear infections, prickly heat, and, in 426 cases, dengue fever.

Darwin is not closely connected with the industrial heart of Australia and cannot readily become so. It is separated from its bases of supply by long, weary miles of sparsely inhabited country. If it is but thirteen hundred miles from the important Indies base of Surabaya, and twenty-three hundred miles from Singapore, it is twenty-five hundred miles from Sydney. Freighters bringing supplies of any kind, from beer to artillery, must come from one of the southeastern cities up the long Queensland coast, around Cape York, across the Gulf of Carpentaria, and along the coast of Arnhem Land. It is an equally long journey up the western coast from Fremantle, port of Perth. Darwin has no direct rail connection with its sources of supply. A poor, badly equipped 3 foot 6 inch railway runs south about three hundred miles to Birdum (population less than one hundred). From thence to Alice Springs in the center of Australia (population, five hundred) there is a six hundred mile all-weather road, completed in February, 1941, as a defense measure. At Alice Springs another 3 foot 6 inch railway is picked up which runs south seven hundred miles until connection is made with the South Australian railways. The troops brought to Darwin in April, 1941, traveled for three thousand miles from their camps in Victoria and New South Wales via Adelaide and this land route.

The importance of Darwin should not be minimized, but it is nevertheless necessary to keep in mind its true relation to the sources of Australian defensive strength. Australian supplies of all kinds must be brought to the town over sea or land routes of upwards of three thousand miles in length. If Darwin is thought of as the northernmost extension of Australia's defenses and the point where they link up with the British and Dutch defenses in the Far East, then its significance will be correctly estimated. But careless deductions based merely on the fact that Darwin is on the continent of Australia will lead one very far astray. Its location in relation to supplies must be clearly seen. Perhaps the best indication of the importance attached to it today is the fact that the United States has stationed a naval observer there.

Two island dependencies off the northeastern coast, New Hebrides, for many years ruled by a joint French-British government, and New Caledonia, a colony of France, have always been of considerable economic importance. With the fall of France their political future became a critical issue. New Hebrides, today regarded as the less valuable, quickly passed to exclusively British control. New Caledonia, incomparably the most valuable French possession south of the equator and far surpassing Tahiti in importance, is now under the control of de Gaulle's followers. New Caledonia is of critical significance in the future of the southwestern Pacific for several reasons: it is a focal point in commercial air transport; its principal harbor is one of the best in the islands; and its mineral resources are a prize to industrialized nations, not to overlook its agricultural possibilities.

When Pan American Airways inaugurated its South Pacific service it selected Noumea, capital city of New Caledonia and the second most populous city in the islands, as a principal station on the run to New Zealand. One day it will be a junction point where passengers for Australia will change planes and, instead of going on to Auckland and thence across the Tasman Sea to Sydney, fly directly to Australia at Brisbane, a run of seven hundred miles. When a call at Suva, Fiji, seat of the British High Commissioner in the Western Pacific, is made on the journey from Canton Island to Noumea, that will also increase New Caledonia's importance. And as British Pacific air services are established, they too will probably use the facilities at Noumea. But bombers can also fly these runs. It is therefore always worth keeping in mind that from Noumea, Australian cities like Brisbane and Sydney could be menaced by a hostile power. Since Australia is the predominant nation of the South Pacific, anything which affects the importance and future of New Caledonia naturally increases its significance to Australia.

The harbor at Noumea could be used as a naval base, possibly by a hostile power. It is but little more remote a possibility than that French islands near the United States might be put to the same use. The point has not been overlooked in Canberra.

The resources of New Caledonia, however, multiply its importance manyfold, for they would be prized even if by location the islands lacked all strategic significance. They are sufficiently valuable to have become, in the prewar years, the cause of competition among the capitalists of France, Britain, Australia, Canada, the United States, and Japan. Of especial value are the actively exploited nickel, chrome, and iron; but there are also deposits of manganese, cobalt, antimony, mercury, cinnabar, copper, silver, lead, gold, and coal, which have potential commercial significance. It is around nickel, chrome, and iron that the international capitalists have conducted their forays. Nickel is of especial importance, for New Caledonia contributes 10 per cent of world production in normal years, ranking second to Canada. Chrome output is also significant, some of it coming to the United States. The Japanese are concerned with both of these ores; and they alone are responsible for the development of the iron. When France fell New Caledonia was, therefore, a prize second only to Indo-China among the French Pacific possessions. Should war come to the South Pacific, Japan would undoubtedly try to "protect" it also. And the pro-Vichy French there wanted to continue the sale of New Caledonia minerals to Japan in order to provide a firm economic base for their regime.

For these various reasons it was important to Australia that New Caledonia stay in friendly hands. Australia was not taking any of New Caledonia's nickel, chiefly because it lacked facilities for working it up from the form in which it was exported, but it was taking chrome for its steel industry. All told, Australia absorbed only 3 per cent of New Caledonia's exports. But it was at the same time supplying about one-third of its imports. The colony was dependent upon Australia for most of its foodstuffs, excepting meat. (It will surprise readers who have romantic notions about the South Seas to learn that New Caledonia exports tinned beef, chiefly to other French possessions.) Australia also supplied coal, for the known New Caledonia deposits are not worked, and miscellaneous metal products, including some machinery. In economic terms, the crisis of 1940 could only be solved by Australia if some way were found to establish larger credits in the Commonwealth than normal trade provided.

Exactly what happened in Noumea at that time has yet to be made public. But in the end the pro-Vichy officials were expelled and a De Gaulle government installed. It is rumored (and denied) that the Australian government actively encouraged this development, which so obviously suited its political book. In any case, once the De Gaulle group was in power, the Commonwealth offered economic assistance and continues to render it. Since August, 1940, an official Australian representative has been stationed at Noumea. A barter arrangement was made whereby a stockpile of nickel was accumulated in Australia as a basis for credits for the purchase of food, coal, and other necessities. The Broken Hill Proprietary played an active role in this transaction, since it is the most likely company to build facilities for handling the ore. But Australia cannot hope to provide the answers to all of New Caledonia's economic problems. It cannot absorb its meat, nor even all its metals. It is therefore serving as an agent for the colony's government, attempting to find new outlets for the exports.

The ultimate fate of New Caledonia is as obscure as the ultimate fate of the French colonial empire generally. But as the United States will never allow French possessions in its area of influence to pass into hostile hands, so the Australian government will keep a close watch over New Caledonia. The New Caledonia French (the white population is about 18,000, of whom 10,000 live in Noumea) are thinking of their future in terms of an autonomous government closely associated with Australia in foreign policy and defense. This might suit the Australians very well. In August, 1940, the Commonwealth formally denied that it aspired to annex the colony. Considering all aspects, it seems likely that annexation would be the last step Australia would want to take. The attitude of the United States is implied by the fact that the first American consul was stationed at Noumea early in 1941.

The case of the New Hebrides is simpler. The joint administration has, since 1906, taken the form of a condominium (the form adopted for the United States-British control of Canton Island). The moth-eaten joke is that it is really a "pandemonium." Of the 1,100 white residents of the islands, almost all are engaged in either agriculture or religious work. Perhaps the majority of the British subjects are Australians.

The Australian missionaries, especially the Presbyterians, have for years kept alive the idea that Australia should assume the authority and burdens of the United Kingdom government under the condominium, thus far with little success. But any attempt to shift the sovereignty to a hostile power would quickly bring the matter to a head. While no minerals are exploited in the New Hebrides, traces of many of value have been found.

The small dominion of New Zealand, twelve hundred miles to the southeast of Australia, is politically and economically an integral part of the British system which heads upon London, but like Australia it is geographically and strategically a South Pacific nation. New Zealand is about the size of the state of Colorado, has a white population of a million and a half, and ninety thousand Maoris, Polynesian aborigines. The economy is based on the cow and the sheep, the products of which go chiefly to the United Kingdom. In the abstract, New Zealand's problems closely resemble those of her nearest neighbor, Australia, but when concretely viewed they are sufficiently different to make reservations of major importance. New Zealand's ultimate fate is bound up with that of Australia. But as long as the British Commonwealth of Nations stands firm, there is no point in bundling these two nations together in one's thinking. Such an action does violence to political, economic, and psychological realities.

New Zealand's outlook was well summarized in an article published by *The Weekly News* of Auckland, September 4, 1940:

New Zealanders are so accustomed to looking first to Britain, their homeland and economic mainstay, that they seldom realize how large a part of the Empire lies in their part of the world. The fact should be constantly remembered as a corrective to any sense of isolation and helplessness, and as an incentive to organize for mutual defence the immense power the Empire commands within the triangle whose points are South Africa, India, and New Zealand.

Thus New Zealand is not, in times of peace, very acutely aware of her near neighbors, even the nearest, which is Australia. Although there are many cultural associations between the two dominions, economically the ties are not as close as one might assume offhand. In 1938 New Zealand sent but 4 per cent of her exports to Australia and drew 13 per cent of her imports from Australia. The disparity between exports and imports is due to the fact that while the exports are competitive, Australia is a source of some of New Zealand's manufactured supplies.

A "White New Zealand" outlook comparable to "White Australia" in emotional force and domestic political significance has never been developed. But New Zealand has nevertheless always considered herself a country reserved for white people. (The native Maori are in no sense immigrants!) Any influx of black or yellow people would be resisted. New Zealand's interest in the Eastern trade has been less active than Australia's, but it exists. On the question of the islands the two dominions agree thoroughly. In times past New Zealand, especially under the leadership of Sir Julius Vogel, took a truly imperialist view of the islands, conceiving herself as the center of a South Pacific commercial empire. Today, in addition to certain small near-by islands, known as "annexed islands," she administers as colonies the Cook Islands and Niue with a capital at Rarotonga and also the Tokelau Islands to the north of the Samoan group. These are governed from Apia, Western Samoa. Western Samoa is, of course, New Zealand's C-class mandate held under the League of Nations. New Zealand and the United States have a common frontier in the Samoas. And the northernmost point under New Zealand's control is actually north of the southernmost point under American control!

Before the present war the government of New Zealand—a Labour government—was the most ardent proponent of collective security of any British dominion. Her spokesman at the League of Nations, W. J. Jordan, gained world-wide fame with his vigorous utterances in favor of this outlook. There can thus be no doubt that New Zealand has always been hostile to Japan's territorial imperialism, but it is nevertheless a fact that she has, until recently, been less fearful of the immediate menace of Japan to herself than has neighboring Australia. Not only is she geographically more remote from Japan and Asia, but she has also, even more decidedly than Australia, failed to take in the full implications of her geographical position. Her contribution of one million pounds to the cost of the Singapore base was a gesture of loyalty to Britain and an insurance payment for general security of the Empire. But it has lately been driven home to the New Zealanders that if the

British bastions to the north of Australia should be destroyed she will, sooner or later, fall victim to the marauding powers which will take advantage of that fact. It has been noted that New Zealand is considered today to be an integral part of the British defense system in the East. She is a participant in the Eastern Group Supply Council.

Equally important is the fact that she has taken steps to strengthen her ties with Australia. What exact conclusion about New Zealand-Australia co-operation was formulated at the British defense conference held at Wellington in April, 1939, is unknown, but presumably it was implemented at the outbreak of the war. There has been co-operation in the patrolling of the Tasman Sea and the islands to the north, both by sea and air. After the fall of France in 1940 when the British situation became critical, a Minister of the New Zealand government flew to Australia to work out an improved program of collaboration; and such collaboration was included in the Australian government's statement of policy for the general election of 1940. Australian Labour took the same attitude. But in mid-1940 it appeared that Australia's resources were fully taken up by the needs of Australia herself and the Empire. There was little to spare specifically for New Zealand. The New Zealand government, therefore, surveyed the country's ability to produce war goods, and early in 1941 it was announced that the dominion was self-sufficient in small arms and ammunition. Plans were formulated for pushing on the production of many types of bombs and shells. The chief reliance is on the railway workshops, but all private engineering works are also co-ordinated under the scheme devised. Beyond this, New Zealand supplies her troops with uniforms and boots. Her great contribution directly to the fighting war is men. Conscription has been instituted in New Zealand both for overseas and home service, in which respect she differs from Australia. She participates in the Empire air training scheme. Her home defense army may one day reach the total of two hundred thousand men. But the cold fact remains that New Zealand, as an agricultural country, is not in a position to sustain mechanized warfare directly out of her own resources.

If her defensive equipment must come from within the geographical area in which she is located, it is only by collaboration with Australia that it can be obtained. It is therefore of great importance that in April, 1941, a permanent consultative committee of Australian and New Zealand Ministers was set up to coordinate the organization of supply and the planning of defense in case of an extreme emergency. Australia is necessarily New Zealand's principal anchor to the windward in case of storm, but as has been emphasized Australia is not herself certain of final survival if she has to stand alone. New Zealand's position is weaker than Australia's from whatever base-line one makes the reckoning.

The Pacific policy of the United States is especially important to Australia, though this is not in any sense to discount the importance to her of American policy *vis à vis* the United Kingdom in the Atlantic. What the United States does that in any measure strengthens the diplomatic and material power of the United Kingdom in southern and eastern Asia redounds to the advantage of Australia, both as a partner of Britain and as an independent nation. Exactly the same is true of American policy with regard to the Netherlands East Indies. When the United States decided to strengthen the defenses of Pago Pago in Samoa, two thousand miles from Sydney, the Australians were vitally interested, for from Pago Pago American seaplanes can readily link up with the Australian island patrol ships. But what measure of direct collaboration between the United States and Australia exists today, or has been planned in the light of possible future developments, is unknown. The diplomats of both countries have refused to admit the existence of any formal arrangements.

Nevertheless the case for political and defensive collaboration between the United States and Australia in the Pacific is very strong. Robert G. Menzies has called this a "functional" relation. Although the United States has not finally shut the door to a negotiated settlement with Japan, she has set her face against unlimited Japanese aggression in southeast Asia and the South Pacific. Where the line will be drawn beyond which Japan cannot go with impunity has never yet been made clear. Probably, however, it will be drawn in the Malaya-Netherlands East Indies region. If so, then the Australians are vitally concerned, and the case for Australian-American collaboration is impregnable.

It is to be hoped that neither party has been persuaded to regard the Australian-American phases of any common action as purely incidental to a British-American scheme. That would be a fatal error. The relative positions of Canada and Australia in relation to the United States are utterly different. Nevertheless it is important that the United States consistently place the British dominions on a plane of equality as far as recognition of their autonomy in foreign relations is concerned. If Canada is prepared to negotiate agreements with the United States, there is no reason why Australia should not do so also. That she will is implicit in the Menzies statement on Pacific policy. Any retreat from that position would be something less than dignified. In insisting on this the United States would not be trying to dissociate Australia from the United Kingdom, whose Far Eastern policy is the bench mark by which Australia still calculates her course. It would rather be insisting that if there is to be collaboration to common ends in the Pacific, all partners should be "equal in status, in no way subordinate one to another."

A "functional" relation between Australia and the United States would be founded on a common aspiration toward certain definite ends. From the American point of view, it would be an indispensable phase of its general Far Eastern policy, not a radical departure. America's Australian policy, insofar as it is differentiated from the policy with regard to the British Commonwealth as a whole, grows out of Australia's geographical position in the Western Pacific and her political orientation. It is a phase of America's general policy in that area—her Far Eastern policy. On no other basis, it seems to me, can the United States calculate a sensible line with regard to Australia. But it should involve more than mere agreement on resisting the aggression of a third power. Such a negative conception might serve the needs of the moment, but it would be a poor foundation on which to build permanent relations. It is therefore important that, apart from close similarities in social outlook, the two countries also agree on at least three points in their view of Pacific affairs. Both countries aspire to control the islands near their shores or see to it that they are in friendly hands. Both countries take a critical view of oriental immigration into their territories, the Australians if possible being more vigorous than the Americans in their opposition. And both wish to found their relations with the Orient on trade designed to serve mutual, as well as individual, interests. These points expand the common ground. A "functional" relationship could be successfully worked out on this basis. But when it comes to the next step—toward what Mr. Menzies has called an "organic" relationship—difficulties are encountered. The economic tie between the two countries is weak, and its strengthening is a puzzling problem. And while their social outlook is similar, the cultural tie is almost as weak as the economic.

The evolution of Australian opinion of the United States would make an interesting study. Some of the attitudes are not necessarily based on sound information. They are mostly prejudices, fortified by stray bits of fact and fiction picked up here and there in the press and the movies and welded into a picture of American life which is apt to be unfavorable. For this the Americans themselves are largely to blame. Most of our "culture carriers" in Australia have been interested in selling something, not in presenting a rounded picture of American civilization. However, the great American industrial enterprises, especially those with Australian branches, like Ford, International Harvester, General Motors, have had great influence on Australian industrial methods. This influence promises to be very strong in the future.

About 1927 Australian labor was especially hostile to the United States, for it was engaged in a campaign of resistance to any move on the part of employers to introduce American methods into Australian industry. Instead of confining themselves to the issues, labor leaders indulged in incredibly splenetic outbursts like the following by Don Cameron, in the *Union Voice* of Melbourne:

. . . the Americanizing of Australia means that . . . as in America, and as the inevitable outcome, we would have here in Australia more of the ignorant and arrogant type of employers and their degenerate progeny; more crime and private murders, such as street executions and mob lynchings; more corruption and immorality both in public and private life; more religious bigotry of the anti-evolution and Ku Klux Klan brand; more sexual grossness and perversity in literature and the theatres; more drug fiends and freak social reformers; more weird Negro jazz music and the antics and dancing of primitive man; more of the extremes of the uncultured wealthy and the cringing poor, and more generally of men and things that are not only positively dangerous, but also the very antithesis of healthy and progressive social life.

This is, of course, outrageous nonsense of the "any stigma will do to beat a dogma" order. But by its very extremity it manages to include almost every hostile observation about the United States heard in Australia in recent decades, with the possible exception of the Uncle Shylock stuff.

But there have always been Australians (other than employers who were traduced by traducing the Americans) to counter such remarks. As conclusive a reply as any is that by Professor G. V. Portus, who wrote in his admirable little book, *The American Background Sketched for Australians* (1928):

There is a fashionable pose of smiling in a superior way whenever the Americans are mentioned. I have no patience with this pose. Whether it comes from a Russian Communist, or an Australian Labour leader, or a British business man, it is a foolish affectation to pretend to despise the United States and things American. For what the Americans are doing, and still more, what the Americans will do, matters, and matters enormously, not only for this country and for the continent of Europe; it matters enormously for the future of the whole human race.

Australian opinion oscillated between these two views during the years between wars. swinging now one way, now the other, as the Americans did things which pleased or displeased the Australians.

Labor slowly lost the extreme hostility to which Mr. Cameron gave voice. The Commonwealth sent a delegation of union leaders and business executives to the United States in 1927 to investigate working conditions. In their report the union delegates expressed the conviction that the key to American industrial success was "the high standard of machinery and equipment, management, organization, and supervision. After visiting America and noting many of her industrial problems, conferring with her leaders representing capital and labour, her economists and students of social progress," they went on, "we are convinced that the great lesson to be learned from that country is the extent to which scientific research has been applied to industry as a whole." This did not lead labor to abate its opposition to certain American practices, notably "payment by results," but it did clarify its view on technological and managerial changes in Australian industry. These were no longer repudiated holus-bolus as "American" and therefore to be blindly opposed. Rather the emphasis swung to the dogma that labor must always share to the full in the increased individual productivity which resulted from the changes. It became not so much a matter of resenting changes designed to bring about higher output per worker, as of kicking against everything that frustrated the workers in their aspiration for higher living standards. With this frustration the Americans obviously had nothing to do, and the anger against them died down.

Among middle and upper class people the anti-American feeling, where it existed, has stayed alive longer, for while it was equally founded on misapprehensions, it was harder to eliminate because it involved conflicting standards of manners and morals (in the widest sense) and especially "racial" ideas. Many of the things Mr. Cameron saw flowing from the American system of industrial relations other Australians saw as the consequences of the mixture of "races" in America, meaning the existence within the population of people of non-British origin even more than the Negroes. They accepted the writings of Madison Grant and still often quote him as an authoritative anthropologist.

From these and other sources, some highly esoteric, flowed those errors about the United States against which Australian public men have lately taken to warning their countrymen. Earlier R. J. F. Boyer's effort to set out the integrating principle in American life, a principle which transcends nationalities and gives no superior place to the group of British origin, has been quoted. Mr. Boyer was seeking to prevent his countrymen from misinterpreting the United States on the basis of their own notions of "race." A complementary approach was recently made by Professor Fred Alexander. He sought to set his countrymen straight on the language question:

. . . a warning against careless use of that phrase "The English-speaking Peoples.". . . . It is true that Americans speak English; it is not true that all Americans are English in racial origin, or that the approach of the majority of the American people to world problems today is similar to the approach of the British peoples. Far from it. . . . The vast majority of the people of the United States today are neither anti-British nor pro-British in their thinking; they are pro-American. . . . In the past we Australians have been too ready to assume that, because Americans speak English, they will approach world problems in the same way as the people of England. When Americans have shown that their approach to world affairs has been very different from the English approach or the British approach we have been too ready to assume that some pro-German or some other evil influence has been at work on the American people. It may be that one of the serious obstacles to an understanding of the United States . . . is the fact that Americans speak English!

This is an extremely interesting contribution to better under-standing between the two peoples, as also is Mr. Boyer's. If they have been widely read and heeded, it will be helpful, but the durability of the habits of mind these writers are combatting should not be overlooked. Moreover, Professor Alexander felt it necessary also to rebuke those entertaining an attitude which I encountered in Australia in 1940: "I have sensed a certain criticism that to stress the importance and the urgency of Australian-American co-operation today is a form of disloyalty to the British connection. If that feeling exists and is widespread, it should be opposed frankly and vigorously." (I can testify that it is amaz-ingly common.)

The fundamental trouble is that the Australians know little about the United States and the Americans even less about Aus-tralia. Reflecting on my own experiences in the two countries I have come to the conclusion that the Americans have a far more flattering general impression of Australia than the Australians have of America. Professor Alexander, who spent 1940 in America, thinks that Australians have a very considerable quantity of superficial and mostly unflattering knowledge of the United States but "have in the past been more or less indifferent to American culture." That is understatement! Rather, it seems to me, the popular disposition has been to conclude from the unflattering information that the United States was totally lacking in culture, especially culture of a specifically American character. A friend of mine who has put in considerable time advocating a free library system in Australia was once told by a "distinguished citizen" of a large town that if "libraries will make Australians like Americans, who seem to like the libraries you want, then I'll oppose libraries."

Only people whose work has required them to gain knowledge of American contributions to certain fields of knowledge, or to visit the United States, have in the past been at all impressed by anything other than America's vulgar power. Few university people in Australia, other than a sprinkling of young men who have not yet risen high in the academic hierarchy, are American-trained. The tradition has been to go to England for advanced work. No Australian university offers even an incidental short course in American history. The joke is that the United States ceased to exist when it dropped out of the Empire. The *Sydney Morning Herald,* the most influential newspaper in Australia, was quite accurately reflecting the situation when it asked rhetorically, ". . . what do we know of the people of this country on whom we rely so heavily now to throw back the tide of barbarism which threatens us, and what can we know unless we know first the background of their lives, institutions, and ways of thought which is, briefly, their history?" The *Herald* concluded, "It is time that this neglect was remedied, and the need to do so is probably greater in Australia than any other part of the Empire." In some measure this is an overstatement, possibly designed to express contrition for ill-founded Australian criticism of the United States in the past, but in essence it is true.

From the American side the situation is not dissimilar. The vital difference is that since Australia has not bulked very large to Americans, their misinformation is less firmly fixed and their general impression more favorable. American impressions are more apt to be based on contacts with individual Australian travelers, whom we usually like, than on any other factor. We do know too much about man-eating sharks and ridiculously exaggerate the importance of the aborigines. The *New York Times* stated the situation accurately when it remarked, "Americans, especially in the East, are apt to dismiss [Australia] as 'a far-away country of which we know nothing.'"

The outbreak of the Pacific war in December, followed almost immediately by the loss of the great British warships *Prince of Wales* and *Repulse* off Malaya as well as land reverses on the peninsula which endangered Singapore and the Netherlands Indies, caused a sharp intensification of Australia's domestic war effort and a dramatic swing toward the United States. Prime Minister Curtin declared that, "I make it clear that Australia looks to America, free from any pangs about our traditional links of friendship to Britain." Although the context of this remark made it plain that Mr. Curtin was emphasizing the Australian need for a close link with America for the successful prosecution of the Pacific war, his phrasing gave an opportunity for old-line politicians and newspapers to assail him bitterly on the ground that he was running out on Britain. Nevertheless he received wide popular support. In his statement on the Roosevelt-Churchill agreement concluded at Washington at the end of the year he said:

It represents a policy of concerted Pacific strategy which the Australian Government has advocated, and amply justifies all that has been said as part of that advocacy. Stern duty made plain speech imperative. . . . In this country there will be a feeling that the defensive interdependence of the United States and Australia has become a tangible thing.

The Australian-American "functional" relationship is now firmly welded. The fortunes of war in East Asia forecast that Australia will become ever more important to America as a base for operations against Japan; and Australian security becomes for that reason an American stake of major magnitude. The war has again emphasized the point that Australia is a *Pacific* nation which must collaborate with all friendly powers in that area—America, Britain, China, Netherlands Indies, U.S.S.R.—for self-protection. It has also underlined for all to see that self-interest equally requires that the United States strongly support Australia against the common enemy to insure that the war is won. Yet it is still true that the "organic" relationship, which is a matter of culture and economics, is as yet only an historical prospect.

Part Four

AUSTRALIA'S TOMORROW

14. AUSTRALIAN DEMOCRACY

WHEN Australians count their blessings they can make an impressive list. Even angry Australians do very well at this fascinating game. Frank Dalby Davison set aside his literary work long enough in 1938 to write an outspoken, acerb pamphlet on the state of the world in general and Australia in particular, which he entitled *While Freedom Lives*. Australia, he said, "is a billabong connected with the main river by a channel, rising and falling with the river, but slightly out of time with it. Our social structure registers repercussions of world events, but never originates them." Then he listed Australia's blessings:

We are few in number, socially flexible, uni-lingual; we have no legacy of ancient hatreds, no distrustful minorities; we have no pressing fear of envious neighbors [forgetting Japan?]; our common people have well-entrenched industrial organizations; they have known severe hardship and bitter industrial struggles, but never the sustained oppression that breeds thirst for revenge; they are accustomed to political power and, most importantly, to its temperate use; we are schooled in the ways of compromise; we are accustomed to the social administration of many large departments of our social and economic structure. The addition of another or several wouldn't alarm us in the least—unless that alarm were deliberately fostered by interested and subversive sections. For these things we can look into our history and learn whom to thank.

With these to work with, Australia faced the future in 1938, when, as Mr. Davison saw it, the issue was radical social change versus Fascism. She will have them to work with in the postwar period. It is an indication of the health and vitality of Australian democracy that "reconstruction" is being vigorously debated while the war is still on.

Not only are the newspapers and magazines discussing the future, but the Commonwealth government is also taking a hand. The war-time Ministry of Labour and National Service includes the Division of Reconstruction Research. However, no plans have yet been made public by this organization. Thus far the best indications of what is in the Australian mind are to be found in newspapers, magazines, and pamphlets.

Brian Penton, the vigorous young editor of the *Sydney Daily Telegraph,* has published a long series of vivid editorial articles and a voluminous selection from the correspondence invoked. Mr. Penton launched his campaign with a pamphlet entitled *Think— Or Be Damned*. That is the keynote of his articles. While he has stirred up controversy, if not much thinking, he is far from satisfied with his results. He has been provoked into making one of the clearest statements I have yet seen of the difficulties confronting any country which seriously undertakes to plan for the postwar world. Mr. Penton had suggested, among other things, that nothing much could be accomplished for Australia if the rest of the world was neglected. Something would have to be done to "rescue nine-tenths of the human race from the bread line."

A fairly noble sentiment which you might expect to evoke a round of humanitarian applause . . . not on your life! From East and West, High and Low, Right and Left, came a hearty bellow of repudiation. For the stockbroker in his castle and the trades-unionist in his cot, for the worker in a tariff-protected factory, and the yeoman on a bounty-protected farm, for boodler and bozo, social justice begins at home *and stays there*. . . . They envision the world after the war as essentially the same kind of world as that of old, only with better pickings.

But Mr. Penton still devotes his great journalistic talents to breaking down this narrow view—to emphasizing that "social justice at home depends upon social justice abroad" because, says he, "however gaseous and beside the point much of the talk has been, involving utopias previsioned by single-taxers, British Israelites, naturopaths, and vegetarians, it has at least affirmed the essential undefeatism of the human spirit."

Postwar tasks in Australia, as elsewhere, fall into two broad divisions, first, rehabilitation, and second, reconstruction. It is much easier to agree on the first than the second. Rehabilitation involves getting the economy back to a peace-time basis, which everybody knows is necessary. Reconstruction means fundamental changes. These may disturb vested interests, who will see, or profess to see, an unwarranted invasion of their "pickings" for what is to them very vague—"the general good."

Rehabilitation in Australia will involve (1) the change-over of the basic industries, primary and secondary, from war-time to peace-time production schedules; (2) the re-absorption of members of the fighting services and almost all munition workers—over five hundred thousand persons—into the peace-time economic structure; (3) the disposition of the war-born industries whether or not specifically established to produce munitions and fighting equipment either by discontinuance or by granting them tariff protection.

Reconstruction will involve (1) reconsideration of the Australian standard of living, the social services, housing and so on; (2) adaptation of the Australian economy to the changing world economic structure; (3) special attention to the position of the agricultural industries; (4) careful consideration of the labor supply, including the employment of women and especially the introduction of immigrants.

At least four general approaches to the problems have been made by interested Australians. These are the continuance of capitalism, the immediate introduction of socialism, more labor "gradualism," and the line taken by the Roman Catholic church.

The case for capitalism comes not as a reasoned statement of conviction, except very occasionally, but as the basic assumption of the conservatives. That for the introduction of socialism comes from the left-wing trade-unionists. The case for "gradualism" is the special property of a large section of the trade unions and a still larger section of political labor. What the Church stands for will be elaborated in connection with its specific, and very remarkable, proposals. It will be possible in postwar Australia, for these various groups to agree upon particular changes which, when added up, may make a considerable difference, even though when taken separately they may seem far from ushering in a "new order."

Writers holding the various points of view come down hard in favor of greater economic security. Professor F. A. Bland—prefacing his remarks, "I assume that the postwar order will comprise a system based on private property and predominantly private enterprise."—has outlined a broad program for planned advances on five fronts:

1. Constructive Community Services: education, libraries, recreation.
2. Social Insurance Services: providing for unemployment, health, and similar problems.
3. Social Assistance Services: pensions, including old-age, widowhood, invalidity, etc.
4. Collective Environmental Services: assistance for drainage, water, sewerage, slum clearance, and town planning.
5. Subsidized Services: assistance for home building; for the purchase of furniture by newly married couples; and in the purchase of milk, fruit, and vegetables.

Many of these services already have a long history in Australia. Professor Bland is obviously thinking of extending them on a Commonwealth-wide scale or increasing the benefits. Others would be new, but all have been vigorously discussed in recent years, as, for example, education and libraries. Professor Bland suggests, "The majority of these services could be covered by some form of contributory insurance; one payment should be made at a central office to cover the lot. Any social service scheme should be made applicable to all persons in the community. If a salary limit is to be imposed, it should not be lower than £400 [about $1,300] a year."

A suggestion about nutrition, tucked away in the fifth category, deserves special attention. Back in 1935 certain Australian leaders became convinced that there was a vital connection between agricultural policy and the food consumption habits of the world's peoples. The Australian government took this idea to the League of Nations. In September, 1935, Mr. S. M. Bruce, Australia's delegate to the Assembly, "won an immediate response when he 'stressed the necessity for marrying agriculture and public health in the interests of the latter; of increasing the consumption of protective foods as a remedy for malnutrition and the agricultural crisis; and of changing the incidence of State protective subsidies so that they should serve to increase consumption rather than to restrict production.'" As a result various technical organizations of the League undertook a world-wide survey of nutrition and published at least six volumes on the matter. The Commonwealth established the Advisory Council on Nutrition, which surveyed Australian conditions and published a report in six numbers. The war brought this work to a halt before it could find much expression in the public policies of most nations. (The so-called food-stamp plan in the United States is, however, related to it.) What is really back of the Australian interest is the strong feeling that if the task of improving living standards should be undertaken on a world scale, the demand for protective foods would rise to such a height that the so-called agricultural surpluses will be eliminated. This would be a boon to Australia. Within her own territory there is, as the Advisory Council's reports show, opportunity for increasing the consumption of such foods. What then must be the situation in less favored lands? This idea is certain to play a central role in postwar plans, but how far it will be implemented and what final effect it will have on the position of the world's agricultural plant cannot be forecast. Professor Bland has wisely provided for its practical application in Australia.

The Catholic churches of Australia observed Sunday, May 4, 1941, as Social Justice Day. All sermons were devoted to explaining the Church's conclusion that the basic wage system of Australia was inadequate. Its replacement by a system of "family wages" was advocated. "There will be no social justice," said a pamphlet issued at that time by the Catholic Bishops, "until recognition of the principle that 'family wages' come before dividends." The ends the Church has in view are these: (1) proper sustenance for the workers and their families; (2) the opportunity to acquire a moderate amount of property so that the workers will not be entirely dependent upon their wages; (3) the ability to make suitable provision through public or private insurance for old age, illness, and unemployment; and (4) the opportunity to improve the cultural condition in which the workers and their families live. The Bishops declared, "It is quite clear that these requirements have not been observed in the fixation of the basic wage in Australia at any time in the past. Nor indeed does the basic wage pretend to fulfill the requirement of a family wage."

If the family wages are to be a first charge on industry, it follows that industry will have to be so governed as to be able to meet them. The Catholic Bishops therefore advocate the formation of industrial councils. These should:

1. determine wages and conditions throughout an industry.
2. fix the prices for goods produced.
3. fix the dividends payable each year.
4. plan the amount and quality of production from year to year.
5. plan employment, social insurance, and pensions for workers.
6. deal with marketing the products.
7. control the number of enterprises in each industry.
8. deal with technical education and apprenticeship.
9. generally have complete control, subordinate only to the ultimate authority of the state, over the policy and development of the industry.

The Bishops concluded, "The wage system in itself is not unjust. But, if its actual working proves incompatible with social justice, the co-operative working of industry, giving the workers an adequate share in the profits, management, and control of industry, may have to be substituted."

The position taken by the Bishops is very remarkable. The Church wields considerable power in the trade unions and the Labour party. The Bishops' program is in no way incompatible with Professor Bland's program, which is, in a sense, included within it. The general approach is easily harmonized with the views of non-Catholic economists. For example, Dr. Herman Black has stated, "We should not have a basic wage, but a basic income—a floor below which income will not fall. Then, year in and year out, we should aim at a higher floor." This idea has the support of all the economists at Sydney University. It thus appears that the leaders of Australian thought on economic security have come around to the idea that until you think in terms of *needs*, which are continuous throughout life, you cannot formulate a satis-factory wage policy. The Church emphasizes *family* needs. Dr. Black extends the emphasis to a yearly income. These are impor-tant conclusions, for Australia has been experimenting with basic wage fixation and minimum margins for almost four decades.

Both the Catholic Bishops and the academic thinkers are, no doubt, enunciating their conclusions without regard to practical politics. Conservative political leaders have not yet spoken very clearly, perhaps because they are accustomed to instituting social reforms in response to Labour pressure. The political and union leaders of labor, however, have done so. A mere listing of some of the reforms mentioned by them will indicate the nature of their thinking. Setting aside declarations in favor of all-out socialism, they have asked for:

Allowances for widows and dependent children on a Common-wealth basis.

Increases in old-age and invalid pensions.

More liberal allowances under the new family-endowment scheme.

An all-around non-contributory national insurance scheme to in-clude health and unemployment protection.

A Commonwealth-subsidized housing program.

The forty-hour week.

Public works to absorb postwar unemployment.

Nationalization of basic manufacturing industries, including the BHP.

Full utilization of the national credit for social purposes through the Commonwealth Bank.

The emphasis in labor thinking is, as always, on a further elabora-tion of the social services and a more intensive control of industry and finance by the government. Labor stands for non-contributory social services. It follows, then, that it favors heavy taxation with the design of redistributing the national income in favor of the workers through governmental channels. It would finance all pub-lic works with Commonwealth Bank credit, along the lines fol-lowed in New Zealand. It would gradually reduce the province of private capitalism by nationalizing industries, probably with compensation for stockholders up to a fixed maximum. Small stockholders, particularly, would be protected. If this presentation of the labor viewpoint accords with the facts, then there is no reason why, in actual political practice, labor should not support the program of the Catholic Bishops, or of Professor Bland. This would create an almost irresistible body of public opinion in favor of at least minimum change. It would be in harmony with the past tactics of the labor politicians. The parting of the ways, within the labor camp and outside it, would come over the issue of socialism. Professor Bland disclaims allegiance to socialism. Without a revolution in Catholic thinking, the Bishops cannot go beyond the "co-operation" they outlined. So the Australian socialists are really left where they were before: a strong, highly vocal, minority pressure group.

Public works as a phase of a postwar plan have received considerable attention. Certain suggestions that have been put forward indicate what can be undertaken with profit to the community. It has been suggested by James Hume-Cook, for example, that:

1. a large-scale public housing scheme be launched.
2. a comprehensive road building plan be executed.
3. the main trunk and strategic railways be converted to a uniform gauge.
4. sewerage schemes be widely undertaken in the country towns.
5. water-storage schemes be carried out on a grand scale.
6. storage buildings for holding stocks of feed for sheep and cattle against drought requirements be built throughout the nation.
7. electric light and power lines be extended to all possible country districts from old and new generating stations.

All of these would, in one way or another, increase the efficiency of the Australian economy and make the country a better place in which to live. They grow naturally out of the needs of the nation. It is difficult to see how some of them can be long postponed. Many of them have long been strongly urged by persons of different political allegiances. They are not expedients designed to provide work during the postwar period of adjustment. In fact, they include most of the suggestions which close students of Australia's needs have accepted long since.

But none of the various schemes, whether to improve the conditions of life or the efficiency of the nation, will be possible if the Australian economy is not in sound working order.

When the war ends, the manufacturing industries will be operating in relation to the needs of the conflict. Many industries formerly engaged in peace-time production will then be fully occupied with war work. These will return to their original use. But there will be new industries established especially for war purposes or to supply from Australian resources goods used in both peace and war but hitherto imported from overseas. National self-sufficiency played a large role in the development of Australian industry between wars. It was often said that anything that could be produced in the Commonwealth should be produced. The war has inevitably increased the feeling that this idea should guide industrial policy. War always intensifies belief in the "economics of siege." There will therefore be small disposition to allow the war-born industries to disappear. And there will probably be a strong effort to convert equipment assembled for war goods to the production of *additional* lines of goods hitherto imported, as for example motor vehicles. The total effect, therefore, will be an increase in the range of industrial capacity far beyond that of 1938. The signs point to the use of the tariff to protect it.

Recalling that the tariff is supported both by the conservatives and Labour, Dr. Herman Black was hardly romancing when he recently said:

I anticipate that at the end of the war we are going to get a tremendous spate of protection. The huge industrial development and the new pattern of employment are going to become a kind of sacred cow to Australians. The policy of protection will be put forward by Left and Right. The result will be that you will have a long ministerial red carpet laid down and along it employer and employee will walk arm-in-arm.

Straws in the wind indicate that Dr. Black's idea is founded on something more than a hunch. But there is no way of telling what the government's policy will be.

In the 1941 *Annual of the Australasian Manufacturer* there are articles which point unmistakably to the conclusion Dr. Black has reached. J. Gordon Jones, President of the New South Wales Chamber of Manufactures, declares, "Already in Australia it is being suggested that 'undesirable' and 'exotic' industries (whatever those terms mean in these modern days) . . . should be scrapped when the war is over. Apparently we will be expected to sell as junk the modern and efficient plant and tools we will have added to our production potential. . . . If that is what is wanted, Australia, as far as Australia herself is concerned, will have fought in vain." In other words, if Australia cannot continue to pursue a strictly nationalistic economic policy after the war, then the war will have been fought in vain.

In harmony with Mr. Jones's view, are the ideas expressed by James Hume-Cook. Mr. Hume-Cook is very much taken with a notion which has considerable vogue among Australians—that after the war there will be a geographical redistribution of industry *within the British Empire,* from which Australia will particularly benefit. Industry will be moved out of the vulnerable British Isles into the safer parts of the British Commonwealth, especially Australia. Not all industries will be moved or even any industry in its entirety. Those parts of industries which are moved will be assigned markets in a particular portion of the globe. Mr. Hume-Cook states that one British concern, apparently the Imperial Chemical Industries, Ltd., has allocated to its Australian plant the Australian, New Zealand, and South African markets. He then says:

By applying the same principle to many more products, and many more factories, Australia would become a secondary base for British Manufacturers and World Trade. . . . For example, the transfer of, say, one-third or one-fourth of Britain's Cotton Textile manufacturing to Australia . . . should result in all round benefits. The cotton—or a great deal of it—could be grown in Queensland. . . .

Mr. Jones is an influential business executive, Mr. Hume-Cook the secretary of the Australian Industries Protection League. Both of these gentlemen, bent on continuing into the indefinite future the task of industry building in Australia, are well aware that only by the use of the tariff can they reach their objective. There can be little doubt that in the postwar period the Australian manufacturers will be as decidedly high protectionists as they have been in the past.

These men will aspire to employ the full powers of the government to accomplish their end, not the tariff alone. There is every reason to suppose that most of the "controls" elaborated in Australia during the prewar years, plus those elaborated during the war, will continue to be used in the postwar period. They cannot very well be abandoned immediately the fighting ceases, for that would result in the intensification of the expected chaos. But there will be widespread support for their continuation indefinitely. After all, Australia has had long experience of them and found that they need not interfere with the fundamentals of the private enterprise system, if they are given the proper slant. The great necessity is to keep the power of governing industry in the hands of the owner-producers. There is little conservative opposition to this kind of organization, except among the wool-growers. There is no Australian conservatism of the laissez-faire variety. Labor is not opposed to controls. It believes that it can protect itself under such a system by insisting upon special controls designed to safeguard its interests. There is a hint of the shape of things to come in Mr. Menzies' statement of August 19, 1941, that the war-time controls of prices and profits will continue after the war.

Of course there is a tremendous political issue concealed in this apparent unanimity. It is not, however, "controls" versus "no controls." The struggle will be over the right to manipulate the controls, for in the manipulation will be found the key to the social future of the nation. Shall they be manipulated to keep the owner-producers in the saddle, or for the good of the whole people—for *power* or *welfare*? That will be the great issue in the bureaucratic state of tomorrow.

If the manufacturers seem to be bracing themselves for a further elaboration of economic nationalism in Australia, what are the primary producers going to do? Their future is uncertain. They face poor marketing prospects in the United Kingdom, except for a temporary upswing immediately after the war. The butter-producers are menaced by margarine, the wool-producers by a variety of substitutes. And the protected primary producers stand to receive a heavier blow than their brethren who have always operated on the basis of the world price. Says Dr. Ian Clunies Ross:

Primary industries will face a black future if postwar reconstruction problems are seen by this or other countries as a means to protect secondary industries. If this is the world approach to a new world order, there is no hope for our primary industries. We shall have reached our peak in this country, and must decline.

Dr. Ross recommends that the primary producers set their various houses in order. Farmers should make full use of latest scientific developments in an effort to rationalize their industries. In this fashion they will be in the strongest possible competitive position. Speaking to the dairy farmers he stated that Australian animal-breeding methods are fifty years out of date; that milk production per cow is very low; that dairymen cannot continue to rely on natural pasture grasses; and that fodder conservation as a protection against slumps in production due to drought is insufficiently practiced. He has also publicly stated that the wool-growers are not making full use of existing scientific knowledge in their field of production. But Dr. Ross recognizes that efficiency without export markets will not help much. He therefore emphasizes that only through international action to raise living standards, including nutritional standards, can Australian primary industries be put on a sound footing. His voice is added to those of other Australians in demanding that his countrymen cultivate a broad outlook on world economic problems, not merely to be generous to others, but in the interest of their own survival. Otherwise, he says, it will be a matter of permanently lowered living standards, in Australia as elsewhere, and periodical rounds of destructive war for the control of resources.

Out of the vexed tangle of "interests" working at cross-purposes no clear trading policy can possibly emerge if all parties are to be fobbed off with unsatisfactory concessions. Secondary industry is unlikely to halt its struggle for full mastery of the domestic market. After this war, it will probably also try for a share of the Eastern trade, bucking Japan, the United States, and others. The primary producers will certainly not beat the retreat Dr. Ross suggests may be inevitable, without a protracted struggle. Australia is rapidly approaching the day when the city and country interests will intensify the battle in which they have been long engaged. Like so many "new" countries—Argentina, for example—Australia has developed a so-called balanced domestic economy, but has failed to think out her problem as a trading nation. The time has now come to do so. The new cry must be for a balanced external trading policy.

Such a policy is exceedingly difficult to formulate. It cannot be glibly phrased by hardened practitioners of political legerdemain. The task of the Australian leaders will be to rise above sectional interests and see the problem whole—whole for Australia and for the world. The criterion must be the welfare of the people, not the aggrandizement of any sectional interest. The postwar slogan must be welfare economics, not power economics. When these two principles conflict, power must give way. All industries will, of course, identify their survival with the national welfare. Such protestations are an expected part of "sectional" ideology. But the job will be to see through these protestations to the truth of the matter. Hard though it may be on those engaged in them, some industries may be assessed too costly in terms of their depressive effect on living standards to be retained by artificial protection. They must go. Australia, particularly, cannot afford to adopt a narrow nationalistic economic policy. It is not only that she lives in an explosive part of the world; it is also that Australia is, by the very structure of her economy, intensely concerned with export trade—with international trading relations. She must "spread" her trade more widely. She simply cannot afford to let the international outlook become the foible of her intelligentsia while her practical men are devoted to an intense economic nationalism. In this respect her problem is analogous to that of the United States. In both countries the "practical" men are the most impractical of theorists, the most dangerous of irresponsible ideologues.

Underlying all arguments about social and economic policy in Australia is the population question. No public issue has been more often canvassed. But it is one of those questions about which men rarely change their prejudices. Both Mr. Jones and Mr. Hume-

Cook state that their programs will increase the population. The same idea is in Professor Bland's mind; it has assuredly not been overlooked by the Catholic Bishops; nor by the labor reformers. The better the living conditions in Australia, the more attractive it will appear to intending immigrants. Nothing would please the Australians more than a *painless* rise in population, anything up to twenty or thirty millions.

There are signs that Australia is reverting during the present war to the easy optimism about immigration prospects (preferably British immigrants) which beguiled her during the last war and on into the ensuing peace. How false those hopes turned out to be, what millions of money were wasted trying to turn them into reality, what a number of disgruntled people were finally assisted to emigrate from Australia—all these things are being forgotten. There will be just as many difficulties after this war. The emigrants from Europe, who will be numerous, will hardly appeal to the Australians. The types they want either will not want to emigrate or will be induced by their governments to stay at home to participate in reconstruction. Englishmen are not fighting today for the privilege of leaving England in favor of Australia, once the fighting is over. However, a good deal depends upon economic conditions in postwar England. It may just be that the "new poverty" which the war is creating, especially among middle-class people, will continue into the peace and act as a stimulus to emigration.

The Australians cannot abandon their hopes of a bigger population. For it is not only economically necessary if they are to make full use of their resources; it is also politically necessary to their survival in a world increasingly hostile to holding resources out of use. Personally I do not think the Australians can be legitimately reproached for holding resources out of use. I think they have done a good job in exploiting their continent. Most of the foreign comments on Australia's resources—her so-called "great-open-spaces"—reflect a comprehensive ignorance about Australian conditions. But it must be recognized that Australia can *theoretically* support far more people than it does at present. This is the criterion by which it will be judged. That is a vital difference between an actual population of seven million and a theoretical optimum of thirty million.

Out of such differences political issues are made. In the postwar period Australia will be thinking hard of how her social and economic policies will influence the growth of population. It is a question from which there is no escape. But what is the practical answer?

AUSTRALIAN foreign policy is not a matter about which the people are universally or consistently alert. There is an upswing of interest in times of acute tension or threat of war, but a decided slump in times of calm and peace. The *Sydney Morning Herald* declared on May 6, 1941—surely a time when all Australians should have been keenly alert—the "Australian public . . . is little interested in foreign policy as such and out of a feeling of complete loyalty to the Mother Country has been disposed to think that major questions affecting the Empire's relations with the rest of the world can be settled well enough in Whitehall." This does not tell us why such an attitude of renunciation of primary national responsibility is widely held. Any explanation would lead us into a Serbonian bog of notes on tradition, newspaper practices, educational foibles, and so on without end. Suffice it to say that the viewpoint is the key to both varieties of Australian isolationism against which the intelligentsia has conducted a vendetta for many years. Its efforts are beginning to bear fruit.

One variety of isolationism arises from the desire to sink Australia's identity in that of the British Empire-Commonwealth as a whole, or even to have Australia, no matter what other dominions may think or do, identify herself with the current foreign policy of His Majesty's Government in the United Kingdom. The political catch-cry is, "Follow Britain!" If Australia did this she would have no *political* foreign policy at all, but would confine herself to trade and technical matters exclusively. She would, in effect, be isolated from the international political world, taking refuge behind the shield of Britain. The other variety of isolationism is less important as a political force. It represents a reaction against the first and expresses itself through the contention that Australia should keep her men and war materials at home in time of universal strife like the present, the better to guarantee Australia's survival. The true partisans of this point of view are remarkably few. Their number is sometimes exaggerated for political effect, especially when the conservatives argue that this represents the logic of the Labour outlook. Labour, as a matter of fact, has tried only to temper the complete identification with the United Kingdom which is advocated by the right-wing conservatives. To them Labour becomes "isolationist" when it says that Australia should express her views on Imperial foreign policy promptly and with emphasis; and that she should take primary responsibility for the defense of Australia, determining the disposition of her men and materials accordingly. During the 1937 general election the Labour party was tagged isolationist. John Curtin replied, ". . . I would say that never, at any time, have I said that Australia, under a Labour government, would not assist Great Britain in time of war. What I have said is that Australia would be rendering a first-class service to the British Empire if she keeps Australia safe for the British Empire." The struggle really boils down, in British terms, to one between the "colonial mentality" and the mentality of the thoughtful dominion nationalists.

In recent years the Australian intelligentsia has striven to find a middle ground between the colonial and the out-and-out nationalist point of view. The successive governments of the Commonwealth have slowly moved in this direction also. Their progress can best be illustrated by recounting the evolution of the Department of External Affairs. This stepchild of the government was first set up in 1901 as a division within the Prime Minister's office. Its functions were very limited. During the First World War it was disbanded. Reconstituted in 1921, it was not definitely separated from the Prime Minister's department until 1935. It was then organized in two principal sections, the Political Section dealing with "foreign policy generally and with Imperial and inter-Dominion relations," and the International Cooperation Section dealing with League of Nations affairs and international treaties. Two years later Australia appointed its first diplomatic officer in a foreign country, an Australian Counsellor in the British Embassy at Washington. But only after the outbreak of the Second World War did Australia begin to appoint ministers abroad, thus trailing years behind Canada, South Africa, and Eire. By the end of 1941 Australian diplomatic representation abroad was:

Minister to the United States, Richard Gardiner Casey.
Minister to Japan, Sir John Greig Latham.
Minister to China, Sir Frederick William Eggleston.
High Commissioner in the United Kingdom, Stanley Melbourne Bruce.
High Commissioner in Canada, Sir Thomas William Glasgow.
Official Representative in New Caledonia, Bertram Charles Ballard.
Official Representative in Singapore, Vivian Gordon Bowden.

There are semi-diplomatic representatives in Egypt and the Netherlands East Indies. Australia has, therefore, developed a fairly elaborate diplomatic service by injecting new elements into its representation abroad. (A special war-time development is the stationing of an Australian Minister in London as a special liaison officer between the Australian and United Kingdom cabinets.)

Nevertheless, in May, 1941, a newspaper described the home office of the service under the headlines: "Cinderella Department —Neglect of External Affairs—Staff Scanty and Underpaid." The Minister, Sir Frederick Stewart, endorsed the article with the words, "It is very correct." In sharp contrast to American practice, where the Secretary of State ranks first among the Cabinet members, the Australian Minister for External Affairs is not ranked as a Senior Cabinet member. When the Cabinet was expanded and reorganized in June, 1941, he was not even included in the inner War Cabinet. There is still a long way to go in Australia toward granting proper recognition to the importance of its foreign relations, not to mention the formulation of unmistakably Australian views and policies on the issues which come up for discussion and settlement.

The problems of external affairs about which Australians must form opinions are divisible into three groups: relations with the British Commonwealth and Empire; relations in the Pacific Basin, especially with the United States, Japan, China, the Netherlands East Indies, and the other islands; and relations with the rest of the world. If the past and present are true guides to the future, Australia will remain closely associated with the British Commonwealth, though not too deeply concerned about the colonial empire of the United Kingdom. It will retain its diplomatic representation in Pacific Basin countries and even raise some of the representatives in rank. As far as the rest of the world is concerned, Australia's attitudes will be determined in large measure by the extent to which she develops trade contacts and the character of the international political machinery that is set up after the war.

Though historically Australia has been slow to take in the full implications of her geographical location, there is every reason to suppose that her position in the Pacific Basin will play a more and more decisive role in the formation of the ideas and attitudes of her people. Although I have been assured again and again during the Second World War that the attention of Australians is riveted on the British Isles, I still interpret this as a logical and inevitable consequence of the fact that what happens to Britain will in very large measure determine what happens in the Pacific. Certainly few writers for the Australian press have any illusions about this, however much they may obscure it by understatement and by an inflexible traditionalism with regard to international affairs. As a leading newspaper writer has put it:

Just look around you. There are 7,000,000 of us occupying the world's Fifth Continent. Next door is the most crowded, poverty-stricken, restless, hungry corner of the globe. China, India, Japan—a thousand million people, half the world's population, living on the world's lowest standard of living, grown aware in the last few decades of better ways of living, grown envious of occidental habits, appetites, and privileges. Are they waiting for something? Have they been waiting for a long time?

This juxtaposition of Australia and Asia is not going to be changed by the war, no matter who wins, or what takes place in the Pacific. Australia is and must remain a nation deeply concerned about what is going on in her Near North. Australia cannot by any stretch of the imagination finish with the Near North during the present war, with Japan making her all-out bid for East Asian supremacy. The prospective defeat of the aspirations of the most aggressive power in the Pacific will not guarantee that

Australia can revert to her curiously unreal attitude of not, after all, belonging in the Pacific context.

The truth that in the end geography always triumphs in the affairs of nations has been resisted by the Australians for a long time, but they are not apt to be allowed to forget it in the years ahead. They must make their future as a Pacific Ocean people— and no matter what happens. Professor A. C. V. Melbourne has put the point with particular vigor: "Australia's interest in the Pacific area differs greatly from the interest of the United Kingdom. Australia is in the Pacific area for all time, but the United Kingdom might withdraw completely from the Far East and still be an influence in world affairs."

In the future Australia need not basically modify her relations with the United Kingdom. She can still base her European policy on that of the United Kingdom. What change in emphasis takes place will naturally reflect Australia's increasing maturity (and Britain's increasing dependence on extra-European support), not any change of heart or of interest. After the war the dominions are going to be much stronger than in the years just passed. Their increasing strength has always resulted in modifications of their relations with the United Kingdom. A Fourth British Empire will certainly emerge from the Second World War.

As to the Pacific, Australia's outlook is bound to differ from the attitudes which sufficed in the past. Has not Robert Menzies, echoing many earlier prophets, declared: "We will never realize our destiny as a nation until we realize that we are one of the Pacific powers"? It is inconceivable, therefore, that Australia will ever again be as divorced from the Pacific context as she was when the Second World War broke out. Just as the First World War made her more conscious of her geographical position than she had ever been up to that time, so the Second World War has further intensified her sense that she is a Pacific nation. The future of the Pacific insures that this sense will continue to be intensified in the years to come. There can be no retreat. Australian representatives have already appeared and will stay in the great capitals where the issues of the Pacific Basin are debated—Washington, Tokyo, Chungking, Batavia. Soon they will appear elsewhere in Asia and perhaps also in South America.

What attitudes does Australia bring to world affairs? The Australians are a pragmatic people, in some respects even more pragmatic than the Americans. They have little taste for abstract ideological exercises, either in their domestic or foreign policies. They often profess not thoroughly to understand the more abstract phases of the American foreign outlook. But they thoroughly understand negotiation and will accept compromises. They are astute actors in public affairs. They will bring to international politics a reasonable willingness to examine problems on their merits, and if they insist on viewing them from the Australian angle, they will be no more guilty of self-regardful thinking than most peoples. They may in the beginning express their views and conclusions with less heed for the feelings of others than is customary with nations of greater diplomatic experience and tolerance for the foibles of foreigners. Their easily forgiven provincialism will slowly diminish as their contacts with foreign nations multiply.

While there are intense "Imperialist-nationalists" of the William Morris Hughes tradition in high places in Australia, and even, here and there, nationalists with little Imperial enthusiasm, it should always be remembered that there are also Australians deeply convinced of the need for broad international co-operation and formal machinery for facilitating it. These men look far beyond the bounds of Australia and the British Empire-Commonwealth. There are among them strong partisans of the League of Nations. There are many who hope for regional machinery to handle Pacific problems. There are more who hope for long-term co-operation with the United States in the Pacific, even though they are not certain as to how to establish it or carry it on. Indeed, it would be extremely easy to conclude on a note of lofty idealism, tricked out with beautifully rhetorical quotations. But it is well to recall the sober words of an Australian scholar who said, in assessing his own nation in 1941, "if Australia, as a victor, will not seek a vindictive peace, neither will she seek to alter the world. Her frame of mind is conservative. She believes in the preservation of democracy, but has not so far shown much inclination to promote far-reaching social revolutions, either at home or abroad."

APPENDIXES

A. CHRONOLOGY

1770 Captain Cook sailed along eastern coast of Australia, then called New Holland.

1788 Arrival of "First Fleet" and establishment of settlement at Sydney, January 26th, now celebrated annually as Australia Day.

1792 Visit of American ship *Philadelphia,* first foreign trading vessel.

1793 Arrival of first free immigrants, eleven in number.

1796 Discovery of coal at Newcastle.

1797 Introduction of merino sheep.

1803 First Australian wool taken to England.
First settlement in Tasmania (then called Van Diemen's Land).

1810 First race meeting.

1813 First crossing of Blue Mountains.

1814 Use of name Australia suggested by Matthew Flinders, explorer. (The name means, "the South Land.")

1824 New South Wales becomes a Crown Colony.
First manufacture of sugar.
First settlement in what is now Queensland.

1825 Beginning of decentralization of government with the proclamation of Tasmania as a separate colony.

1827 First official claim of British sovereignty over all Australia.

1829 First settlement in Western Australia, at Perth.

1831 First assisted immigration.

1834 First settlement in what is now Victoria, at Portland Bay.

1835 Foundation of Melbourne by John Batman, who, tradition

has it, selected the site with the remark, "This is the place for a village."

1836   First settlement in South Australia, at Adelaide.

1839   Discovery of Port Darwin.

1840   Abolition of transportation to New South Wales.

1843   First Representative Constitution, New South Wales.

1846   Initiation of meat preserving.

1847   First iron smelting, New South Wales.

1849   Heavy emigration to California gold fields.

1851   Payable gold discovered, New South Wales. Beginning of rushes.
       Victoria proclaimed a colony, formed from part of New South Wales.

1855   First railway opened for traffic.

1856   Responsible government initiated in New South Wales, Victoria, South Australia, and Tasmania.

1858   Sydney, Melbourne, and Adelaide in telegraphic communication.

1859   Queensland proclaimed a separate colony, also formed from part of New South Wales. With the proclamation of Queensland, all the present-day Australian states had been established.

1860   Center of continent first reached, by McDouall Stuart.

1861   Anti-Chinese riots on New South Wales gold fields. Beginning of efforts to restrict Chinese immigration.

1862   Continent first crossed from south to north.

1864   First sugar made from Queensland cane.

1867   Victoria imposes first protective tariff.

1870   Imperial troops withdrawn.

1872   Cable connection with Europe established.

1873   Mail service to San Francisco established.

1876 Australia and New Zealand connected by cable.

1877 Western Australia connected by telegraph with South Australia and the other eastern colonies.

1879 First artesian bore driven.

1880 First Australian telephone exchange, Melbourne.

1883 Discovery of silver at Broken Hill.

1888 Centennial celebrations at Sydney.

1890 Western Australia granted responsible government, the last Australian colony to win this form.

1891 Labor elects 35 members of the lower house, New South Wales. Beginning of labor's real political power.

1901 Proclamation of Commonwealth. First Federal Parliament opened.

1907 Sydney and Melbourne connected by telephone.

1908 Theodore Roosevelt's "Great White Fleet" visits Australia.

1911 First Federal Census. Northern Territory taken over by Commonwealth. Compulsory military training begins.

1914 Outbreak of First World War.

1915 First steel produced by Broken Hill Proprietary at Newcastle.

1918 Australian population reaches 5,000,000.

1919 Peace Conference.

1921 First wireless press message received from England.

1925 American fleet visits Australia.

1927 Seat of Federal Government transferred to Canberra.

1930 Export prices reach half 1928 level.

1931 First England-Australia air mail. (On regular basis, 1934)

1932 Imperial Economic Conference at Ottawa.

1938 Sesquicentennial celebrations, New South Wales.

1939 Outbreak of Second World War.

B. STATISTICS

AREA

Commonwealth:	2,974,581	square miles	(39% tropical)
New South Wales:	309,442	"	"
Victoria:	87,884	"	"
Queensland:	670,500	"	"	(53% tropical)
South Australia:	380,070	"	"
Western Australia:	975,920	"	"	(37% tropical)
Tasmania:	26,215	"	"
Northern Territory:	523,620	"	"	(81% tropical)
Australian Capital Territory (including Jervis Bay)	940	"	"

POPULATION
(*1938 figures*)

Commonwealth	6,929,671
New South Wales	2,735,695
Sydney	1,288,720
Victoria	1,873,760
Melbourne	1,035,600
Queensland	1,004,150
Brisbane	325,890
South Australia	595,109
Adelaide	321,410
Western Australia	462,461
Perth	220,330
Tasmania	241,407
Hobart	63,250
Northern Territory	5,645
Darwin	1,600 (approx.)
Austral. Cap. Terr.	11,464
Canberra	10,000 (approx.)

NATIONALITY (i.e., ALLEGIANCE), 1933

The census of 1933 showed that 99.1% of the people living in Australia, excluding fullblood aborigines, were British subjects. Of these 86.3% were native-born Australians. The 99.1% included 6,569,518 persons, leaving but 60,259 (plus 62 "not stated") in the "foreign" category, as follows:

Chinese	7,792	Norwegian	1,238
Danish	1,279	Polish	1,757
Dutch	915	Russian	2,055
Estonian	838	Spanish	596
Finnish	1,062	Swedish	1,307
French	1,647	Swiss	952
German	3,672	U. S. A.	2,557
Greek	5,652	Yugoslav	2,826
Italian	17,658	Other	4,309
Japanese	2,084		

ABORIGINAL CENSUS, JUNE 30, 1938

	Fullblood	Half-Caste	Total
New South Wales	809	9,611	10,420
Victoria	92	647	739
Queensland	12,160	6,461	18,621
So. Australia	2,081	2,148	4,229
West. Australia	21,882	4,602	26,484
Tasmania	1	256	257
No. Territory	14,354	907	15,261
Austral. Cap. Terr.	.....	86	86
Commonwealth	51,379	24,718	76,097

LABOR FORCE

Although based on the census of 1933, the following analysis is still given in the Official Year Book for 1939.

Industry Group	Persons
Fishing & Trapping	14,611
Agricultural, Pastoral, Dairying	547,787
Forestry	26,133
Mining & Quarrying	68,520
Industrial	
Manufacturing	511,511
Building	107,466
Roads, Earthworks, etc.	217,656
Other	29,588
Total Industrial	866,171
Transport & Communication	233,893
Commerce & Finance	451,172
Public Administration & Professional	232,212
Entertainment, Sport, Recreation	24,250
Personal & Domestic Service	242,378
No Industry or Industry not stated	172,403 *
Pensioners	286,091
Total Breadwinners	3,155,621
Dependants	3,474,218
Total	6,629,839

Professor F. R. E. Mauldon and Associates in their *Mechanization in Australian Industries* (1938) make the following general comments on the labor force:

As between 1901 and 1933 the occupied or breadwinning population increased by 93%. Breadwinners in rural occupations were 23.5% of the total in 1901 but had fallen to 20.5% of the total in 1933. Breadwinners in manufacturing, building, and constructional occupations were 28% in 1901 but had increased to 32% of the total in 1933. The actual increase in the rural group between the two years was by 29.2% (i.e., from 424,000 to 548,000), the actual increase in the manufacturing-building-constructional group by 100.9% (i.e., from 431,000 to 866,000). These two groups account for more than half the breadwin-

* Includes unemployed persons for whom industry not stated.

ning population at any time. Their changing numerical relationship is the most outstanding feature in the occupation-composition of the Australian population since the beginning of the century.

In short, Mauldon and Associates find, in the figures covering a very long term of years, clear evidence of the rise of manufacturing to a place of great importance in the Australian economy. Really to define when it made its greatest advances would require the breaking down of the figures into shorter periods than 1901-1933. For some indications on this point, the reader can recall the remarks in the text of this book. These figures also bear out the point that if Australia wants rapidly to increase her population (and is able to do so), manufacturing development is a more hopeful course than further elaboration of rural industries, especially when there are large possibilities of increasing rural productivity without increasing the number of farm units.

Colin Clark in his Joseph Fisher Lecture for 1938, entitled *Australian Economic Progress Against a World Background,* points out that the distribution of the occupied population in several countries is as follows (table shortened here):

	Primary (Agric., Pastoral, etc.)	Secondary (Manufacturing)	Tertiary (Services)
Australia	24.4	29.4	46.2
Great Britain	6.4	43.9	49.7
New Zealand	25.7	24.3	50
U. S. A.	19.3	31.1	49.6
Japan	36.4	25	38.6

Many conclusions can be drawn from this table, but for our purposes it will suffice to quote the following from Clark:

In a progressive modern community, adequately supplied with natural resources, the labour of 10 per cent, or less, of the population ought to suffice to produce the community's whole requirements of primary produce. If the proportion of primary producers in the working population is much above that, the country will have to export a large part of this primary output. Australia, employing only 24 per cent of its population in primary production, exports half its output of primary produce.

This goes far to explain what has seemed inexplicable to many Americans to whom I have talked about Australia: that a country chiefly known to the world as an exporter of foodstuffs and raw materials nevertheless employs but a small proportion of her workers in primary production. It also explains why so many Australians are town and city dwellers and why, with increases in rural productive efficiency, this will continue to be the case in the visible future. The only escape from this is to establish by fiat a rural subsistence peasantry, which I regard as a madhouse, hopelessly retrogressive idea, though it is solemnly advocated by the Catholic writer Paul McGuire in *Australia, Her Heritage, Her Future* (1939). McGuire wants a subsistence peasantry to breed soldiers to defend Australia, and for other purposes.

PRODUCTION

AREA UNDER CROP, 1937-38. ACRES.

New South Wales	6,470,160
Victoria	4,662,354
Queensland	1,618,738
So. Australia	4,736,428
West. Australia	4,201,548
Tasmania	255,260
No. Territory	1,612
Austral. Cap. Terr.	5,631

Total 21,951,731

PRINCIPAL CROPS AS PERCENTAGE OF CROPPED AREA, 1937-38

	Wheat	Hay	Oats	Barley	Sugar Cane	Corn	Potatoes
New South Wales	69	12	4	.1	.3	2.	.4
Victoria	58	23	8	3	—	.5	.8
Queensland	23	5	1	.5	21	11	.8
So. Australia	67	12	7	9	—	—	.1

	Wheat	*Hay*	*Oats*	*Barley*	*Sugar Cane*	*Corn*	*Potatoes*
West. Australia	72	10	9	1	—	—	.1
Tasmania	8	29	13	4	—	—	13
No. Territory	—	—	—	—	—	—	
Austral. Cap. Terr.	36	49	3	—	—	.2	.6
Commonwealth	63	14	6	3	1.6	1.4	.5

WHEAT YIELD PER ACRE, 1937-38. BUSHELS.

New South Wales	12.3
Victoria	17.9
Queensland	10
So. Australia	13.7
West. Australia	11.9
Tasmania	24.9
No. Territory	—
Austral. Cap. Terr.	24.
Commonwealth	13.6

Total wheat production, 1937-38: 187,255,673 bushels.
Net wheat exports, 1937-38: 124,764,592 bushels.

LIVESTOCK, 1937.

	Horses	*Cattle*	*Sheep*	*Pigs*
New South Wales	528,625	3,019,581	51,563,181	356,765
Victoria	359,106	1,880,429	18,863,467	285,259
Queensland	445,916	5,959,165	22,497,970	282,941
So. Australia	197,334	324,163	8,904,402	66,647
West. Australia	151,067	740,241	8,732,076	64,598
Tasmania	31,578	254,812	2,520,950	43,067
No. Territory	31,662	891,640	28,856	388
Austral. Cap. Terr.	1,225	8,325	263,616	417
Commonwealth	1,746,513	13,078,356	113,372,518	1,100,082

WOOL PRODUCTION, 1937-1938. POUNDS.

New South Wales	496,824,150
Victoria	178,890,131
Queensland	174,751,280
So. Australia	86,606,388
West. Australia	70,684,855
Tasmania	15,598,500
No. Territory	35,000
Commonwealth	1,023,390,304

LIVESTOCK SLAUGHTERED, 1937

	Cattle	Sheep & Lambs	Pigs
New South Wales	1,223,320	6,875,496	537,038
Victoria	971,338	8,128,544	509,041
Queensland	1,266,412	1,120,729	513,369
So. Australia	167,451	1,588,507	167,997
West. Australia	145,375	1,227,843	104,918
Tasmania	48,451	372,547	68,823
No. Territory	2,456	——	——
Austral. Cap. Terr.	2,693	25,375	1,244
Commonwealth	3,827,496	19,339,041	1,897,430

DAIRY COWS, 1937

	Total	Milking
New South Wales	1,047,332	757,714
Victoria	952,906	784,369
Queensland	958,858	701,258
So. Australia	164,903	122,447
West. Australia	124,278	94,116
Tasmania	92,493	77,325
No. Territory	——	——
Austral. Cap. Terr.	1,129	845
Commonwealth	3,368,899	2,538,074

DAIRY PRODUCTION, 1937-38. POUNDS.

	Butter	*Cheese*	*Cond's'd Milk, etc.*
New South Wales	120,882,732	8,004,873	4,066,123
Victoria	141,321,445	16,466,038	52,064,898
Queensland	118,244,260	11,963,445	——
So. Australia	22,428,298	15,516,879	——
West. Australia	15,373,334	885,418	——
Tasmania	11,997,323	3,370,189	——
No. Territory	——	——	——
Austral. Cap. Terr.	14,218	——	——
Commonwealth	430,261,610	56,606,842	incomplete

SECONDARY INDUSTRIES, 1937-38.

New South Wales	Factories	9,097
	Hands	224,861
Victoria	Factories	9,241
	Hands	201,793
Queensland	Factories	3,063
	Hands	52,119
So. Australia	Factories	1,890
	Hands	44,084
West. Australia	Factories	2,066
	Hands	23,133
Tasmania	Factories	948
	Hands	13,170
Commonwealth	Factories	26,395
	Hands	559,160

Factory: "an industrial establishment in which four or more hands are employed or in which power other than hand is used."

MINERAL PRODUCTION, 1937

Mineral	Unit	N.S.W.	Vic.	Q'land.	S.A.	W.A.	Tas.	N.T.	Com.
Antimony	ton	144	295	1	—	565	—	—	1,005
Chromite	"	459	—	—	—	—	—	—	459
Coal	"	10,051,519	257,945	1,120,179	—	553,510	91,121	—	12,074,274
Brown Coal	"	—	3,393,919	—	—	—	—	—	3,393,919
Copper	"	3,627	—	5,149	340	35	12,420	7	21,578
Gold	troy oz.	68,607	145,799	127,281	6,962	1,000,647	20,276	11,563	1,381,135
Iron	ton	677	—	4,479	1,866,414	—	61	—	1,871,631
Lead	"	*	—	38,474	12	—	9,117	—	incomp.
Manganese	"	107	—	1,035	—	—	—	—	1,142
Mica	cwt	—	—	—	840	—	—	832	1,672
Crude Petrol	gal	—	9,372	—	—	—	—	—	9,372
Salt	ton	—	—	—	73,558	—	—	—	incomp.
Scheelite	cwt	202	—	38	—	—	—	—	240
Silver-Lead	ton	281,624	—	—	—	6,163	—	26	287,813
Tin	"	1,143	218	1,171	—	80	1,090	41	3,743
Wolfram	cwt	915	—	1,963	—	—	5,820	5,831	14,529
Zinc	ton	219,838	—	27,598	—	—	23,481	—	270,917

* Mined in N.S.W., but treated outside state, see silver-lead and zinc.

CLASSIFIED BY NUMBER OF HANDS, 1937-38

	Under 4	4	5-10	11-20	21-50	51-100	101 up
New South Wales	2,616	878	2,431	1,289	1,054	435	394
Victoria	3,229	741	2,221	1,267	1,008	405	370
Queensland	1,081	309	812	385	266	109	101
South Australia	481	211	625	280	237	90	56
Western Australia	979	104	508	215	180	55	25
Tasmania	257	133	355	107	66	16	14
Commonwealth	8,643	2,376	6,952	3,543	2,811	1,110	960

FACTORY EMPLOYEES BY AGE, 1938, PERCENTAGE.

	Under 16	16-21	Adult
New South Wales	6	26	68
Victoria	6	25	69
Queensland	6	22	72
South Australia	6	22	72
Western Australia	5	23	72
Tasmania	6	21	73
Commonwealth	6	25	69

VALUE FACTORY OUTPUT, £ A., 1937-38

New South Wales	214,883,557
Victoria	157,050,725
Queensland	59,639,403
South Australia	36,239,937
West. Australia	19,643,960
Tasmania	11,321,559
Commonwealth	498,779,141

HORSEPOWER IN FACTORIES USING STEAM, GAS, OIL,
ELECTRICITY, OR WATER POWER, 1937-38

	Ordinarily in use
New South Wales	604,522
Victoria	353,189
Queensland	178,344
So. Australia	96,285
West. Australia	61,544
Tasmania	42,367
Commonwealth	1,336,261

CENTRAL ELECTRIC STATIONS, 1937-38

	Effective Capacity, H.P.
New South Wales	769,377
Victoria	421,851
Queensland	152,056
So. Australia	158,569
West. Australia	88,605
Tasmania	117,843
Commonwealth	1,708,301

SAWMILL OUTPUT OF NATIVE TIMBER, 1937-1938

	1,000 sup. ft.
New South Wales	168,042
Victoria	141,439
Queensland	208,098
South Australia	16,167
Western Australia	129,986
Tasmania	83,009
Commonwealth	746,741

C. READING LIST

It is an unfortunate fact that American libraries have generally failed to build up satisfactory Australiana sections. The Library of Congress has a rich collection of Australian government papers, but its book collection is not of equivalent standard. Other large libraries are rich in specialized directions; that of Harvard University has an excellent collection of Australian law material, and Stamford has a collection of early Australian pamphlets. In general, however, most public and university libraries have only small collections of Australiana, and the books are apt to be of uneven value. The publication of Australian books in America has been similarly haphazard, though New York publishing concerns like Macmillan, Longmans, Green, and Oxford University Press, whose London houses have published numerous Australian books, often can supply these for American purchasers.

The writer owns what is considered to be the largest collection of Australiana in private hands in America. It includes many books, pamphlets, etc., not available elsewhere in this country. For conditions under which this collection may be consulted, write the author setting out purpose and needs.

The reading list that follows is based, with the exceptions specified, on books published in the United States and presumably available in a large number of American libraries.

Reference: The Australian Encyclopedia, edited by Jose, Carter, and Tucker (latest edition, Sydney, 1927) is a two volume work found in many libraries. It contains a wide range of factual material necessary for the formation of judgments on Australian affairs. *The Cambridge History of the British Empire,* Volume VII, Part I, deals with Australia. It was published in New York in 1933 and also provides an immense quantity of facts, though it is sparing in interpretation. *The Official Year Book of the Commonwealth of Australia* is the indispensable statistical record. It also includes some factual articles and a short bibliography. The Commonwealth National Library publishes an *Annual Catalogue of Australian Publications,* which materially assists the foreign student in keeping up to date. *The Economic Record* (Journal of the Economic Society of Australia and New Zealand) is found in some American libraries. Also occasionally to be found is the most distinguished Australian magazine of general circulation, *The Australian Quarterly*. The former began publication in 1925, the latter in 1928. In 1937 the *Austral-Asiatic Bulletin* was launched as a periodical primarily concerned with presenting the point of view on Pacific problems of the Australian intelligentsia. The historians established a journal for the cultivation of their interests in 1940: *Historical Studies, Australia and New Zealand*. Australian popular weeklies are rarely available in America. *The Bulletin,* which older Americans recall as the most original and most Australian of Australian weeklies, has drifted away from its old moorings and now presents a minority point of view, though with much of its characteristic vigor. There is no Australian daily paper which gives a "national coverage." Perhaps the *Sydney Morning Herald* is most frequently found in American libraries.

American Magazines and Newspapers: Occasional articles on Australian affairs are found in many American magazines, but none pretends to cover the subject comprehensively or with regularity. These articles are listed in *Readers' Guide to Periodical Literature*. It is my impression that *Asia* publishes articles on Australia most regularly of all the magazines of general circulation. Newspaper coverage of Australian affairs is erratic. I have long been of the opinion that only those rare persons who have a working knowledge of the Australian background and foreground can derive much useful information from the items printed. Personally I rely upon the *New York Times* for my current information on Australia, though occasionally I pick up items from other papers. The *Christian Science Monitor,* the *Baltimore Sun,* the *Chicago Tribune,* and the *New York Herald Tribune* also publish special Australian correspondence. But most American papers depend upon the great press services. There has been a marked improvement in the quantity and quality of the news items coming from Australia since the outbreak of the present war.

Books of Historical, Interpretative, or Informational Character:

The best book on Australia by an Australian published in an American edition is *Australia* by W. K. Hancock (1931). Professor Hancock is well known to students of British affairs as the author of those indispensable books, *Survey of British Commonwealth Affairs*, Volume I, *Problems of Nationality, 1918-1936*, and Volume II, Part 1, *Problems of Economic Policy, 1918-1939*, which also contain valuable material on Australia, critically presented. Paul McGuire's *Australia, Her Heritage, Her Future* (1939) is another discussion of Australia by an Australian. It is brilliantly written and a delight to read, but it is the reverse of systematic and on controversial points presents only the Roman Catholic outlook. *Australia Advances* by David M. Dow (1938) is of lighter weight than either of the two books just mentioned, but it is worth reading because it presents the views of a man who represented Australia in the United States for many years. *Australia in the World Crisis* by Douglas Copland (1934) recounts the measures taken to combat the Great Depression and has the added interest of presenting the views of an economist who took a conspicuous part in formulating the various schemes. (To my mind a better book on this period is *Economic Planning in Australia*, 1929-1936 by W. R. MacLaurin (1937), an American economist, but unfortunately the book has only had an English edition.) A survey of the Australian position *circa* 1931 is *An Economic Survey of Australia*, published as the November 1931 number of *The Annals*. It includes valuable articles by various Australian economists, historians, and publicists.

Australian Discovery is a two volume compilation by Ernest Scott of narratives by the explorers of Australia, published in New York in 1929. *Human Australasia* by Charles F. Thwing (1923) is an informal account of the education systems of Australia and New Zealand by an American. *The Life of Vice-Admiral William Bligh* by George Mackaness (1936) is the most comprehensive biography of this famous navigator. Dr. Mackaness is an Australian. (If it can be found, *Rum Rebellion* by Dr. H. V. Evatt deals in greater detail with Bligh's unfortunate experiences as governor of New South Wales. It was published in Sydney in 1938. The foreword was contributed by the present writer.) Ellsworth Huntington's *West of the Pacific* (1925) presents the views of the well-known American geographer. *White Settlers in the Tropics* (1939) by

A. G. Price contains material on the white workers in the Queensland sugar-cane fields. *The Labour Movement in Australasia* by V. S. Clark (1906) is still rewarding reading. Dr. Clark is an American, author of the monumental *History of Manufactures in the United States. Speeches and Documents on the British Dominions,* edited by A. B. Keith for the "World's Classics" series, contains Australian material. Some valuable maps are to be found in *Literary and Historical Atlas of Australasia* which is included in Everyman's Library. Also in this library are *Voyages of Discovery* by Captain Cook, and *A Letter from Sydney* by Edward Gibbon Wakefield, whose ideas on land settlement had considerable influence in Australia.

Sir George Wilkins, the well-known explorer, is an Australian. In 1929 he published *Undiscovered Australia,* an account of a collecting expedition into the back country. *Flying Fox and Drifting Sand* by Francis Ratcliffe (1940) is an immensely engaging account of Mr. Ratcliffe's experiences while carrying out work in Australia for the Council for Scientific and Industrial Research. *The Flight of the Southern Cross* by C. E. Kingsford-Smith and C. T. P. Ulm (1929) is an account of the first flight across the Pacific. Thomas Wood's *Cobbers* (1934) is probably the most popular book on Australia ever written by an Englishman. It is a delightful account of the surface of life in Australia, telling very accurately what it is "like" there. Unfortunately it has worn out its welcome with me because so many Australians had no other answer to my inevitable query, "Well, what do *you* think I should read?" *Koonwarra* by Charles Barrett (1939) is an Australian naturalist's notebook which will please nature lovers. It also contains some pointed reflections on the incredibly bad hotels found in the Australian "outback."

Of varying value are such books as *Knocking About* by Augustus Baker Peirce (1924), the reminiscences of an American who spent from 1860 to 1890 in Australia; Jack McLaren's *My Odyssey* (n.d.); Robert Macdonald's *Opals and Gold* (n.d.); and *Adventures of an Outlaw* by Ralph Rashleigh (1929). The latter purports to be an account of the experiences of a convict in Australia in the early days.

Americans will be interested to know that *A Black Civilization* by the American anthropologist, W. L. Warner (1937) is considered the best account of a tribe of Australian aborigines ever written.

Representative Ph.D. theses on Australian subjects, written by American students attending our universities, are *Australian Social Development* by C. H. Northcott (1918), *British Imperial Preference in Relation to Australia* by V. F. Cleary (1934), *An Introduction to Some Problems of Australian Federalism* by K. O. Warner (1933), and *American Precedents in Australian Federation* by E. E. Hunt (1930). *Nationalism and Education in Australia* by T. F. Mackenzie was published in England in 1935, but the author teaches in America. The late Professor C. D. Allin's *Australasian Preferential Tariffs and Imperial Free Trade* (1929) is far from being a Ph.D. thesis, but rather is an excellent example of an academic monograph.

(Older Americans may wonder at the absence of the books of Henry Demarest Lloyd. Mr. Lloyd's books, excellent studies of experimental social legislation, deal with New Zealand, not Australia.)

Two books not directly concerned with Australia, but containing indispensable information for all who want to understand the problems of the part of the world in which Australia is located, are *The South Seas in the Modern World* by F. M. Kessing (1941) and *The Dutch East Indies* by A. Vandenbosch (1941 edition). Other books which may profitably be read for the same reason are *Labor Problems in the Pacific Mandates* by J. A. Decker (1940), *Savage Civilization* by Tom Harrisson (1937), a study of the New Hebrideans, and Dr. S. M. Lambert's amusing *A Yankee Doctor in Paradise* (1941).

The Institute of Pacific Relations publishes or distributes important books on Australia, including *Australian Standards of Living* by various Australian hands, unfortunately more a general discussion than a specific analysis, and *Land Utilization in Australia* by Professors Wadham and Wood of the University of Melbourne, a detailed survey of a semi-technical character. Jack Shepherd's excellent *Australia's Interests and Policies in the Far East* is included in the I.P.R. Inquiry Series. The World Peace Foundation publishes Fred Alexander's *Australia and the United States,* a pamphlet. Shepherd and Alexander are both Australians.

Little Australian poetry has been published here and, to my knowledge, no drama. Exceptions with regard to poetry are two small pamphlets containing poems by William Baylebridge published in New York in 1935 and 1940. The song "Waltzing Matilda" is available in an American edition. The following is a list of Australian novels which have been published in the United States in recent years.

Katherine Susannah Prichard:
>Working Bullocks (1927)
Coonardoo (1930)
Fay's Circus (1931)

Henry Handel Richardson:
Fortunes of Richard Mahoney (1 vol. ed. 1931)
The Getting of Wisdom (rev. ed. 1931)
The End of a Childhood (short stories, 1934)
Maurice Guest (1908 and later ed.)
Young Cosima (1939)

Frank Dalby Davison:
Red Heifer (1934, Australian title, "Man Shy")

M. Barnard Eldershaw:
A House is Built (1929)
Green Memory (1931)

Leonard Mann:
A Murder in Sydney (1937)

Eleanor Dark:
Return to Coolami (1936)
Sun Across the Sky (1937)
Waterway (1938)
The Timeless Land (1941)

Kylie Tennant:
The Battlers (1941)

Henry Kingsley:
Geoffry Hamlyn (Everyman's Library)

Louis Stone:
Larrikin (1933, Australian title, "Jonah")

Brian Penton:
  Landtakers (1935)

Norman Lindsay:
  Every Mother's Son (1930, English title, "Red Heap")
  Mr. Gresham and Olympus (1932)
  The Magic Pudding (1936)

Novels by Australian writers not mentioned in the text but published in America include *Salute to Freedom* (1938) and *Framed in Hardwood* (1940) by Eric Lowe; *Seven Poor Men of Sydney* by Christina Stead (1935); *Pageant* by G. B. Lancaster (1933); *The Singing Gold* (1929) and *Tharlane* (1930) by Dorothy Cottrell; *Boomerang* by Helen Simpson (1932); *The Madeleine Heritage* (Australian title, "The Montforts") by Martin Mills (1928); and *Happy Valley* by Patrick White (1940).

The above lists do not pretend to be exhaustive surveys of the various fields but are rather designed to suggest that an American reader wishing to lay the foundations of a knowledge and understanding of Australia will find to hand a variety of books published in America. It is when he wishes to go beyond the limits imposed by the resources of American public libraries and publishers that he will find himself handicapped. If he plans to go deeply into any one phase of Australian life, he will soon encounter insuperable obstacles to satisfactory progress.

INDEX

Aborigines, 39-40, 307
Adelaide, 30, 145, 262
Advisory Council on Nutrition, 283
Aeronautical Research Laboratory, 203
Agriculture: beginnings of, 49-50; post-war crisis, 289-291; production and export percentages, 96; protection of, 102-106. *See also* Appendix B
Agricultural Council, 53
Alexander, Fred, 273, 274
Alice Springs, 5, 262
Aluminum, 60, 63
American Revolution, 41
American Rolling Mill Co., 77
American Smelting and Refining Co., 38
Anderson, Judith, 183
Anglo-Japanese Alliance, 221, 248
Animals, native, 34-35
Antimony, 63, 313
Anzac, 224-225
Arbitration Courts, 128-129, 134-142
Archibald, J. F., 168
Armaments Industry, 236-239
Army, 222-223, 224-225, 239. *See also* Anzac, Australian Imperial Force, World War, First, World War, Second
Art, 34, 36, 40, 51, 174-181
Art Galleries, 186-7
Ashton, Julian, 178, 179
Atherton, Tableland, 38
Australia: As Australians see it, 9-25; economic growth, 43-56; exploration of, 43; history, 41-56; name of, 41; population growth, 42
Australian Capital Territory. *See* Canberra
Australian Council for Civil Liberties, 245
Australian Council for Educational Research, 183
Australian Council of Trade Unions, 131, 133, 142, 143, 246
Australian Imperial Force, 225
Australian Workers Union, 68
Aviation, 82-83, 238, 240

Balfour Declaration, 213-214, 215
Ballard, B. C., 296
Bank of New South Wales, 90
Banks, Sir Joseph, 41
Baker, David, 76
Banksia, 36
Barley, 59, 310-311
Bartlett's *Familiar Quotations*, 194
Barton, G. B., 165-166, 167
Baylebridge, William, 169-170, 322
Baynton, Barbara, 169
Bean, C. E. W., 70, 169
Bedford, Randolph, 169
Beef, 59, 95, 195. *See also* Appendix B, 311-312
Birds, native, 35
Birdsall, Paul, 229
Black, Herman, 284, 287
Bland, F. A., 143, 161, 282, 283, 284, 286, 292
Bligh, William, 44-45
Blunden, Godfrey, 172, 173
Boer War, 222
Boldrewood, Rolf, 3, 167
Boote, Henry, 131
Borden, Sir Robert, 214
Boronia, 35
Botany Bay, 41, 42
Bourke, 6
Bowden, V. G., 296
Bowerbird, 35
Boxing, 199
Boyer, R. J. F., 189, 273, 274
Brennan, Christopher, 169, 170
Brent of Bin Bin, 171, 172
Brisbane, 30, 161, 306
Broken Hill, 5, 71ff
Broken Hill Proprietary Ltd., 54, 246, 265, 285; history of, 71-79, 93; 1892 strike, 124-126
Brooke-Popham, Sir Robert, 251, 256, 259
Brownlee, John, 181
Bruce, Stanley Melbourne, 229, 282, 296
Bull, John W., 50

Bulletin, The, 168, 318
Bunny, Rupert, 178
Burdett, Basil, 176
Burma Road, 251
Bush, 32-34
Business concerns, 93-94
Butler, I. A., 114
Butter, 95, 195. See also Appendix B, 312, 314
Buvelot, Louis, 178

Cabinet, 149, 150, 152
Cables, 82, 260
Cairns, 6, 38, 79
Cameron, Don, 271-272, 273
Canada, 61, 92, 95, 97-99, 149, 150, 163, 212, 213, 215, 216, 232, 264, 270, 296
Canberra, 205-208, 223, 306
Canton Island, 83, 240
Carnegie Corporation, 183
Casey, Richard Gardiner, 241, 296
Chaffey Bros., 70
Chanak, 214
Chartists, 10, 117
Chemicals, 61
China, 249, 296, 297
Chinese, 119, 220, 307
Chromite, 62, 313
Chronology. See Appendix A, 303-305
Church of England, 184, 198
Civil Servants, 164
Clark, Colin, 95, 109-110, 142, 309
Clarke, Marcus, 3, 34, 167
Clark, Dr. Victor, 119-120
Climate, 31
Clothing, 195
Clune, Frank, 260
Clunies Ross, Dr. Ian. See Ross, Dr. Ian Clunies
Coal, 62, 313
Coates, George, 178
Collins, Tom, 3, 168, 174
Colonial Sugar Refining Co. Ltd., 69, 93
Condor, Charles, 178
Commonwealth Bank, 90-92, 156
Commonwealth Grants Commission, 143-144, 147, 161-162
Communications, 82
Communist Party, 130, 156

Connolly, J. V., 201
Conscription, 227, 229
Constitution, 100, 149, 205, 222-223
Convicts: arrival of, 41; as a labor force, 116-117; in history, 10-11; transportation, 41, 48
Cook, James, 41, 43
Cook, Sir Joseph, 224
Copland, D. B., 88, 95, 111
Copper, 62, 313
Corn, 59
Cotton, 59, 62, 288
Council for Scientific and Industrial Research, 203
Country Party, 152, 153ff, 241
Crawford, John G., 95, 142
Cricket, 199
Crown, 215, 216
Curtin, John, 242, 243, 276, 295
Cusack, Dymphna, 172, 173
Cultural life, 12, Chapter 9

Dairying, 59, 96, 290, 312, 314
Dampier, William, 43
Dark, Eleanor, 173, 174, 322
Darling, John, 125-126
Darling River, 70, 72
Darwin, 5, 247, 256, 257, 259-262
Davies, David, 178
Davison, Frank Dalby, 173, 174, 279, 322
Defense, 222-224, 251. See also World War, First; and Second
Delprat, G. D., 76
Dennis, C. J., 169, 193-4
Depression, Great, 52, 55, 185, 237
Development policy, 85-86
Diet, 195-6
Dominion, status of, 211-217
Drake-Brockman, Henrietta, 182
Dutch, 220, 252; discoveries, 42, 43. See also Netherlands East Indies
Duntroon, 223
Dyson, Will, 180

Eastern Supply Group Council, 255
Education. See Schools, Universities, etc.
Eggleston, Sir F. W., 296
Eighteen-nineties, 51-52, 123
Eire, 212, 213, 216
Eldershaw, Barnard, 173, 174, 322

Elkin, A. P., 39
Ellis, Havelock, 167, 169
Emeny, Brooks, 60
Emu, 35
Esson, Louis, 182
Eucalypts, 36, 177
Eureka Stockade, 118-119
Evans, Ivor, 204
Evatt, Dr. H. V., 45, 119, 229
Exports, 95-98
External Affairs, Department of, 295-296

Fadden, Arthur William, 242, 243
Far East, 6-7. See Chapters 12, 13, 15.
    See also Japan, etc.
Farrer, W. J., 50
Federal Loan Council, 89-90
Federal-state relations, 161-163
Federalism, 19-20, 149, 207
Finey, George, 180
Fisher, A. G. B., 106, 187
Fisher, Andrew, 224, 226
Fisher, Thomas, 186
Fishing, 59, 96, 308
Fitzgerald, Robert, 169, 171
Fitzpatrick, Brian, 93, 94, 229
Fiji, 82, 220, 263
Flag, 204
Flannel flower, 35
Flowers, native, 35-36
Flynn, Erroll, 183
Foreign policy, 22-23, 218-222, 235-236,
    247-252, 294-299
Foreign Private Investments, 92ff
Franklin, Miles, 168, 172
Free Library Movement, 183
Fremantle, 81, 262
Fruit production, 59, 95

Galahs, 34
Gallipoli, 225, 226
Gambling, 200-201
Geelong, 81
Gepp, Sir Herbert, 110, 111
General Motors Holden Ltd., 78
Gilbert, Web, 178
Glasgow, Sir T. W., 296
Glynn, Patrick McMahon, 124
Gold, contemporary production, 59, 313
Gold rushes, 49, 117-119
Gordon, Adam Lindsay, 167-8, 194

Government: federal, state, local, Chap-
    ter 8; local, 184, 197; state, 183, 197
Governor-General, 149-150, 151
Governors, state, 150, 160
Grainger, Percy, 181, 182
Great Barrier Reef, 32, 37
Great Britain: tie to, 21, 22, 78-79, 85ff,
    92-95, 211-217, 218, 235-236. See also
    United Kingdom
Green, Paddy, 73
Griffin, Walter Burley, 206, 207
Griffith, Sir Samuel, 139
Gruner, Elioth, 178, 179
Gum trees. See Eucalypts
Gunn, Mrs. Aeneas, 173

Hargrave, Lawrence, 240
Hay, 59, 310-311
Heggie, O. P., 183
Herbert, Xavier, 172, 173
Heysen, Hans, 178, 179
Higgins, H. B., 139, 140, 141
High Commissioner, 150
High Court, 89, 149
Hill, Alfred, 182
Hobart, 30, 306
Hoff, Rayner, 178
Holman, W. A., 228
"Home," 202
Hong Kong, 261
Hopkins, Livingston, 180-181, 203
Horses, 59, 311
House of Representatives, 149, 151, 206
Housing, 145, 146-7, 196-7, 285
Hughenden, 5
Hughes, William Morris, 188, 223, 226-
    234, 243, 248, 249, 298
Hume-Cook, James, 286, 288, 291
Hutcheson, Ernest, 181

I.W.W., 130
Imperial Chemical Industries, 78, 94,
    288
India, 214, 215
Indian Ocean, 6, 30, 39, 224
Industrialization, 16. See also Appen-
    dix B
Industries, 57-60; location of, 57-60. See
    also Appendix B
Iron, 61; ore, 62; production figures,
    313

Irrigation, Murray River, 69-71
"Island policy," 219-220, 256
Isolationism, 294-295

Japan, 81, 85, 269, 290, 296; and airline, 83, 257; Anglo-Japanese Alliance, 221, 248-249; attitude toward, 22, 247, 249-252, 297; and German Islands, 231; and New Caledonia, 264; and Pacific Islands, 253-255; and racial equality, 233; trade with, 97-98, 107
Jarrah, 36
Jones, J. Gordon, 288, 291
Julius, Sir George, 200

Kangaroo, 34, 35
Karri, 36
Katanning, 5
Kawai, Tatsuo, 252
Keane, R. V., 143
Kendall, Henry, 167
Keynes, John Maynard, 230
King George VI, 206, 213
Kingsley, Henry, 166, 171, 322
Kingsford-Smith, Sir Charles, 240
Kingston, Charles C., 128, 129
Kitchener, Lord, 223
Koala, 34
Kookaburra, 35

Labor force, 116-118, 308-310
Labor Movement, 17-19; ideology of, 127
Labour Party, 10, 11, 17, 52, 54, 87-88, 90, 91, 100, 109, 128, 152ff, 223, 224, 228-9, 240, 241-244, 245, 248, 268, 281, 285
Labor Unions, 17, 50, 54, 245-246, 272-273, 281, 285. See also Chapter 7
Lamb, 59, 95, 195, 312
Lambert, George Washington, 178
Land: "good country." See map p. 58; tenure, 198; under crop, 310
Lane, William, 127
Lang, John Thomas, 87-88, 89, 156
Latham, Sir John G., 232, 296
Lawlor, Adrian, 177
Lawrence, D. H., 167
Lawrence, Marjorie, 181
Lawson, Henry, 3, 168, 169, 174, 194-5

Lead, 63, 313
League of Nations, 214, 230, 295, 299
Lemons, 38
Liberal Party, 224, 228
Libraries, public, 184, 186, 207
Lindsay, Sir Lionel, 177-8, 179
Literature, 3, 51, 165-174
Lindsay, Norman, 172, 173, 180, 323
Livestock. See Industries, also Appendix B
Loan Expenditure, 86
Locarno, 215
London, as mecca, 175, 202
Longstaff, Sir John, 178
Low, David, 180
Lumber, 59, 71, 96, 316
Lyons, Joseph, 241, 250
Lyrebird, 35

Macarthur, John, 44, 45
MacDonald, James S., 175-6, 177, 186
Machinery, 61
Mackay, 50
Malaya. See Singapore
Mallee, 36, 70
Mandated Territory of New Guinea. See New Guinea
Manganese, 62, 313
Manjimup, 71
Mann, Leonard, 172, 173, 322
Manufacturing: efficiency of, 109-111; future of, 114, 288-289; location of, 59-60; progress of, 54-55; and tariff, 108-111; statistics, 314-316
Martens, Conrad, 178
Matsuoka, Yosuke, 252
Maurice, Furnley, 169, 170-171
May, Phil, 180
McCrae, Hugh, 169
McCubbin, Fred, 178
McCulloch, George, 73ff
Melba, Nellie, 181
Melbourne, A. C. V., 298
Melbourne, 6, 30, 145, 167, 204-5, 206, 306
Meldrum, Max, 178
Menzies, Robert Gordon, 240-44, 250, 251, 269, 271, 289, 298
Mercury, 63
Mica, 63, 313
Mildura, 70

Minerals, 38-39, 59, 313
Ministry of Labor and National Service, 53, 280
Mitchell, A. G., 191
Mitchell, David Scott, 186
Moore, John, 178, 179
Mt. Isa, 5, 38
Mt. Kosciusko, 31
Movies, 201
Muller, Baron Ferdinand von, 50
Murdoch, Sir Keith, 176
Murray River, 5, 72
Murrumbidgee River, 59
Music, 181-182
Muskett, Philip E., 195
Mutton, 59, 95, 195, 312

Napoleonic Wars, 43, 45
National Standards Laboratory, 203
National War Council, 244
Nationalist Party, 228
Nationality, 188-191, 307
Natural resources, 13-14, 30-31, 38-39; critical raw materials, 62-63; great essentials, 61-62. *See also* Appendix B
Nauru, 63, 232-233, 254-255
Navy, 223-224, 239-240
Near East. *See* Chapters 12, 13
Near North. *See* Far East
Neilson, Shaw, 3, 169, 170
Netherlands East Indies, 23, 247, 249, 255-259, 262, 269, 296
New Caledonia, 40, 61, 82, 83, 263-265, 296
New Guinea, 40, 61, 82, 83, 220, 225, 226, 231, 240, 247, 252-254, 257
New Hebrides, 220, 262, 263, 265-266
New Holland, 41
New South Wales, 30, 33, 57, 60, 87-88, 100, 128, 241, *passim;* discovery of, 41; settlement of, 42. *See also* Appendix B
New Zealand, 83, 91, 97, 98, 129, 163, 180, 212, 213, 219, 231, 232, 233, 259, 263, 266-269, 285, 288
Newcastle, 54, 61, 81, 161, 237
Newspapers, 83, 157
Nickel, 63, 264
Nitrates, 62
Northern Territory, 30, 37, 39, 198, 260.
See also Appendix B

Noumea. *See* New Caledonia
Nutrition, 144, 282-283

Oats, 59, 310-311
Oberon, Merle, 183
O'Dowd, Bernard, sonnet, vi, 3, 168, 169, 174
Official Opposition, 151
Oil. *See* Petroleum
Opals, 59
Oranges, 38
O'Reilly, Dowell, 169
Ottawa Agreements, 98, 109

Pacific, Southern, 22-23, 218, 222, 224, 228, 236, 247ff, 263, 264, 297-298
Pago Pago, 7, 220, 269
Palmer, Vance, 173-4
Pan American Airways, 263
Papua. *See* New Guinea
Paterson, A. B., 169
Pearl Shell, 59, 247
Penton, Brian, 172, 173, 280, 323
Perth, 30, 78, 262, 306
Petroleum, 62, 253, 256
Phar Lap, 200
Phillip, Capt. Arthur, 42, 55, 219
Phosphates, 63. *See also* Nauru
Platypus, 34
Politics, 19; federal, 152ff; state, 158ff
Population: question of, 291-293; statistics, 306
Pork, 59, 311, 312
Port Kembla, 81, 237
Port Moresby, 253, 254
Port Pirie, 75, 76, 78
Portuguese, discoveries, 43. *See also* Timor
Portus, G. V., 143, 272
Potash, 63
Potatoes, 59, 311
Pragmatic outlook, 118, 299
Preston, Margaret, 178
Prichard, Katherine Susannah, 171, 172, 182, 322
Prickly pear, 37
Priestly, R. E., 187
Prime Minister, 149, 150, 151, 154, 160
Privy Council, 22, 149
Public health, 144-145
Public works, 50, 286-287

Queensland, 30, 31, 32, 33, 37, 38, 57, 306, *passim. See also* Appendix B

Rabbits, 37
Race. *See* Nationality
Racing, 199-200
Recreation, 145-146. *See also* Sports, Movies, etc.
Radio broadcasting, 82, 158
Railways, 79-82, 86, 162, 223; problem of gauges, 80
Rasp, Charles, 73
Reconstruction, post-war, 24-25, 187, 203, 279-293
Referendum, 104-105, 149
Religion, 12-13, 198-199
Renmark, 70
Rice, 59
Richardson, Henry Handel, 171-172, 322
Ridley, John, 50
Rivett, Sir David, 203
Roads, 81-82
Roberts, Tom, 51, 178, 179
Roman Catholic Church, 10, 128, 184, 198, 199, 281, 284-285, 292
Rosevear, J. S., 106
Ross, E. A., 190
Ross, Dr. Ian Clunies, 114-115, 290
Ross, Dr. Lloyd, 127
Ross, Robert, 119
Rubber, 63, 253

Samoa, Western (German), 231, 267. For U.S. Samoa. *See* Pago Pago
Schools, 184
Scott, Sir Ernest, 230
Senate, 149, 151
Sheep: shearing, 66-68; station, 64-68; statistics, 311
Shipping, 80-81, 258
Singapore, 248, 256, 259, 261, 269, 296
Slang, 192
Sleath, Richard, 125, 126
Smith, R. B., 50
Social services, 143-147, 282-285
Socialism, 17, 131, 245-246, 286
South Africa, 212, 213, 215, 231, 288
South Australia, 30, 38, 57, 161, 166, *passim. See also* Appendix B
Speech, 191-194

Spence, Catherine H., 166
Spence, W. G., 121
Sports, 13, 199-201
States: area under crop, 57; economic importance, 30. *See* map p. 58. *See also* Government
Statistics (text tables): commodities as percentage of total exports, 96; consumption foodstuffs, 195; destination of exports 97; loan expenditure, 86; origin of imports, 98; production exported, 96; total debts, where redeemable, 87. *See also* Appendix B, 306-316
Statute of Westminister, 212-213, 215, 230
Steel, 54, 61, 77-78
Stephens, A. G., 168, 190
Stewart, Nellie, 182
Stivens, Dal, 172, 173
Stone, Louis, 168, 322
Streeton, Sir Arthur, 178, 179
Strikes, 137, 138
Suez, 81, 239. *See* Map 210
Sturt, Charles, 72
Sugar, cane, 37, 59, 69, 95, 195, 310-311
Sulphur, 63
Sutcliffe, J. T., 142
Swearing, 192-3
Syme, David, 100
Sydney, 6; founding of, 42; harbor, 29, 30; *vs.* Melbourne, 204-205; population, 306; port, 81; recreation, 145

Tariff, 50, 53-54, 100-102; preference, 108
Tariff Board, 109, 112
Tasmania, 30, 31, 43, 57, 161, 200, *passim. See also* Appendix B
Tate, Henry, 182
Taxation, 197-8
Taylor, Griffith, 30, 39
Tea, 195, 256
Tennant, Kylie, 172-3, 192, 322
Tennis, 199
Theatre, 182-183
Timor, 220, 257
Tin, 63, 313
Tinney, Frank, 183
Tobacco, 59

Townsville, 79, 81
Trade policy, Chapter 6, 221, 249, 291
Trade unions. *See* Labor unions
Trees, native, 36
Tropics, 37-39, 69
Tudor, F. G., 228
Tungsten, 63, 313
Two-up, 200

Unemployment, 142, 147
United Australia Party, 152ff, 228, 241
United Kingdom: and defense, 223-224, 236, 247, 255; and government debt, 87; political relations, 211-217, 222, 294, 298; private investments, 92-95; trade with, 97-99, 105, 112-114, 221, 289; and U.S., 269, 276
United States, 81, 116, 149, 163, 164, 207, 240, 258, 262, 264, 296; airline from, 83; attitude toward, 23-24, 189, 269-276, 290, 299; diet compared, 195; indebtedness to, 87; investments, 92; Pacific possessions, 7, 220; trade with, 97-99
Universities, 185-186
Urban-Rural conflict, 15-16, 80
Urbanization, 15, 48

Van Dieman's Land. *See* Tasmania
Van Kleffens, 259
Versailles Peace Conference, 214, 218, 229-234
Victoria, 30, 38, 57, 118, 166, *passim.* *See* Appendix B
Voting, compulsory, 154

Wage fixation, 138-142
Wallaby, 34
Waratah, 35
Ward, Hugh, 203
Washington Conference, 248-249
Water: artesian, 65; conservation of, 65-66
Wattle, 35
Wentworth, W. C., 166
Western Australia, 30, 35, 36, 37, 38, 57, 60, 71, 132, 161, *passim. See also* Appendix B
Wheat, 59, 95, 105, 310-311
White Australia policy, 50, 53, 69, 189, 220-221, 228, 230
Wilson, Woodrow, 229, 230, 233
Whyalla, 76
Wine, 95
Withers, Walter, 178
Wombat, 34
Wood, G. L., 95
Wool, 59, 63, 95, 312
Wool-broking, 93, 94
Wool industry, 15, 44, 45, 46-49, 64-68, 290; and tariff, 106-108; 290
World War, First, Chapter 12; action in, 225-226; casualties, 225; debt, 234; effects of, 52, 54, 185; and Pacific outlook, 298; reparations, 234
World War, Second, 52, 235-276, 298
Wyndham, 5, 261

Yampi Sound, 62

Zinc, 62, 313